WRITING
FOR SCHOLARLY PUBLICATION

BEHIND THE SCENES
IN LANGUAGE EDUCATION

WRITING FOR SCHOLARLY PUBLICATION

BEHIND THE SCENES IN LANGUAGE EDUCATION

Edited by

Christine Pearson Casanave
Teachers College, Columbia University
Tokyo, Japan

Stephanie Vandrick
University of San Francisco

LAWRENCE ERLBAUM ASSOCIATES, PUBLISHERS
2003   Mahwah, New Jersey   London

Lawrence Erlbaum Associates, Inc., Publishers
10 Industrial Avenue
Mahwah, NJ 07430

Cover art by Christine Pearson Casanave

Cover design by Kathryn Houghtaling Lacey

Library of Congress Cataloging-in-Publication Data

Writing for scholarly publication : behind the scenes in language education / Christine
   Pearson Casanave and Stephanie Vandrick, editors.
      p. cm.
      Includes bibliographical references and index.
ISBN 0-8058-4243-8 (alk. paper)
ISBN 0-8058-4244-6 (p : alk. paper)
      1. English language—Study and teaching—Foreign speakers 2. English language—Rheto-
      ric—Study and teaching 3. Academic writing—Study and teaching 4. Learning and schol-
      arship—Authorship 5. Immigrants—Authorship 6. Scholarly publishing 7. Authorship I.
      Casanave, Christine Pearson, 1944-   II. Vandrick, Stephanie.

PE1128.A2 W758 2003
808'.02—dc21   2002190771
                                                                         CIP

Books published by Lawrence Erlbaum Associates are
printed on acid-free paper, and their bindings are chosen for
strength and durability.

Printed in the United States of America
10   9   8   7   6   5   4   3   2   1

I dedicate this book to my sister, Martha Casanave, who has bravely taken risks in her field of fine art photography all her life. It has taken me a while to catch up.

• *Christine Pearson Casanave*

I dedicate this book to my very dear daughter, Mariam Missaghi, who is the joy of my life. She keeps me honest, makes sure I don't get too settled and staid, and opens up my world in wonderful ways.

• *Stephanie Vandrick*

CONTENTS

APPENDIXES

Preface

Writing for publication is becoming increasingly important in language education, as fields such as composition and rhetoric, teaching English to speakers of other languages (TESOL), and multicultural studies become both more professional and more competitive. Researchers and practitioners face pressures to publish as a way to secure or keep a job, to move up in rank, and to contribute to the field by sharing knowledge and communicating critically with interested readers. It is equally important for graduate students wishing to enter a tight marketplace to understand and experiment with writing for publication. Writing researchers and scholars, too, are curious about what happens behind the scenes in the construction of the artificially seamless published product. Yet few scholars talk candidly about their experiences negotiating a piece of writing into print. This collection of first-person essays by established authors and editors in second language and multicultural education begins to fill this gap by providing needed support and insights for new and experienced academic writers. We believe the essays will help readers expand their understanding of both what it means to write for publication in language education fields and what writing for publication can mean to them personally.

Writing for Scholarly Publication thus doubles as a professional book for language educators and a resource book for graduate students and novice writers. First, it is especially appropriate for graduate students and novice professionals in language education who are just beginning to write for publication or who may be having trouble getting published. The book is both a personal and a practical resource book for this group—a "textual mentor" in the sense that published academic writers share their own experiences and insights with readers. Second, it will appeal to scholars of academic and disciplinary discourse, both graduate students and faculty, who are researching the social, political, and personal aspects of academic writing. Third, it will be of interest to experienced academic writers who wish to reflect in a personal way on their own publishing experiences. The collection helps readers achieve these goals by demystifying the practice of writing for publication from the inside. For instance, the essays provide insights into how and why writers choose to write for publication, how writing that is targeted for publication is negotiated with gatekeepers, what some of the issues of voice and identity are in writing for publication, and what kinds of challenges face writers on the periphery. The main value of the essays will be in the reflections and discussions they spark and the connections readers can make with their own issues, curiosities, and practices in writing for publication.

Many of the essays in this book portray hardship and struggle that are not obvious in a finished piece of writing. The invisible aspects of the process of writing for publication are not always comfortable ones. They are, however, aspects that need to be made more transparent than they currently are. In working toward this transparency, the contributions are carefully crafted, engagingly written, issue-oriented essays and narratives that are focused and provocative. They document authors' experiences with a range of practical, political, and personal issues in writing for publication. With the perspectives of the authors taking center stage, readers are urged to connect the narratives to their own lives and to participate in and resonate with events and issues in the authors' lives. Practical information such as contact information for journal and book publishers, manuscript guidelines, and useful reference books is included in appendixes. The unconventional author biostatements include many authors' favorite readings that have inspired their writing.

STRUCTURE AND SUMMARY OF CHAPTERS

Writing for Scholarly Publication consists of an introductory essay by the editors and sixteen essays by contributors, organized into four thematic parts: Newcomers, Negotiating and Interacting, Identity Construction, and From the Periphery. Although arranged by theme, the essays overlap in many ways because each author considers multiple issues. In the introductory essay (chap. 1), the editors discuss some of these key issues related to writing for scholarly publication, such as writing as a situated practice, issues faced by newcomers to writing, the construction of professional identity through writing, writing and transparency, aspects of the interactive nature of scholarly writing, and political issues intertwined with writing for publication.

Part I contains four essays written by newcomers to academic writing and publishing. The essays demonstrate that newcomers come in many shapes and sizes and face issues that differ in interesting ways. Ena Lee and her graduate supervisor, Bonny Norton (chap. 2), offer readers a dialogue in an engaging mix of scholarly and conversational prose that covers basic questions about writing for publication that many graduate students ask. What is the connection between term papers and a paper for publication? How do writers choose a journal to submit their articles to? How do PhD students turn their dissertations into books? How do processes of collaboration, coauthorhsip, and revision work? These and other questions are explored from the perspectives of both graduate student and supervisor. Paul Kei Matsuda (chap. 3), on the other hand, describes his gradual immersion, beginning with his MA studies, into his field of specialty, second language writing. Readers will note how central the activity is for him of engagement with ideas, other scholars, and literature in the field as he found his "voice" in the transition from graduate student to young scholar. Stephanie Vandrick (chap. 4) narrates a tale of a late bloomer. She tells how she had been in the field of English as a second language (ESL) for many years but began seriously writing and publishing only after age 40, when events in her professional life gave her the confidence and the resources to begin writing, an activity she had previously thought that only others did. Ryuko Kubota (chap. 5) takes readers through some of her first efforts at publication as a new faculty member, under pressure to write a great deal in her first several years on her road to tenure, a "publish-or-perish" nightmare faced by assistant professors at many universities. As a second language speaker of English and a new scholar with strong ideas, Ryuko found that she had to work exceptionally hard to retain what she calls her "original voice" in these early publications.

In Part II, Negotiating and Interacting, four essays examine especially closely the interactions among authors, editors, readers, manuscript reviewers, and collaborators. These interactions tend to be the least often discussed in print, and these essays therefore offer readers fascinating insights into the sensitive social, political, and personal relationships among the many players in the scholarly writing game. George Braine (chap. 6) takes readers on a long and painful journey that documents the birth, development, and final publication of an article. We see close up how editors, author, and reviewers interact, miscommunicate, and negotiate in order to resolve misunderstandings and to find a home for an article. Sandra Lee McKay (chap. 7) writes a double-voiced essay from her position as former editor of a major journal. We see from the inside not only how complex and labor intensive the job of journal editor is, but also how delicate and problematic her multiple relationships are with authors, reviewers, editorial boards, and executive boards. Likewise, Ilona Leki (chap. 8) narrates some of the complexities she faces in her job as editor of another major journal. Like Sandra McKay, she is also an author, so feels torn in her role as an editor who at times has to reject articles that authors feel strongly should not have been rejected. She discusses in particular how difficult it is to negotiate with unhappy authors and with reviewers whose reviews are late or unnecessarily harsh in tone. In the final essay in this section, John Hedgcock (chap. 9) offers a series of anecdotes that document some of his experiences writing with coauthors and collaborators. His analogy of collaboration and traveling with a companion brings to light countless social and interpersonal details of the collaborating process that the inexperienced and unwary may never have considered. His final checklists provide sound advice for all readers who are writing or wish to write for publication with friends and colleagues.

In Part III, Identity Construction, four authors write about their experiences with and reflections on the ways that professional writing helps construct their identities as writers and scholars. These essays share a theme of multivocality in the sense that questions of voice, identity, and construction of a professional persona are never portrayed as unified, unambiguous, or fully under control of the writer. In chapter 10, Christine Pearson Casanave deals with her own sense of multiple selves with the metaphor of narrative braiding, finding that her conflicting relationships with her field do not need to be resolved, but to be woven and rewoven as needed into different wholes. Linda Lonon Blanton (chap. 11), too, narrates stories about her conflicted relationship with the very public nature of published academic writing. Her writing only gradually flourished as she became able to put herself into, and indeed liberate herself from, her previously sometimes sterile academic prose. In chapter 11, Dwight Atkinson discusses the notion of voice, both abstractly and personally. He asks himself whether he has a voice in his scholarly writing, and if so, what that voice might consist of and how it interacts with other published voices in his field, particularly over controversial topics. In the last essay in this section, Aneta Pavlenko (chap. 13) takes us on the journey that began with her refugee flight from the Ukraine and ended up at Temple University. We see the early roots of her courageous academic identity and the events, encounters, and drive that contributed to the shape that identity took as she discovered the passions that continue to drive her as a scholar.

Part IV of this collection, From the Periphery, brings together four very different essays that help redefine what the notion of "periphery" might mean, from a concept with a negative connotation of "outsider" to a positive connotation of active and unconventional participant. A. Suresh Canagarajah (chap. 14) takes us back to his homeland in Sri Lanka, where scholars who lack resources still find ways to write and publish. The strategies used by the author and his colleagues, though rarely discussed in print, show from the inside how conventional rules for writing and researching are adapted and manipulated to the authors' advantage under these difficult circumstances. Miyuki Sasaki (chap. 15) reveals another sense of the concept *periphery scholar*. Although not from a developing country, she sees herself at the periphery of her field by virtue of her commitment to her family life in addition to her participation in her scholarly community. Confessing that she publishes less than some of her colleagues, she admits nevertheless to deep satisfaction with her choices, which the editors note include writing at least one superb article for publication each year. Her essay will be inspiring for any readers who are similarly torn between scholarly and nonscholarly pursuits. Another sense of "periphery" can be seen in Brian Morgan's essay (chap. 16), which links scholarly writing to real-life issues in the lives of practitioners. Morgan, as a committed and politically astute practitioner himself, found himself resisting the power that the printed scholarly word can have over marginalized classroom teachers and students. He shows how he gradually developed a sense of self as an academic writer without losing either his belief that practitioners' knowledge remains undervalued or his commitment to the practitioner side of scholarship. The collection ends with an essay by Martha Clark Cummings (chap. 17), who reminds people in academia that if they wish to write, options other than scholarly writing and publishing exist that they may find deeply satisfying. A prolific writer of fiction, she finds ways to maintain her ties with academia without falling into the publish-or-perish trap and without needing to limit herself to the identity of the stereotypical academic researcher and writer.

Acknowledgments

Perhaps more than many other scholarly books, this one came to life through the efforts of people who were willing to do things a bit differently. As editors, we are indebted above all to the contributors to this volume, many of whom had never written publicly in such candid and personal ways before. Without their risk-taking, this book would still be just an idea. Similarly, our editor at Lawrence Erlbaum Associates, Naomi Silverman, joined us in taking a chance with the book and provided support and guidance during the entire process. Jodi Nelms and Betsy Rymes, the reviewers of earlier ideas and drafts, helped shape the book as well, offering critical commentary while still conveying their own excitement about the project. We are also grateful to our production editor, Sarah Wahlert, for her meticulous editing and her assistance throughout the later stages of this project. Finally, our deepest thanks go to friends, relatives, and colleagues who listened to our ideas, offered advice and support, and were patient with us when we were buried in the details of the work.

1

Introduction:
Issues in Writing for Publication

Christine Pearson Casanave
Teachers College, Columbia University, Tokyo, Japan

Stephanie Vandrick
University of San Francisco

It is increasingly important, even critical, for those in language education to write for scholarly publication, and not only for the obvious purpose of securing or keeping an academic position. Researching and writing about teaching and related topics also allows educators to grow professionally and intellectually, to share their ideas with peers, and to become better teachers through the reflective and critical processes of writing for a public readership. Yet many language educators, particularly but not only newcomers, resist the challenge of preparing work for possible publication, feeling intimidated by an activity that seems fraught with obstacles. These obstacles include the sense that getting into print is an accomplishment that only a few insiders with insider knowledge manage to achieve, that the process threatens egos and individual voice, and that people who get published somehow find it easier to write than those who do not. Our major aim in this book is to help demystify the activity of writing for publication, demonstrating that the obstacles are surmountable. We do not claim that such writing is easy, or that we have any easy shortcuts to doing such writing. But we do believe that by gathering and sharing the stories of well-published scholars in language education and English as a second language (ESL) in a book like this, we can begin to make the process of scholarly writing, in all of its aspects, more transparent, more accessible, less overwhelming, less intimidating.

In sharing their stories, our contributors reveal that they did not start off with any natural ease at writing, or take any uncomplicated or direct paths to writing and publishing. Each contributor has struggled, has overcome obstacles, has made difficult choices, and has experienced rejections and discouragement. In addition to revealing some shared issues in their stories, the contributors show in the specifics of each narrative that they have found different issues to be salient in their experiences of writing for publication. What the authors have in common is a willingness to pull the curtain aside, revealing that there is no mystery, no magic. However, our message is not as simple as "if you only try hard, you too can write and publish like these contributors." We acknowledge that some readers face particular obstacles that may be hard to overcome. But we want to convey our belief that knowing something about other people's paths to publication can contribute to how we understand our own writing issues, that most often obstacles can be overcome, and that there are many ways to reach one's goal of contributing to a scholarly field through writing.

We are particularly interested in issues related to inclusiveness. We believe that scholarly writing should not be an insiders' club for those already "in the know." Issues of gender, race, national origin, and class, among others, can and do influence access to the world of scholarly publishing. Some of our contributors discuss being marginalized or being on the periphery and talk about how they have addressed writing from those positions. However, they have not allowed perceptions of insider privilege to dissuade them from participating in the increasingly diverse scholarly conversations in language education. Our group of contributors is multicultural, multiliterate, as are many in language education fields, and we believe that such diversity adds richness to our field and to its publications.

We asked contributors to write narratives illustrating issues they have encountered in writing for publication. We believe that the explication of the issues is important; we also believe that the narrative form has its own power in exemplifying the issues, and that narratives allow for understanding and connection in ways that straight exposition does not. Truth in academic writing, particularly in the more scientific fields, has been characterized as objective, as written in the third person, as distanced from personal feelings and experiences. Language education, especially ESL, was grounded in applied linguistics, which considered and perhaps still considers itself a science, so these attitudes have been the foundation of scholarly writing in many language-related fields. Yet we contend, as do an increasing number of scholars in our field as well as related fields, that there is another kind of truth to be obtained from narratives, stories, and first-person viewpoints, which people use to construct their realities and interpret their experiences (Bruner, 1991; Polkinghorne, 1988).

In the remainder of this introductory chapter we briefly discuss a number of issues that help frame our contributors' narratives: academic writing as a situated practice, the invisible challenges of writing for publication, identity and voice, and power and position.

ISSUES

Writing as a Situated Practice Within Academic Communities

For a framework for understanding the practices of writing for scholarly publication we can turn to the notion of situated learning and situated practice. By focusing on scholarly writing as a situated practice we emphasize the importance of the very local and concrete interactions that take place in academic communities rather than broader theoretical abstractions about social practices. Much of our understanding of situated practice comes from the work of Jean Lave and Etienne Wenger (Lave, 1997; Lave & Wenger, 1991; Wenger, 1998). Several interrelated concepts from this work relate to how we wish to conceptualize the activity of writing for publication. The main concept is that of participation as a mode of learning, as opposed to learning as the acquisition of knowledge (Lave, 1997). The second concept is that of changing patterns of participation as indications of evolving membership in specialized communities (Lave & Wenger, 1991; Wenger, 1998). The third is the notion of peripherality, which we believe is treated somewhat apolitically and simply in the work of Lave and Wenger. They do stress, as we will too, that they wish the term to have a positive connotation (Lave & Wenger, 1991, p. 37).

First, it is unarguable that learning to write for publication necessarily involves engaging in, rather than just learning about, this scholarly practice. It is paradoxical in this regard that we feel strongly that a book of collected essays about writing for publication can contribute to readers' own writing practices. It is perhaps by revealing practices that usually remain hidden that the authors can contribute to our understanding of how central the activity of participation is in learning to write for publication (see the discussion below on invisible challenges), and how important it is for writers to understand the local and concrete nature of that participation.

Participation in scholarly writing practices, in the first place, refers to interactions with people. When inexperienced writers consider what kinds of interactions are central to their writing, they may think of interactions with teachers and peer readers above all. The academic writing community, however, consists of many more players than these. It may include a tenure review committee made up of individuals who agree on some criteria for the kinds and numbers of publications a tenure-track faculty member needs but not on other criteria. It includes the authors that a graduate student or teacher reads and interacts with as part of a discussion in a literature review section of an article. And it includes above all the many and sometimes difficult interactions among authors, production editors, journal editors, and critical reviewers. Guiding a piece of writing into print requires knowing how to participate in all of these interactive practices in ways that do not jeopardize a writer's chance of success. Although it may be possible to characterize such participation in general ways, the most consequential kinds of participation will be those in a writer's immediate environment, the details of which can be learned only in situ.

Throughout an academic career, beginning in graduate school, scholars who write for publication change the patterns in which they participate in their academic communities. As documented by Lave and Wenger (1991) in their studies of apprenticeship and identity development in communities of practice, as people learn to participate in a community's defining practices, they change their locations within the community, gradually taking on roles of more experienced members, whose patterns of participation differ from those of newcomers. In an academic setting, a graduate student might participate in data collection and analysis on a research team led by a principle investigator, but not actually write significant parts of the published report until dissertation time, if then (Prior, 1998). Graduate students who wish to use dissertations for future publications participate in very different ways with journal and book editors than they do with graduate advisors (Lee & Norton, this volume). Young faculty members who are not encouraged to write by a supportive administration, a situation that Stephanie Vandrick (this volume) experienced, participate in very different practices, and develop different academic identities than do faculty who receive strong support for participating in professional practices (see also the discussion of identity and voice, below). People who coauthor articles with colleagues develop particular social skills and sensitivities needed to bring a work into print (Hedgcock, this volume). Scholars who participate in local academic writing practices in their home countries develop the local expertise they need to bring their work into print but then must learn new participation practices when they move into a new academic community (Canagarajah, this volume). More experienced academic writers in general learn to take on increasing amounts of responsibility for their writing, which does not mean becoming a more solitary or independent writer. It means, on the contrary, becoming a writer who knows how to participate skillfully in the many subtle social, political, and linguistic practices needed to write for publication.

The notion of peripheral participation, first described by Lave and Wenger (1991), concerns the amount of engagement a person has with the defining practices of a particular community. Not meant to describe either a literal center or an edge, the concept of periphery (or location more generally) instead refers metaphorically to the ways community members participate (Lave & Wenger, 1991, p. 37). No community is made up of only core members or full insiders. As can be seen in any academic community, the community itself will be defined by multiple ways of participating by newcomers and oldtimers, and even by oldtimers who may reside permanently and by choice on the periphery. As described by Wenger (1998), the periphery of a practice is thus "a region that is neither fully inside nor fully outside, and surrounds the practice with a degree of permeability" (p. 117). People have "multiple levels of involvement" in a community, rather than simply belonging or not belonging. In Wenger's conceptualization, those who are prevented from belonging are constrained by boundaries, not by peripheries, which are permeable. Important for the authors of the essays in this volume, Wenger notes that "the periphery is a very fertile area for change" given the many layers and more or less engaged ways of participating in any community of practice.

But as Suresh Canagarajah (this volume) notes, there must be enough transparency even in peripheral participation for (potential) members to become legitimate participants. He highlights the fact that the metaphorical periphery in academic communities is not a neutral place, but a political and a social location. The essays in this volume attest to the fact that the multiple ways that people participate in the practices of writing for publication and other professional practices cannot be separated from influences of power and expertise, many aspects of which are not transparent to outsiders. Nevertheless, those who feel marginalized or far from the metaphorical center of mainstream practices, such as Canagarajah's Sri Lankan colleagues, "late-blooming" women scholars (Vandrick, this volume), women with families (Sasaki, this volume), and "practitioners" (Morgan, this volume), can sometimes find cracks in the system and can change and shift the rules of the game. In other words, changing locations as an academic writer involves far more than developing one's writing skills. It demands that writers see the multiple layers of their academic communities, understand the many ways they can strategically participate in different layers of the peripheries, and hone their interactive political skills for finding their ways into and through the layers. Transparency of social and political processes helps, and this volume of essays contributes to this transparency.

Invisible Challenges

Many of us began to learn to write for publication by modeling our submissions on articles we were reading. This system has its advantages, of course, in that we learned what topics were being talked about in the literature, how people were talking about them, and conventions of style and form for particular journals that could be imitated easily. The system also deceives novice writers into believing that the polished nature of a published work results from the writer's knowledge of the topic and expertise in writing, and that these two work together somehow to make the process of writing for publication relatively smooth and trouble-free.

This mistaken perception leads some novice writers to conclude that "others" write for publication—others who know more (Vandrick, this volume), or others who can write better, more "academic" English even when that prose may not be fully comprehensible to us as readers (Blanton, this volume; Cummings, this volume). It also ensures that novice writers will be shocked, dismayed, or outraged at some of the hidden processes, such as the time it takes from the first draft to publication, the bluntness of some critical reviews, and the need to go back to a piece of writing they thought was finished, not once, but multiple times in order to shape it into what may feel like someone else's work (Braine, this volume; Kubota, this volume).

In composition and rhetoric studies and in education, the call has gone out by a number of people for more transparency in writing processes, identities, and agendas in research and writing (e.g., Bishop, 1999; Bridwell-Bowles, 1995; Burdell & Swadener, 1999; Geisler, 1992, 1994; Kirsch & Ritchie, 1995). In multicultural studies and second language education, authors are beginning to reveal their own previously hidden writing processes and professional experiences as well (Belcher & Connor, 2001; Braine, 1999; Casanave, 2002; Casanave & Schecter, 1997; all the essays in this volume). These authors believe that greater transparency of the invisible facets of professional development in general and writing for publication in particular can ease the transition for novices into the practices of their academic communities. Having a look behind the scenes in writing for publication may not make the process of learning to participate in professional practices easier: As Lave and Wenger (1991; Wenger, 1998) remind us, learning takes place via participation, and there may be no way to shorten this process. The greater ease of transition comes about as novice writers come to understand and thus not summarily reject the lengthy social, political, and sociolinguistic processes that lie hidden behind the polished product that we finally see in print. By offering writers the views of editors as well as authors, we believe that the essays in this volume contribute to our agenda of making the processes of writing for publication more transparent than they typically are (Braine, this volume; Leki, this volume; McKay, this volume).

Identity and Voice

In writing for publication, authors construct identities for themselves, resulting in different "voices." Their published writing creates a representation of self which then influences how they see themselves and how they are seen by others. We mention two important ways this happens that have been discussed in the literature on communities of practice and on writing and identity and then comment briefly on the notion of voice.

First, from Lave and Wenger (Lave, 1996, 1997; Lave & Wenger, 1991; Wenger, 1998) comes the idea that we become certain kinds of people as we learn to participate in a community's practices. Lave and Wenger (1991, p. 53) phrased it as follows:

> Learning ... implies becoming able to be involved in new activities, to perform new tasks and functions, to master new understandings. Activities, tasks, functions, and understandings do not exist in isolation; they are part of broader systems of relations in which they have meaning.... Learning thus implies becoming a different person with respect to the possibilities enabled by these systems of relations.

Referring to identity as a "negotiated experience" in which we "define who we are by the way we experience our selves through participation as well as by the ways we and others reify our selves" (Wenger, 1998, p. 149), Wenger is especially interested in how people change over time as they change their "trajectories"—where they have been and where they are going (p. 149).

In academic settings, not everyone participates in the same ways. Not everyone writes for publication, and some who do write do not necessarily write academic pieces. Who is Martha Clark Cummings (this volume), for example—an academic or a fiction writer? She asserts she is both, and her essay reveals how her identity is constructed by different kinds of writing activities that take place nearly simultaneously within the same setting. In another example, the stereotypical identity clash persists between those who consider themselves primarily practitioners (teachers) or researchers (Morgan, this volume). No matter how false this dichotomy, it captures an identity dilemma that emerges from the kinds of activities these two broad groups of people are thought to engage in. The former group, the stereotype goes, teaches and the latter does research and writes. In learning to participate in an academic community through the activity of writing for publication, the stereotype breaks down, and people who previously identified themselves in one way come to see themselves in new ways (Blanton, this volume; Morgan, this volume; Vandrick, this volume). Similarly, graduate students who begin writing for publication gradually shift their identities from that of student to that of scholar and author, often with associated anxieties and tensions, by virtue of the changing ways they participate in the activities and conversations of their fields (Lee & Norton, this volume; Matsuda, this volume).

Second, from the work of Roz Ivanič (1994, 1995, 1998) is the notion of the discoursal self, namely, the self that intentionally or not is constructed through the linguistic and other semiotic resources available to writers. In the simplest of examples, the discoursal self that is created through a writer's use of passive voice throughout a research or academic article differs greatly from the self that is created through first-person pronouns and active voice. Both Linda Lonon Blanton (this volume) and Martha Clark Cummings (this volume) give examples quoted from the applied linguistics literature of dense nominal prose (including a passage that Blanton herself wrote) that reflects discoursal selves that these authors feel alienated from, and other examples that they identify with more compatibly. Their sense of alienation does not have to do with prose alone but with identity: Do I want to represent myself as this kind of person in my published work? If not, how do I want to be identified? Dwight Atkinson (this volume) addresses the same issue in his coda. He comments, in response to our request as editors that he shift the tone of his essay from one that was quite densely theoretical to one that was more personal, that he had represented himself accurately in the original draft, as an academic and a researcher socially positioned within the white, male, middle class. This self was the discoursal self he had intended.

In all the essays in this volume, we can see authors aligning themselves through the discourse they use with different "socioculturally shaped possibilities for self-hood, playing their part in reproducing or challenging dominant practices and discourses, and the values, beliefs and interests which they embody" (Ivanič, 1998, p. 32). As the work of Ivanic with inexperienced writers shows, and as many essays in this volume attest to as well, it takes time and effort for many writers to develop control and agency over how they use discourse to forge these alignments, which may never be fully free of tensions and conflicts (Casanave, this volume). Whether writers exude confidence from early on in a career (Matsuda, this volume; Pavlenko, this volume) or begin writing for publication with doubts and anxieties (Blanton, this volume; Vandrick, this volume), their identities as people who contribute to academic conversations develop and shift along with their public discourse.

As for the complex issue of voice, Dwight Atkinson (this volume) reviews some of the historical background and comments as well on some of his previous work on voice, so we will not belabor a topic that he has covered thoroughly. We are interested, however, in the links between identity and voice in published writing and note that several other authors in this volume seem to be interested in these links as well (e.g., Blanton, Canagarajah, Kubota). Atkinson struggles with the question of whether he has an individual voice in his academic writing, concluding mainly from his responses to editors rather than from his theorizing that he probably does. Ryuko Kubota, too, mixes theory and personal response to editors and reviewers in her search for what at some level she feels is "original voice"—though as is the case with Atkinson she cannot justify this feeling theoretically. In the view of Ivanič and Camps (2001), however, "voice" is not an "optional extra" (p. 4). Rather, it is displayed by writers whether they wish it to be there or not in the form of the self-representation that writers construct from the semiotic resources available in our cultures and communities. Voice as self-representation, they note, is inherent in all writing, whereas "voice" in the sense of speaking one's mind it is not (p. 7). Communicating both authoritatively and deferentially in writing are aspects of voice as self-representation (p. 8).

The important issue for those who wish to write for publication, we believe, is not whether inexperienced writers have no voice and experienced writers do. Rather it is how all writers can put their semiotic resources to work for them, to construct a self-representation—both a voice and an identity—that suits their purposes (whether that purpose is to come across as authoritative, deferential, impersonal, personal, or some combination of these). Important as well is for writers to construct a self-representation that can interact successfully with other members of the academic community, accommodating, challenging, resisting, and contributing to knowledge. In describing some of the behind-the-scenes processes they have experienced in writing for publication, the authors in this volume reveal some of the linguistic, social, and political challenges they faced in learning to represent themselves (and helping others represent themselves) in their writing by negotiating their voices and identities with the many players in the publishing process.

Power and Position

As difficult as writing appears to all newcomers, it seems even more so if one is not a member of the most privileged group in academe: white middle-class heterosexual men born in the countries where they are teaching, brought up speaking the language they are teaching, and following the ideal academic path through graduate school and into positions at institutions where research is valued and supported. Some newcomers start at the periphery (see earlier discussion); gender, class, sexual identity, nationality, ethnicity, race, language, education, and professional status are just some of the factors that may influence one's likelihood of publishing. If a teacher or researcher does not have all of the characteristics of the privileged individual outlined earlier or if material resources for publishing are scarce (Canagarajah, 1996), the path to writing and publishing is harder. First, it may in some cases be harder because of discrimination, both active and passive. Especially in the past, but even now, professors, editors, reviewers, and other relevant participants may—sometimes without realizing it themselves—be less likely to see the ideas and writings of women and of those of various ethnicities or minorities in academe as legitimate and publishable. Second, it is harder because of all the ways in which someone not in these privileged positions is—directly or indirectly—not steered toward scholarship. Third, it may be harder because many who are not located in these favored positions may lack a sense of confidence or entitlement to be part of a community of scholars.

Some obstacles are less obvious than others and may well be internal and invisible (e.g., learning disabilities, psychological problems, trauma caused by criticism of one's early scholarly efforts). Because they are hidden and generally unacknowledged, such invisible obstacles are often the most difficult hurdles to address and overcome. Again, by talking about and writing about these issues, we hope to reduce their mystery and their harmfulness.

Some obstacles come about because of a writer's desire to write about "difficult" topics, topics that are very controversial, that are considered inappropriate for academic venues, or both. Until the past few years, such topics included gender, class, and sexual identity as they affected language education and students, and even now such topics are somewhat marginalized. But changes in what are considered "acceptable" topics for academic writing do come about, so we encourage writers interested in writing about unorthodox subject matter to pursue these interests with enthusiasm and resolve.

As stated earlier, we believe that many of these obstacles can be overcome, and many of our contributors' chapters testify to this overcoming of obstacles. In fact, some scholars, including some of our contributors, have clearly turned what might normally be viewed as obstacles or disadvantages into strengths or advantages (Canagarajah, this volume; Pavlenko, this volume; Sasaki, this volume).

Fortunately, in recent years some scholars in ESL and applied linguistics have addressed many of these issues of ways in which power and position influence teachers, students, classroom interactions, institutional priorities, disciplinary focuses, and scholarly work. The work of these scholars has provided a context for examining the role of power and position in scholarly writing as well. Benesch (1993, 1999, 2001), for example, reminds us that all educational interactions are political, whether consciously perceived as such or not. Pennycook (1994, 1998) and Canagarajah (1993, 1999), among others, use the lens of postcolonial theory to demonstrate that the international contexts of English language learning must be understood, and other scholars (e.g., Phillipson, 1992; Tollefson, 1995) write on related language policy issues. Still other scholars, many of whom are associated with the study of critical pedagogy (e.g., Auerbach, 1991, 1995; Auerbach & Burgess, 1985; Cummins, 1996; Kubota, 1998; Morgan, 1998; Norton, 2000; Vandrick, 1995, 1997) point out ways in which those with power in setting educational policy, and teachers who follow such policy, can fundamentally and often very detrimentally affect classroom interactions and students' lives and learning. These and other scholars' discussions of power and privilege in language education have led a few, though so far only a few, scholars to examine how these issues also affect language education scholars and their research and writing (e.g., Canagarajah, 1996; Morgan, 1997). We believe that one of the contributions this book makes is to forward the discussion of how power, privilege, and position affect scholars and scholarly publication.

CONCLUSION

As readers peruse the following chapters, we as editors of this volume hope that they will find that the contributors' thoughts and experiences shed light on some of the many dimensions of writing for publication, such as the reasons why people write; the contexts for their writing; the challenges they face in getting started and in continuing to write and possible ways to deal with those challenges; the processes that go into scholarly writing and publication; and the roles of identity, voice, politics, power, and position in scholarly writing for publication. We further hope that this book will in some small way encourage readers to plunge in, to participate in their academic communities of practice, and thus to contribute their scholarly expertise and their ideas to their communities. Most of all, we hope that such participation will allow readers to experience the great privilege of living the life of the mind and sharing that life with others.

REFERENCES

Auerbach, E. R. (1991). Politics, pedagogy, and professionalism: Challenging marginalization in ESL. *College ESL, 1*(1), 1–9.

Auerbach, E. R. (1995). The politics of the ESL classroom: Issues of power in pedagogical choices. In J. Tollefson (Ed.), *Power and inequality in language education* (pp. 9–33). Cambridge, England: Cambridge University Press.

Auerbach, E. R., & Burgess, D. (1985). The hidden curriculum of survival ESL. *TESOL Quarterly, 19,* 475–495.

Belcher, D., & Connor, U. (Eds.). (2001). *Reflections on multiliterate lives.* Clevedon, England: Multilingual Matters.

Benesch, S. (1993). ESL, ideology, and the politics of pragmatism. *TESOL Quarterly, 27,* 705–717.

Benesch, S. (1999). Rights analysis: Studying power relations in an academic setting. *English for Specific Purposes, 18,* 313–327.

Benesch, S. (2001). *Critical English for academic purposes.* Mahwah, NJ: Lawrence Erlbaum Associates.

Bishop, W. (1999). Places to stand: The reflective writer–teacher–writer in composition. *College Composition and Communication, 51*(1), 9–31.

Braine, G. (Ed.), (1999). *Non-native educators in English language teaching.* Mahwah, NJ: Lawrence Erlbaum Associates.

Bridwell-Bowles, L. (1995). Freedom, form, function: Varieties of academic discourse. *College Composition and Communication, 46,* 46–61.

Bruner, J. (1991). The narrative construction of reality. *Critical Inquiry, 18,* 1–21.

Burdell, P., & Swadener, B. B. (1999). Critical personal narrative and autoethnography in education: Reflections on a genre. *Educational Researcher, 28*(6), 21–26.

Canagarajah, A. S. (1993). Critical ethnography of a Sri Lankan classroom: Ambiguities in student opposition to reproduction through ESOL. *TESOL Quarterly, 27,* 601–626.

Canagarajah, A. S. (1996). "Nondiscursive" requirements in academic publishing, material resources of periphery scholars, and the politics of knowledge production. *Written Communication, 13*(4), 435–472.

Canagarajah, A. S. (1999). *Resisting linguistic imperialism in English teaching.* New York: Oxford University Press.

Casanave, C. P. (2002). *Writing games: Multicultural case studies of academic literacy practices in higher education.* Mahwah, NJ: Lawrence Erlbaum Associates.

Casanave, C. P., & Schecter, S. R. (Eds.) (1997) *On becoming a language educator: Personal essays on professional development.* Mahwah, NJ: Lawrence Erlbaum Associates.

Cummins, J. (1996). *Negotiating identities: Education for empowerment in a diverse society.* Ontario, CA: California Association for Bilingual Education.

Geisler, C. (1992). Exploring academic literacy: An experiment in composing. *College Composition and Communication, 43*(1), 39–54.

Geisler, C. (1994). *Academic literacy and the nature of expertise: Reading, writing, and knowing in academic philosophy.* Hillsdale, NJ: Lawrence Erlbaum Associates.

Ivanič, R. (1994). I is for interpersonal: Discoursal construction of writer identities and the teaching of writing. *Linguistics and Education, 6,* 3–15.

Ivanič, R. (1995). Writer identity. *Prospect, 10,* 1–31.

Ivanič, R. (1998). *Writing and identity: The discoursal construction of identity in academic writing.* Philadelphia: John Benjamins.

Ivanič, R., & Camps, D. (2001). I am how I sound: Voice as self-representation in L2 writing. *Journal of Second Language Writing, 10*(1–2), 3–33.

Kirsch, G. E., & Ritchie, J. S. (1995). Beyond the personal: Theorizing a politics of location in composition research. *College Composition and Communication, 46*(1), 7–29.

Kubota, R. (1998). Voices from the margin: Second/foreign language teaching approaches from minority perspectives. *The Canadian Modern Language Review, 54*(3), 394–412.

Lave, J. (1996). Teaching, as learning, in practice. *Mind, Culture, and Activity, 3,* 149–164.

Lave, J. (1997). The culture of acquisition and the practice of understanding. In D. Kirshner & J. A. Whitson (Eds.), *Situated cognition: Social, semiotic, and psychological perspectives* (pp. 17–35). Mahwah, NJ: Lawrence Erlbaum Associates.

Lave, J., & Wenger, E. (1991). *Situated learning: Legitimate peripheral participation.* Cambridge, England: Cambridge University Press.

Morgan, B. (1997). The politics of publishing: Positioning critical voices in an ELT journal. *College ESL, 7*(1), 14–31.

Morgan, B. (1998). *The ESL classroom: Teaching, critical practice, and community development.* Toronto, Ontario, Canada: University of Toronto Press.

Norton, B. (2000). *Identity and language learning: Gender, ethnicity and educational change.* White Plains, NY: Longman/Pearson Education.

Pennycook, A. (1994*). The cultural politics of English as an international language.* London: Longman.

Pennycook, A. (1998*). English and the discourses of colonialism*. London: Routledge.

Phillipson, R. (1992). *Linguistic imperialism*. New York: Oxford University Press.

Polkinghorne, D. E. (1988). *Narrative knowing and the human sciences*. Albany, NY: State University of New York Press.

Prior, P. A. (1998). *Writing/disciplinarity: A sociohistoric account of literate activity in the academy*. Mahwah, NJ: Lawrence Erlbaum Associates.

Tollefson, J. (Ed.). (1995). *Power and inequality in language education*. New York: Cambridge University Press.

Vandrick, S. (1995). Privileged ESL university students. *TESOL Quarterly, 29*, 375–381.

Vandrick, S. (1997). The role of hidden identities in the postsecondary ESL classroom. *TESOL Quarterly, 31*, 153–157.

Wenger, E. (1998). *Communities of practice: Learning, meaning, and identity*. Cambridge, England: Cambridge University Press.

I

Newcomers

2

Demystifying Publishing: A Collaborative Exchange Between Graduate Student and Supervisor

Ena Lee and Bonny Norton
University of British Columbia, Canada

Bonny: Hi Ena. I have an idea I'd like to share with you. I've been invited to contribute to a collection of articles in an edited volume, *Writing for Publication: Behind the Scenes in Language Education.* Because the audience for this publication includes graduate students, I wonder if you'd like to coauthor the chapter with me. I'm hoping we can enter into a discussion about some of the questions that you have about writing for publication. I'm sure that your questions would echo those of many graduate students in the field of language education. Also, writing on this topic with a real person in mind will help make my writing a lot more focused and enjoyable. Are you interested?

Ena: Of course! This is a great way to clear up what I'm sure are my own misconceptions about the world of publishing. It'll also compel me to face (and, I hope, resolve) my own fears about publication and graduate studies—fears that I know, talking with my fellow classmates, are not just my own. If you ask graduate students interested in pursuing academic careers what one of their greatest worries is, I wouldn't be at all surprised if the word *publishing* was at the top of the list. Hearing such phrases as *publish or perish* constantly reminds us how integral this activity is to our future careers and forces us to face this fact. What is it about publishing that causes so much anxiety and panic in students?

Bonny: If it's any consolation, when I was a graduate student, I had exactly the same fears as you. When I had completed an honors thesis in applied linguistics in South Africa, I was encouraged to publish it. However, I had no idea where to start—and I was doubtful that anybody would be interested in the work of an unknown student in an isolated region of the world. I had done a good deal of reading and knew the work of many scholars, but everybody seemed so remote—geographically and intellectually. It was difficult for me to connect with a larger scholarly community. This is why, in my graduate classes, I show videos of scholars that are well-known in the field; I discuss the scholars I have met and talked to; I examine the controversies around published work. My purpose is not only to demystify publishing, but to demystify authors.

Ena: It's comforting to hear that you had the same concerns about publishing when you were a grad student. Most of the time when I read articles or books, I don't think about the processes the authors went through to get to this point in their writing and publishing careers. I forget that at one point they were graduate students like me trying to find their own niche. I guess I'm fortunate in my opportunity right now to be able to talk with someone who has been there and has gone through the very same process that I'm about to embark on. But where to begin?

Bonny: I wonder if it's helpful to think about publishing without first thinking about ideas. For me, publishing is the final part of a process that begins with an idea, a question, a desire to understand. As I have moved from place to place during my academic career, I've been confronted with questions about the way learning and teaching are structured in the diverse communities I have lived in. I've always asked myself whether I can make a difference to the opportunities to learn in that community—whether I'm working with children, adolescents, or adults. It's been through grappling with the complexities of teaching and working in a given place, at a particular time, that I have sought to document, reflect on, and investigate my practice. The rigor involved in attempting to articulate my ideas through the written word helps me to make sense of my teaching, my community, and myself.

Ena: I know that your current research interests revolve around issues of identity and language learning. So you're saying that you look at your publishing as a means of reflection or self-reflection—as a way of sorting through issues like these that are important to you?

Bonny: Yes, I think that moving from one place to another, one country to the next, has led me to question where I belong; how I can meet my different responsibilities as scholar, mother, teacher, daughter, friend; what contribution I can make to both my local and international community. Because I have worked with diverse groups of immigrants, younger and older, I have seen them grappling with similar issues. It was access to poststructuralist theory that liberated me from the desire to make my life coherent and reconcile my multiple identities. And it was a great relief to know that I did not have to abandon my history as I moved from place to place! Because such theory was so influential in my own life, I wondered to what extent it might be helpful in understanding the experiences of diverse language learners. When I saw how powerful the theory was in relation to my research, I wanted to share my insights with a larger community.

Ena: I guess publishing is one way that we communicate with others, especially in our field. It's a way of sharing our interests and our research findings. It's this open forum, however, that worries me! I know for myself, my fear of publishing stems from my fear of being revealed for the fraud that I am. After all, what makes me think I have anything of worth to say, let alone anything people would actually want to read about? Perhaps even more frightening, what happens if what I write is wrong? That is, what if someone well-respected in my field reads my work and feels compelled to respond to it only because they can't believe that someone would say such dumb things? Who knows? Maybe I'm being a bit too melodramatic, but these are the concerns I've been grappling with for a while. There are also a lot more basic concerns that prevent me from even getting anywhere near my fear of rejection and ultimate "exposure." For example, what do I write about? How do I write? Where do I write? There are so many questions I want to clear up.

Bonny: I'm not sure that all the questions you have will be cleared up. If the answers were simple, somebody would have retired early with a how-to book! Although I've learned a great deal through experience, I've found that learning to write for publication is an ongoing process, involving constant surprises. But I do understand how vulnerable you feel as a newcomer to the publishing community. Every time we enter new communities, whether they are publishing communities, sporting communities, or workplace communities, we take risks. We don't know how much of our history will be valued, and we are uncertain about the contribution we can make to the new community. And just when we think we have a handle on the community, it changes! The publishing community is no more stable than other communities: debates shift; editors come and go; editorial boards change. So how do we proceed, Ena?

Ena: I guess I'd like to start off with questions about the writing process, since that's where it all logically starts. Thinking about what to publish is probably the most difficult part of the process. Then I'd like to investigate more closely the contentious (at least for me) issues of authorship and ownership and the politics of publishing. I would think that publishing involves going through a certain amount of red tape. And finally, there are so many details about publication structure and even etiquette that, although mundane, seem important to ask …

Bonny: I also have some questions for you. What has been your experience of writing thus far in your career? It would be good to know your own particular history with research and collaboration. Could you fill me in as we go along?

FROM TERM PAPER TO PUBLICATION

Ena: Okay, well, so far, my writing experiences have been limited to term papers and other types of writing that students have to do for courses. But since the beginning of my graduate program, I've been told that whenever we have to write a paper for a course, we should approach the task as if it were potentially publishable. Talk about pressure. Most students have enough trouble writing term papers as it is without having now to worry about trying to get them published. This might explain, however, why, in most cases, we've been given the liberty to choose our own topics of research for term papers. In a small way, this freedom makes the challenge of writing that much more bearable. I'd like to think that I choose topics for term papers that I'm personally interested in learning more about; however, if I think about term papers as potential journal articles, then all of a sudden choosing a topic isn't just about what interests me. Perhaps my first question then is: When students write papers for courses, what is more important to consider: our own interests, publishers' interests, what's currently being researched in the field, or new innovations (which can be difficult)?[1]

Bonny: I am guilty of advising students to write a potentially publishable paper for their term papers. I do this because when I entered the PhD program at the Ontario Institute for Studies in Education (OISE) of the University of Toronto, I had already completed an undergraduate degree, an honors degree, and an MA degree, and I had spent many years agonizing about what my professors thought of me and my work. By the time I reached the PhD, I wanted to wean myself from dependence on the views of my professors. It wasn't that I didn't care what they thought, I simply wanted to enter into a healthier relationship with them. The only way I could do this was to widen the audience for my work: Instead of writing for my professors, I tried to write for a larger community. I saw each graduate course as a window on a different scholarly community within the larger field of language education, and as I read diverse texts from that community, I felt more comfortable about contributing to it. Clearly, the challenge was to see whether there was a match between my own interests and the interests of this community. When I encourage students to write a term paper that is potentially publishable, I'm trying to encourage students to think of themselves as members of larger scholarly communities, and I'd also like students to think about the possible contributions they can make to such communities.

Ena: Hmm … "members of larger scholarly communities" … I've always felt so overwhelmed by the whole concept of being a part of a scholarly community. You read so much throughout your academic studies, and although not all of it is absolutely profound, sometimes you read something that's just amazing. "Wow!", you know? And then you think, "I'll never be able to match that." It sets up almost impossibly high publishing standards in grad students' minds. Yeah, but then again, afterwards you'll read other articles that are NOT so great and you realize, "Oh. My mistake."

But seriously though, I assume that writing for a general audience is a lot different from writing for your professor or for yourself. Up to now, I've written term papers with a closed audience

---

[1]In an aside, though, are there such things as new innovations anyway? Pennycook (1996) argued that "language use is marked far more by the circulation and recirculation of words and ideas than by a constant process of creativity" (p. 207). He quoted Goethe, who said, "everything clever has already been thought; one must only try to think it again" (cited in Pennycook, 1996, p. 208).

in mind. I've depended on knowing that the professor has a pretty good grasp on what I'm writing about. That is, although writing clearly and concisely is never far from my mind during my writing process, I know that there is a certain amount of information that I don't need to touch on in my paper or include for reasons of brevity or redundancy. However, now that I have to worry about readers who may not come from the same field or have the same knowledge base as me, I wonder how I need to adapt my writing process. This relates to my next question: How does writing for publication differ from writing a term paper? For example, how much theoretical background or history do you need to give your readers in order to set up your current work? Does any of this depend on which journal you choose to submit to?

Bonny: To some extent, writing a term paper is not very different from writing for publication. Even if you have your professor in mind, you still need to make assumptions about what that professor does or doesn't know. In fact, most professors don't want you to make assumptions about what they know; they want to know if you, as the graduate student, are familiar with the literature the professor knows and whether you can integrate it with your own research. So when I wrote my term papers at graduate school, I tried not to rely on the professor's background knowledge. Instead, I always tried to link my experience with the broader literature—not only to gain a better understanding of my own work, but also to find out where the gaps in the literature might be. In general, I would identify one or two journals that might be interested in the topic of my term paper. Because each journal already has a broadly defined audience, I would write the term paper with this broadly defined audience in mind and provide as much background as I thought the average reader would need to have in order to make sense of my paper. Simple, eh?

WHICH JOURNAL?

Ena: Yeah, right. Easier said than done! Anyway, I see that you've touched on my next question about choosing journals for publication. I mean, there are so many different journals out there. Where does one begin? I doubt that in the publishing world, all journals are created equal. I think it goes without saying that if a journal is published with the same paper, format, or tone as the *National Enquirer* as opposed to in a more permanent (and more respectable, in some readers' opinions) bound form, we can safely assume that they are held up to different standards. That said, I guess the question is: How does one choose a journal to submit to? Or, alternatively, how does a journal choose you?

Bonny: On the question of the *National Enquirer*, you'd be interested to know that the research I've been doing with *Archie* comics is considered by some scholars as not "real" research because comics are deemed educationally undesirable. Not properly bound! It's been a bit of a battle to convince some colleagues that this is respectable research. So to gain legitimacy, I feel a need to have the research published in a journal that is particularly well-respected in the field. Much research, however, is not this contentious. The way I see it is that different journals represent different communities, and when I choose to submit my work to a particular journal, it's because it represents a community I would like to have some affiliation with. Because I enjoy being part of a variety of communities, I send different aspects of my work to different journals. For example, if I'm working on a project that has particular relevance to language education in Canada, I would submit my work to the *Canadian Modern Language Review* or the *TESL Canada Journal*. If I'm working on a project that may have broader relevance to the field of language education, I would submit my work to the *TESOL Quarterly*, *Applied Linguistics*, or the *Harvard Educational Review*. Clearly, whenever I choose a particular journal, I try to ensure that I am up to date with current issues in that journal and that I can link my work to existing debates.

Ena: That sounds pretty overwhelming. As much as I'd like to have my hands in as many cookie jars as possible, I'm intimidated enough about just getting into one journal, let alone a number at the same time! It sounds like there are so many publishing opportunities we can choose from, but for some reason, I always thought that for a graduate student, it would be next to impossible to get published because of stiff competition and incredibly high publishing standards. Because of this, I always fear that my work is destined to occupy the pages of only the most obscure journals in my field. And with the mantra publish or perish, I'm torn about whether this is a good or bad thing. I figure at some point, I'll just have to take what I can get; however, my question is: If your work is only being accepted and published in journals with limited distribution, is that bad? As they say, any publicity is good publicity, but when publishing is so crucial, to what degree should we be more concerned about quality versus quantity?

Bonny: An "obscure" journal to one person is very central to another, and I think all writing should reflect our very best efforts. I think that no matter where we publish our work, the quality should be never be in question. It may be that one publication turns out to be more significant than another, but I think every publication should reflect careful and meticulous scholarship. Having said this, I don't think every written contribution needs to be ground-breaking. There are many ways that both novice and established scholars can contribute to a field: Book reviews are central in many journals; forum pieces are important; "notes from the classroom" are welcome; published interviews are engaging. All of these contributions reflect a scholar's interest in and commit-ment to a field.

Ena: Interesting—I never thought about publishing in this way. I al-ways had this vision that because I'm a graduate student, I would need to prove myself through groundbreaking research, and it's this pressure to produce seminal work that has made me so ner-vous about publication. I must admit, I'm very relieved to hear that this isn't the case.

Bonny: But Ena, I expect you to produce seminal work!!

PHD THESIS TO BOOK

Ena: Umm ... let's just start with that "publishable term paper" and work from there, okay?! Anyway, Bonny, I understand that your book *Identity and Language Learning* (Norton, 2000a) is based on your doctoral thesis. I know that this sort of publishing (from a thesis to a book) has been done by many people. So I'm wondering, what is the process one goes through to pub-lish a thesis (either a master's or a PhD) into a book or into arti-cles? I know this is a broad question, but if most of what we write for a course should be geared towards publication, it only makes sense that your most ambitious research paper would be aimed for some degree of major publication. Also, related to this question, I've wondered about issues of recy-cling and reusing previously published work. I ask this ques-tion because a colleague and I have noticed that a particular prominent professor in an English as a second language (ESL) field turned his thesis into a seminal book. However, we have since noticed that many of his articles in different journals seem eerily similar to chapters of his book. This leads me to ask: Can you submit the same article to other journals even after it's been published somewhere else? Or do you have to re-work it to some degree first?

Bonny: As you suggest, Ena, it certainly makes sense to publish aspects of your PhD thesis in article or book form. Since PhD work is expected to make a contribution to a given field, it would be a waste not to seek publication in some form or other. The advice that was given to me was to publish different aspects of my thesis in the form of a number of refereed journal articles, and then, if there was interest in my work, rewrite the thesis as a book. The important point is that refereed journals seek work that has been previously unpublished, while publishers of books are somewhat less stringent. In fact, book publishers prefer to publish authors whose work has already been well-received by peers.

Sometimes, when I'm invited to write on a previously published topic for an edited collection of book chapters, I ask if I can submit a reprint. I do this not because I am unwilling to make changes to a previously published article, but because I don't want to pass off previously published work as original. For this reason, my practice is to keep the original title and text so that there can be no confusion in the reader's mind. Reprints, however, are often not considered desirable to publishers. As far as refereed journals are concerned, the accepted practice is that work that has been submitted for publication should not have been published elsewhere. Clearly, however, one project can have different facets to it and thus more than one publication associated with it. Each publication, however, would assume a distinct scholarly community and a different set of research questions, review of the literature, and analysis.

Ena: Okay, so there should be new angles to our research—looking at it through different lenses. Also, your answer reminds me of how important it is to think about the journal's potential audience when writing anything for publication. I guess a change in audience alone warrants reanalysis and a certain degree of rewriting of your research. Going back to the thesis-to-book question for a moment though, in trying to get our theses published, is there anything we can do—like make connections with editors or network with others in the field? That is, besides schmoozing like a pro, do you have any other suggestions for graduate students?

Bonny: I think that if you want to have your work taken up by a field, whether you wish to publish a thesis or write a journal article, it helps to show a certain commitment to the field. I am always amazed when people turn up at conferences, expecting a full house at their own presentations, but then spend the rest of the conference on the beach! I see the networking you talk about as an opportunity to share ideas and discuss issues relevant to the field. Presenting at conferences is an important part of this process. I think that if editors and publishers see that you have an active interest in the field, they are more likely to show an interest in your work. Sometimes, however, a publisher might consider the topic of your thesis alone sufficiently interesting to warrant publication, even if the author is not particularly active in the field.

OWNERSHIP OF WORK

Ena: Onto more political matters: So Bonny, if I produce a publishable thesis, and you supervise it, who "owns" it? Alternatively, if I help you on one of your research projects, can I claim to "own" at least some of it? This relates to an issue I've thought a lot about: authorship and ownership in publishing. The notions of authorship and ownership are especially important to me because of the high regard I have for intellectual integrity and my awareness of the debate around the concept of intellectual property.[2]

Bonny: Talk about a can of worms! This is such an important question, with few guidelines available. My colleagues and I sometimes talk about this issue in the "corridor chats" in our building, but it seems everybody has their own take on what is appropriate practice. I also think that acceptable practice differs from one field to another, and from one discipline to the next. I've come to the conclusion that one has to make decisions on a case-by-case basis and be creative in trying to meet the needs and investments of all parties. I am sensitive to the fact that there is an unequal relation of power between graduate students and their supervisors or principal investigators and that graduate students may be reluctant to raise the issue of ownership with faculty. So in my meetings with graduate students and research assistants, I always put publishing on the agenda and try to have a frank discussion of the issues. Some students welcome the opportunity for joint authorship be-

---

[2]I recognize that it has been argued that words and ideas cannot or should not be "owned." Miller (1990) argued against this commodification of language when he asserted, "words are shared assets, not personal belongings" (p. 79). Further, Pennycook (1996) asked, "in terms of what is understood as shared language or knowledge and particular language or knowledge: At what point does a phrase or an idea become owned? And at what point does it become public?" (p. 204).

cause they see this as part of the mentoring process; others prefer to take sole ownership of their particular contributions. I also recognize that although two people can set a particular agenda and define a set of expectations at the outset of a project, events may change in the process of data collection, analysis, and writing. During the course of a project, and particularly when preparing work for publication, I generally find it useful to revisit the original plan and determine if relative contributions have shifted.

Ena: There seem to be many complex issues involved in the ownership and publication of work, but there's also another issue: What about the way the work is read and interpreted by the larger community? Whenever I write a paper, it's obvious to the reader that I hold particular beliefs (usually strong) about what I'm researching. I'm not afraid to take very clear stances on issues. However, because of the nature of language itself and because published work is in the public domain, I would think that some people are inevitably going to misinterpret my beliefs or my work in general.[3] I know that misunderstandings happen all the time; however, I'm concerned about misunderstandings in such a public forum where people may start putting words into my mouth. What do you do when people misinterpret what you're trying to say?

Bonny: This is a very complex area. I know how disturbed I was when I read the *TESOL Quarterly* responses to my articles published in 1989 and 1995 (see Norton Peirce, 1989, 1995; see Dubois, 1990; Price, 1996). "How could the articles be read this way?" I asked myself. It should not have come as a surprise to me, however. In my own work (see Norton, 2000b; Norton & Stein, 2001; Norton Peirce, 1992), I've seen much evidence to the effect that the way an article is read may not necessarily be consistent with the way the author intended it to be read. Thus, in my view, the issue is not necessarily about misunderstanding, but about investment. Differ-

---

[3]I relate this possibility of misinterpretation to Bakhtin's (1986) notion of "heteroglossia":

> Heteroglossia ... is *another's speech in another's language*, serving to express authorial intentions but in a refracted way.... It serves two speakers at the same time and expresses simultaneously two different intentions: the direct intention of the character who is speaking, and the refracted intention of the author. In such discourse there are two voices, two meanings and two expressions. (p. 324)

Thus, words and utterances can carry many different meanings and interpretations depending on the context and the people involved. Every time the words are said, they have the possibility to take on entirely new meanings.

ent readers have diverse investments in a given text, and the way that they read the text is partly determined by their own histories, identities, and desires for the future. This is why Foucault (1979) talked of the death of the author. The larger question is one of meaning construction. Where does meaning originate? In the text, in the author, or in the interaction between reader, text, and author within a larger social context? The answer to this question depends to a large extent on which theories of meaning you consider most persuasive. It was from this perspective that I re-read the critiques and was thankful that I had been given the opportunity to elaborate on my research and theories.

I also got another nasty shock when I was doing some work on what I thought was an original idea: imagined communities. I had been working on the notion of resistance in language learning and had read some of Wenger's (1998) work on the role of imagination in learning. As I reflected on my data and his theories, I wondered to what extent language learner investments in what I called *imagined communities* were important in language learning. I was excited by this idea and wrote a paper on the topic (Norton, 2001). After the article was published and began to circulate, it was brought to my attention that Benedict Anderson (1983/1991) had written a whole book on imagined communities! Clearly, his context was very different from mine, but the notion of imagined communities was not as original as I had initially thought. After my initial embarrassment, I have found ways of incorporating Anderson's work into my research, and I've benefitted greatly from his insights.

JOINT AUTHORSHIPS

Ena: I think that to a certain degree, many, if not all, of the ideas we now hold have been shaped by those around us, especially in an academic setting. For example, whenever I write a term paper, I see so many different readings, professors, and colleagues reflected in my work.[4] If we relate this to the process of writing for

---

[4]Bakhtin (1981, 1986) has written extensively on the notion of language appropriation and "dialogization":

> Our speech, that is, all our utterances (including creative works), is filled with others' words, varying degrees of otherness or varying degrees of "our-own-ness," varying degrees of awareness and attachment. These words of others carry with them their own expression, their own evaluative tone, which we assimilate, rework, and re-accentuate. (1986, p. 89)

Currie (1998) further pointed out, "the intertextuality of discourse renders it difficult indeed for any writer to be the sole originator of his or her words or ideas" (p. 1), thus challenging the notions of textual authorship and ownership. (For an interesting analysis of how children appropriate language, see Lensmire & Beals, 1994.)

publication, the circumstances of joint authorship, and the notions of authorship and ownership, it leads me to ask this burning question: At what point does a person's contribution warrant joint authorship? For example, people thank others in the acknowledgments section of an article. To what degree these people aided in the writing process, I don't know. Perhaps it was with words of encouragement; perhaps it was in the initial development stages; perhaps it was in the editing process. No matter what these circumstances may be, though, I think it's important to ask: What is the quantifiable boundary (if there is one) between a thank you and joint authorship?

A related question is whether it's easier to get published by doing joint work with an established person (case in point). I acknowledge, however, that opportunities such as these don't appear every day for most graduate students. Perhaps then, the question I should be asking is: Does one have a better chance of being published writing a joint paper? Or, more broadly, what is the industry view on jointly authored work? I ask this question from personal experience as I've written many term papers with other school colleagues. I've always wondered, from a publishing point of view, are two heads really better than one?[5] I realize that joint authorship doesn't always result in a good writing experience (spoken from experience), but when it does, the writing process is so much more rewarding (also spoken from experience). No matter what the result of the joint authorship experience, however, one is left with some serious implications around issues of authorship and ownership.

Bonny: Let me deal with the simpler question first. I don't think it's necessarily easier to get your work published if you write with an established person. This may be the case for an edited collection of articles, but not for a refereed journal article. Refereed journal articles are generally blind reviewed (i.e., the author doesn't know the reviewer, and the reviewer—generally—does not know the author). The question of a quantifiable boundary between a thank you and joint ownership is far more challenging. If a student, for example, makes a unique contribution to a given project, is active in data analysis, and contributes to the writing of a paper, the student can expect to be a coauthor; if the student only transcribes or proofreads transcripts (difficult though this is!), the student may

---

[5]Roen and McNenny (1992), for example, seem to outline only negative attitudes toward jointly authored works in academia. In their arguments, adjectives such as "dishonourable and treasonable" (p. 2) and "suspicious" (p. 5) abound.

simply be acknowledged by the author. There are many grey areas between these two extremes, however, and these often need to be negotiated. On the question of thank you's, however, don't forget to acknowledge your funding sources!

One particularly successful example of how three of us resolved joint authorship challenges was the study on Levi Strauss that I undertook with Barbara Burnaby and Helen Harper while Helen and I were still graduate students at OISE (see Burnaby, Harper, & Norton Peirce, 1992; Norton Peirce, Harper, & Burnaby, 1993; Harper, Norton Peirce, & Burnaby, 1996). Barbara, a member of the faculty and principal investigator, had invited us to help her on a research project that investigated the workplace literacy practices at three Levi Strauss jeans factories in Canada. Helen and I did most of the data collection, but we met with Barbara on a regular basis. At the conclusion of the project, we produced three jointly authored publications. The first publication, in which Barbara was first author, described the study and summarized our central findings. The second article, with me as first author, provided a focus on second language learner issues in the three respective factories. The third article, with Helen as first author, focused on gender issues in literacy practices. All three researchers contributed to each of the three articles, but it was the first author who took on the major responsibility for writing, revising, and submitting the article for review.

CHALLENGES OF COLLABORATIVE RESEARCH

Ena: That sounds both fair and logical. I posed the question about authorship and ownership because I am currently grappling with my own dilemma about joint authorship. Three years ago, I coauthored a paper with another student in my class. We had similar research interests and held similar stances on educational issues. We decided that it would make sense to work together on a major term paper, and so our process of joint authorship began. Each of us would do some readings and then make sense of the issues through constant dialogue with each other. We would then put our ideas into writing by dialoguing all the way through the typing process, taking turns typing while the other played devil's advocate in the constructing of each and every sentence. It was a collaborative paper in every sense of the word.

Three years have passed and we remain good friends. We both continue to pursue graduate studies, but our research interests have since diverged from the original paper three years earlier. Although our general research interests remain the same, the major topic that once brought us together is no longer a common interest. I have since revised the paper so it now reflects my current interests. Some of the ideas are still recognizable from the original paper we wrote together; however, they have been modified, and new directions have been added. I have discussed issues of authorship and ownership with my colleague and we have agreed that we can use the original paper however we see fit; from an ethical standpoint, though, I am still torn. It would be nice to publish the paper as a sole author, but at the same time, I realize and admit that I wouldn't have had anything to revise or rework in the first place if it weren't for the ideas that my colleague and I originally developed together. The fate of the paper is still in limbo, in part because of this situation.

Bonny: I can understand your dilemma. When I was in graduate school, I had a slightly different experience, but one that also left me in a quandary. I developed a term paper that drew on my research with a practicing teacher. We each had a different perspective on and experience of the topic in question, and my term paper compared our two approaches. When it came to preparing the paper for publication, I thought the ethical approach would be to submit it as a joint authorship. My colleague was excited by this idea and offered to revise the paper so that his voice could be more appropriately represented. After many months and numerous reminders, no revision was forthcoming. The paper would have been stronger with my colleague's contribution, but I felt unable to speak on his behalf. I decided in the end to simply rewrite the paper, focusing on my work alone. It was a frustrating and time-consuming experience. Since then, I have approached collaborative research with greater care. Whereas collaborative research can be a pleasure, we all know it can cause tremendous hardship if different parties do not contribute actively to the project. Because research and writing is so time-consuming, I try to work with people who are responsible, creative, and not overly sensitive. A good sense of humor is a major plus!

THE REVISION PROCESS

Ena: No kidding! I think not being sensitive and having a good sense of humor will help with dealing with publication rejection as well. As a graduate student just starting my career in academic publishing, I expect rejection to be a huge part of my publishing experience (unfortunately). However, I need to know what rejection really means. When it comes to getting rejection letters from publishers, does rejection always mean that your attempts at publication are hopeless, or does it simply mean that you need to rework your paper from another perspective? How do you know whether it is the former or the latter situation? The optimist in me would like to think that the work just needs some fine-tuning; however, at the same time, I realize that fine-tuning may not always be enough. Therefore, I feel that it's also pertinent to ask how many times should you attempt to resubmit a piece to the same publisher or journal before figuring that, for one reason or another, it's just not going to be accepted? I don't ask this question to imply that all rejection letters are hints that you're just not cut out for this sort of thing; rather, I ask this because I realize that the revision process plays an important role in the scheme of publishing and that revising the paper could mean the difference between an acceptance letter and a rejection letter.

Bonny: I can say unequivocally that the review process is the most important practice in writing for publication. At the outset of this discussion, you expressed concern that you might write something that is "wrong," something that might heap scorn on you as a novice scholar. If there is a fair and thorough review process, most egregious errors would be identified at the review stage, prior to publication. I am always impressed by the meticulous care that has been taken in the review of articles I have published, and my publications have benefitted greatly as a result of careful and sympathetic reviews. I have found editors in the field of language education to be very supportive people who consider it part of their responsibility to encourage and mentor graduate student writing. Many academic conferences offer symposia in which editors discuss the mandates of their respective journals and offer advice on the submission process.

   Having said this, it is also true that different journals may value one kind of research over another. For example, qualitative research has, until recently, struggled for legitimacy. Furthermore, some controversial topics may invite critical reviews. However, if the author of a controversial paper defends her or his claims with careful analysis and thoughtful argument, there's a good chance that the paper will be published. Clearly, a great deal depends on the orientation of the editor and the willingness of the editor to take some degree of risk. It is important for authors to recognize that if a poorly researched and incoherently written article is published, the reputation of the editor, the journal, and, ultimately, the field suffers. On the other hand, if the editors reject a well-researched paper, simply because it challenges received wisdom in the field, the author is faced with a choice. The author can defend her or his views in a carefully written letter of rebuttal, or the author can submit the work elsewhere.

As to your specific question about the nature of the rejection you might receive: I think editors try to be as explicit as possible about journal expectations. Very few submissions are accepted "as is," and most papers require at least some revision before they are published. You may get a letter that says "accept with revisions." If you do the required revisions, the paper is generally sent to the same reviewers who initially reviewed the paper. If your revisions are satisfactory, your paper should be accepted for publication. You may, however, be asked to "revise and resubmit." In this case, you have a reasonable chance at publication, but the review process will be lengthier. If you receive a rejection letter, the editor may suggest other venues for the publication of your work.

When I receive a letter that says "accept with revisions," I am sometimes caught between contradictory advice from reviewers. One reviewer might say that a particular idea is not central to the paper and should be deleted; another reviewer might say that the idea is important and should be developed. I take each reviewer's comments very seriously and try to revise the paper with a view to improving its overall logic and coherence. Where I have followed the advice of one reviewer and not another, I explain this in a covering letter to the editor.

Ena: Okay, now that I understand that the review and revision processes are key steps in publishing, it brings up important issues for me that relate back to issues of authorship and ownership.[6] Although some revisions are expected to a certain degree, Brian Morgan (1997) raised the issue of more political types of revisions when he recounted his own experiences with the revision process. In a recent article, he talked about his own experiences publishing in an English language teaching journal and how he felt that many of his key theories and conclusions about issues of social justice and language teach-

---

[6]I think it is interesting and pertinent to point out that Scollon (1995) also questioned these notions in publishing when he called attention to the fact that

> by the time the public sees [his] article, other readers will have read it and made suggestions for editing. A single person has referred to himself as *I* throughout [the] article, and in doing so has taken responsibility for its positions.... But again, by the time the public sees it, the article will have involved other animators. (p. 13)

Thus, besides the potential political nature of the review and revision processes, it is the very processes themselves that call into question issues of sole authorship.

ing were trivialized in the editing process.[7] Taking his revision experiences into account, I'd like to know: What do you do when the suggested or mandated revisions don't remain true to what you're wanting to say (i.e., to what degree, if any, do you have to compromise or water down your original ideas?)? Do you ever have to fold under the demands of publishers just because publishing is so imperative?

Bonny: I'd like to think that I wouldn't compromise the central arguments in a paper just to get it published. I try to distinguish between what I think of as substantive and relatively minor changes to a text. While I am happy to compromise on relatively minor changes, I resist compromising on fundamental issues. However, I've come to realize that if what I say is controversial, I shouldn't expect a universally sympathetic audience. It's incumbent on me to provide much evidence to support my ideas and findings. In general, providing more evidence and tightening an argument strengthens rather than weakens a paper.

WHAT TITLE?

Ena: Bonny, I just have a few more questions about the more minute details of publication. First of all, how important is the title of your paper? I figure that it is the first thing people will read, and therefore I assume that one should give it some degree of thought.[8] I've read articles with the longest, most boring titles ever, and I seem to carry that impression with me while I read the article. On the other hand, when I read a title that seems to defy convention (i.e., like a successful ad slogan, it's snappy and catches my eye), this also seems to have an effect on my reading of the article. A fellow graduate student even told me once that what she chooses to read is almost entirely dependent on whether the article or book considered has a good title! (Talk about literally "judging a book by its cover.")

Bonny: I do think the title is a very important part of a paper, and I spend a good deal of time thinking of appropriate titles for my articles. In

---

[7]Morgan (1997) wrote, "to my mind, these edits seemed to be at some variance with the staff editors' claims that they were only concerned with 'sentence structure' and to 'make my work clearer'" (p. 23); however, he would later qualify that he did not necessarily believe that this was a deliberate effort to alter his ideas.

[8]Morgan (1997) pointed out that "titles, layouts, fonts, and highlighted quotes ... are not entirely neutral in formulating a superficial impression of an article" (p. 25).

fact, as I plan the publications for a given research project, I find experimenting with titles a very helpful way of trying to consider the project from different angles. I remember how devastated I was when the title of my very first publication (Norton Peirce, 1989) was changed without my knowledge. I had wanted the article to make a general argument about the need to rethink notions of communicative competence in the teaching of English internationally, and it was my first attempt to bring poststructuralist theory to the field of ESL. To strengthen my arguments, I drew on research in South Africa. My original title was "Toward a Pedagogy of Possibility in the Teaching of English Internationally." This was already a long title, and, in retrospect, I could have reworded it "Power and Possibility in Teaching English Internationally." When the journal arrived at my home, I opened it with great excitement only to find the following title: "Toward a Pedagogy of Possibility in the Teaching of English Internationally: People's English in South Africa." Not only was the title a very long one, but I was convinced that the focus of the article had shifted from a more general argument about the politics of teaching English internationally, to a focus on the teaching of English in South Africa.

WHAT'S IN A NAME?

Ena: On another note, I've read a bit of your work and have wondered about the varying forms of the name you have chosen to use in each of your publications. Peirce, Norton Peirce, Norton—I'm sure there is some significance to this, and I'm curious to find out more about this: What is the significance (if any) of the names we use when we publish? Are there any implications for the names that we choose to write under?

Bonny: I can't really speak for others, Ena, but I can tell you that my name has given me a few sleepless nights. And I often wonder if other female academics have had similar experiences. I certainly doubt that Chris Candlin or Jim Cummins has agonized about his name! But I'm getting ahead of myself. For a number of complex reasons, I added my partner's name (Peirce) to my name when we got married. Norton, my original surname, became a middle name. At first, I thought it wouldn't be a problem in publishing, thinking of people like Shirley Brice Heath as role models. However, because of the way that a person's work is referenced, the name Norton seemed to have less and less significance. As a feminist, I was in a quandary. Apart from which, copyeditors kept changing Peirce to Pierce! After much agonizing, I decided to go through the whole bureaucratic process of dropping Peirce from my name. Although some people warned me that this was professionally risky because the scope of my research would be lost, I figured that I'm the only person who has my life to live. Further, the changing nature of identity is central to my work—and I'm living proof!

During the process of dropping Peirce from my name, I discovered at the passport office that I could choose any middle name I liked. So, Peirce is now a middle name and I've regained Norton as a surname (though my children did ask me if I was still a member of the family!). By the time I did this, I had published many articles and book chapters under Peirce, and I reference these as Norton Peirce in an attempt to inform readers that we are one and the same person (but with multiple identities!).

PUBLISHING ON PUBLISHING

Ena: Well, Bonny, this discussion has clarified a lot of issues about publishing for me, and I'm glad (and pleasantly surprised!) to say that it has really quelled a lot of my fears as a graduate student embarking on the next level of my academic career. Although I can attribute this change as due partly to the content of our conversation here, I have to admit that, for the most part, it's due to the very writing process I went through for this paper.

It's interesting that you mentioned the notion of academic "legitimacy." You talked earlier about how you had a hard time convincing people that your research on *Archie* comics was really research. Ironically, I was wondering whether we'll have to do the same for this paper.[9] After all, looking at the "academic" articles and books that I've read, none of them read like the way we've written this chapter. To say that it's unorthodox would be an understatement. However, I'm glad that we decided to maintain the conversational tone throughout the text. I think this experience has really helped me to reflect on what publishing is all about—and to me, it seems that it's about finding my own voice. I guess this is what you meant when you talked earlier about issues of identity and publishing. Here I thought that academia and publishing was all about theories and other "serious" stuff. Who

---

[9]Academic researching and reporting against the grain is what Canagarajah (1996) focuses on in his thought-provoking article. He advocates "energetic experimentation with alternate forms of research reporting that would better reflect our emerging realizations on the nature of research and knowledge production" (p. 321).

knew that "academic" writing could actually be enjoyable? Having fun publishing—that's allowed, right?

Bonny: Yes, if I didn't find writing enjoyable, I doubt that it would be worth all the time and energy. Just think how many drafts of this chapter we have written, Ena! And I think what you say about finding your own voice is crucial. This IS serious stuff!

ACKNOWLEDGMENT

We gratefully acknowledge financial support from a UBC–HSS grant and a Social Sciences and Humanities Research Council of Canada grant.

REFERENCES

Anderson, B. (1991). *Imagined communities.* London and New York: Verso. (Original work published 1983)

Bakhtin, M. (1981). *The dialogic imagination.* Austin, TX: University of Texas Press.

Bakhtin, M. (1986). *Speech genres and other late essays.* Austin, TX: University of Texas Press.

Burnaby, B., Harper, H., & Norton Peirce. B. (1992). English in the workplace: An employer's concerns. In B. Burnaby & A. Cumming (Eds.), *Sociopolitical aspects of ESL education in Canada* (pp. 304–329). Toronto, Ontario, Canada: OISE Press.

Canagarajah, A. S. (1996). From critical research practice to critical research reporting. *TESOL Quarterly, 30*(2), 321–331.

Currie, P. (1998). Staying out of trouble: Apparent plagiarism and academic survival. *Journal of Second Language Writing, 7*(1), 1–18.

Dubois, B. L. (1990). Comments on Bronwyn Norton Peirce's "Toward a pedagogy of possibility in the teaching of English internationally: People's English in South Africa." A reader reacts. *TESOL Quarterly, 24*(1), 103–104.

Foucault, M. (1979). What is an author? (Kari Hanet, Trans.). *Screen, 20*(1), 13–33.

Goethe, J. W. (1963). *Maximen and reflexionen.* München, Germany: Deutscher Taschenbuch Verlag. (Original work published 1829)

Harper, H., Norton Peirce, B., & Burnaby, B. (1996). English for garment workers: A feminist project? *Gender and Education, 8*(1), 5–19.

Lensmire, T. J., & Beals, D. E. (1994). Appropriating others' words: Traces of literature and peer culture in a third-grader's writing. *Language in Society, 23,* 411–426.

Miller, K. D. (1990). Composing Martin Luther King. *Publications of the Modern Language Association of America, 105*(1), 70–82.

Morgan, B. (1997). The politics of publishing: Positioning critical voices in an ELT journal. *College ESL, 7*(1), 14–31.

Norton, B. (2000a). *Identity and language learning: Gender, ethnicity and educational change.* Harlow, England: Longman/Pearson Education.

Norton, B. (2000b). Writing assessment: Language, meaning, and marking memo-
    randa. In A. Kunnan (Ed.), *Fairness and validation in language assessment* (pp.
    20–29). Cambridge, England: Cambridge University Press.
Norton, B. (2001). Non-participation, imagined communities, and the language class-
    room. In M. Breen (Ed.), *Learner contributions to language learning: New direc-
    tions in research* (pp. 159–171). Harlow, England: Longman/Pearson Education.
Norton, B., & Stein, P. (2001). Why the "Monkeys Passage" bombed: Tests, genres,
    and teaching. In S. Beck & L. Olah, Perspectives on language and literacy: Be-
    yond the here and now. *Harvard Educational Review Reprint Series, 35,*
    419–434. [Reprinted from Why the "Monkeys Passage" bombed: Tests, genres,
    and teaching, pp. 50–65, by B. Norton Peirce & P. Stein, 1995, *Harvard Educa-
    tional Review, 65*(1).]
Norton Peirce, B. (1989). Toward a pedagogy of possibility in the teaching of English
    internationally: People's English in South Africa. *TESOL Quarterly, 23*(3),
    401–420.
Norton Peirce, B. (1992). Demystifying the TOEFL reading test. *TESOL Quarterly,
    26*(4), 665–689.
Norton Peirce, B. (1995). Social identity, investment, and language learning. *TESOL
    Quarterly, 29*(1), 9–31.
Norton Peirce, B., Harper, H., & Burnaby, B. (1993). Workplace ESL at Levi Strauss:
    "Dropouts" speak out. *TESL Canada Journal, 10*(2), 9–30.
Pennycook, A. (1996). Borrowing others' words: Text, ownership, memory, and
    plagiarism. *TESOL Quarterly, 30*(2), 201–230.
Price, S. (1996). Comments on Bonny Norton Peirce's "Social identity, investment,
    and language learning": A reader reacts. *TESOL Quarterly, 30*(2), 331–337.
Roen, D. H., & McNenny, G. (1992, March). *Collaboration as plagiarism: Cheating is
    in the eye of the beholder.* Paper presented at the Annual Meeting of the Confer-
    ence on College Composition and Communication, Cincinnati, Ohio.
Scollon, R. (1995). Plagiarism and ideology: Identity in intercultural discourse. *Lan-
    guage in Society, 24,* 1–28.
Wenger, E. (1998). *Communities of practice: Learning, meaning, and identity.*
    Cambridge, England: Cambridge University Press.

3

Coming to Voice: Publishing as a Graduate Student

Paul Kei Matsuda
University of New Hampshire

In December 1998, I was attending the Modern Language Association conference in San Francisco. I sat in the back of a crowded room where presenters were using literary theories in contemplating the depleted academic job market. Although they were talking mostly about literary fields—the market seemed far from depleted for composition specialists and applied linguists—I decided to let myself be amused by a prominent literary scholar's psychoanalytic reading of how her own experience of being on the job market was akin to being castrated. Another speaker argued that early professionalization had become the norm, allowing institutions to expect more from graduate students without also increasing compensation. He also suggested that the pressure to publish was taking time away from graduate students who should be reading more widely.

"Let them be students" was the message.

I didn't like what I was hearing. I didn't like it because it reduced academic publishing to mere production of intellectual capital. I didn't like it because it placed the blame on hard-working graduate students rather than on the institutional practices that exploited knowledge workers. I didn't like it because it assumed that those who professionalize early do not read widely. I didn't like it because it suggested that being a graduate student somehow precluded me from being a professional.

"Too late," I thought. I had already published two refereed journal articles, and I wasn't about to yank back those forthcoming articles and book chapters. By the time I left Purdue with my PhD in August 2000, I had six journal articles in print in addition to a number of forthcoming works, including articles and book chapters as well as two coedited books.

Why did I try to publish so much while still in graduate school? It was not really the pressure of the job market or the anxiety over the tenure process. To me there were other more important reasons for publishing. My drive to publish had to do mostly with what I wanted to do *to* the profession as well as *in* the profession. Publishing, to a large extent, was a means to an end; it was a way of reaching out to a wider audience in order to make a difference. As a former English as a second language (ESL) student who learned to write in U.S. higher education and as a non-native-English-speaking (NNES) graduate student who strived to grow as a professional in fields that had traditionally been dominated by native English speakers, I felt the need to contribute my voice to the profession.

Of course my attitude toward publication was not always this way. Nor was it typical, as I was reminded when another graduate student invited me to collaborate with him on a project while I was finishing my dissertation at Purdue. As we began to develop ideas, I felt the need to clarify our goals in collaborating on the project.

"Let's think about what we are trying to accomplish here—why do we want to do this project?" I asked.

"Uh, a vita line?" he said.

"I mean, what do we want our presentation to do? What do we want to contribute to the field?"

"I don't know. You tell me."

I wanted to smack him, but then I realized I was just like him when I first became a graduate student. I wanted to publish because that was what scholars were supposed to do. I wanted to publish for the sake of publishing.

A (NOT SO) HUMBLE BEGINNING

When I began my MA studies at Miami University of Ohio in August 1993, I already "knew" publishing was for me. I had just received my BA in communication with a journalism emphasis. I also had five writing-intensive courses and a dozen writing-related courses on my transcripts. I regularly published news and feature articles in the college newspaper—many of which I had written for my journalism classes. In addition, I had 4 years of experience as a writing tutor, and two of my short essays on tutoring ESL writing had become required readings for the tutoring practicum. So when I started working on the major paper in my first graduate seminar, Theory and History of Composition and Rhetoric, there was no question in my mind that I would submit it to a journal at the end of the semester. Even before I had decided on a topic, I asked Bob Johnson, my teacher for the seminar, to comment on my paper with the possibility of publication in mind.

I have to admit, however, that the thought of writing a 20-page paper seemed a bit daunting—I had never written anything longer than 8 pages as an undergrad. I remember discussing the length issue with a classmate, a doctoral student, in the stairwell of Bachelor Hall. When I lamented that 20 pages seemed like a lot to write, he replied that 20 was barely enough for him to say what he wanted to say. I stared at him with the mixed look of admiration and disbelief. He thought of the length requirement as a constraint; in contrast, I was still tweaking fonts and margins to make my paper look longer. I wondered whether I would ever be able to say something like that.

The length was certainly intimidating, but even more frightening was the amount of reading I would have to do just to find a suitable topic. I didn't know enough about the field to identify important issues, much less to contribute new knowledge. I didn't even fully understand what constituted a significant contribution except that it had to be new, original, and interesting—just like those news stories I used to write. Had someone asked me, "Why do you want to do this project?" I would probably have said, "Because I want to publish." (I wouldn't have said "a vita line" because the concept of an academic vita had not entered my consciousness yet; it was not until the beginning of my second year in the MA program that I began to develop my vita, which consisted of only one page.) I wanted to publish articles just because that was what scholars were supposed to do. Publishing was the goal in and of itself.

With the same kind of journalistic zeal that had contributed to my success as an undergraduate student, I went into the library, searching for a "scoop." With the same kind of persistence and thoroughness that I was taught to practice in an investigative reporting class, I went through all the journals I could find that had anything to do with writing. What I discovered was that the field of composition and rhetoric was a vast territory. Amidst the days of struggle, I went to a bookstore in Cincinnati to take a break and found Andrea Lunsford's 1992 essay, "Rhetoric and Composition" in *Introduction to Scholarship in Modern Languages and Literatures* (Gibaldi, 1992). In a desperate attempt to understand the scope of the field and to find a place for me, I bought the book and made a copy of Lunsford's bibliography to check off those books and articles I had already read. I was pleased that I was able to check off quite a few of them; I was determined to read everything else in the bibliography before I left Miami University with my degree.

As I explored the field, I ran across a few articles that particularly piqued my interest in composition journals such as the *Journal of Basic Writing* and *The Writing Instructor*. They were articles on ESL writing by Ann Raimes (1986) and Vivian Zamel (1990); their articles resonated well with my frustration with what seemed to me at that time to be an overemphasis on sentence-level error correction in many ESL writing classes. At the same time, I was troubled by my fascination with ESL writing. I already seemed to know a lot about the topic from my experience both as an ESL writer and as a writing tutor for both native and nonnative English speakers, but I wanted to find something that didn't have anything to do with ESL. I didn't want people to think that I was interested in the topic just because of my background as a nonnative speaker of English. I thought it would draw too much attention to the part of my identity that could put me at a disadvantage in the profession. I also feared that it might be seen as an easy way out—something a real scholar wouldn't do.

Yet I was not able to find other topics that intrigued me as much, and Thanksgiving break—which I was planning to devote to my seminar papers—was quickly approaching. In the interest of time, I reluctantly decided to write a paper on ESL writing "just this time," thinking that I would find myself a real field of specialization over the winter break. I went back to the library, where I spent many hours looking through the pages of *TESOL Quarterly* and *Language Learning*. I searched for and checked out all the books that had anything to do with ESL writing, including *Writing Across Languages and Cultures* (Connor & Kaplan, 1987), *Writing Across Languages* (Purves, 1988), *Richness in Writing* (Johnson & Roen, 1989), and *Coherence in Writing* (Connor & Johns, 1990). At the recommendation of Kim Murray, a doctoral student who had taken a course in ESL writing at her MA institution, I ordered *Second Language Writing* (Kroll, 1990) through the campus bookstore. Looking at a growing number of books neatly lined up on my bookshelf, I was beginning to realize that second language writing was evolving into its own field of study.

Among various topics in second language writing, one that caught my attention the most was the notion of contrastive rhetoric. Even as an undergraduate student, I had been exposed to Bob Kaplan's (1966) diagrams of "cultural thought patterns" several times. I had seen them in some books on cross-cultural communication (e.g., Singer, 1987). I had attended a talk where the guest speaker displayed Kaplan's "doodles" before presenting her study of differences between Japanese and English business letters. It also came up in a conversation with one of the teachers at the English Language Institute, who mentioned that Bobbie Stokes, one of my mentors at the writing lab, might have a copy of the original article. When I asked Bobbie about it, she said I should be careful with it because it had been critiqued. "Sure," I said, but I had no idea what it was all about.

After all the readings I did for the seminar paper, I finally understood what Bobbie meant. The notion of contrastive rhetoric had been hotly contested from various perspectives, and the field had gone through many important changes as a result. Even then, there seemed to be some truth to the notion that some ESL writers organized their texts in ways that deviated markedly from the way native English speakers would in a similar situation. In fact, I was tutoring a Japanese student that semester whose paper seemed to follow the *ki-shoo-ten-ketsu* pattern of organization, which John Hinds had documented in a series of articles (1983, 1987, 1990). With the permission of the Japanese student, I decided to write about the issue of teaching organization to ESL students.

In that seminar paper, I considered the extent to which the transfer of "rhetorical structures" occurred in the Japanese student's texts and proposed the discussion of possible rhetorical transfer as a step in the revision process. Using a case study approach, I described how the student and I noticed the need to work on the organization of her paper, how we discussed the organization of the text, and why it might have been confusing to the native-English-speaking teacher. I included the comments and scores the teacher provided for each draft to show how her original draft was considered to be lacking in organization and how the focused revision improved coherence in the teacher's eyes. I also discussed how it was important for the discussion of organizational structures to take place in the process of revision rather than at the beginning of the writing process so as to avoid prescription and appropriation.

The project was helpful for me as a writing tutor because it gave me some insights into the frustration my student and I experienced as we tried to figure out what the problem was that made her text "unacceptable" to some native-English-speaking readers. It was a solid pedagogical application of insights from contrastive rhetoric research; it was also a good example of action research. Most important of all, I didn't overgeneralize. But I didn't feel I was ready to publish it because of many issues and controversies that surrounded the notion of contrastive rhetoric. That is, I didn't feel I had read widely enough to know all the arguments for and against the notion and to anticipate possible responses from my audience. In addition, I didn't have a specific audience in mind; if anybody, I was my own audience. The seminar paper certainly helped me develop some insights that seemed helpful to me, but I didn't know whether it was news to the field.

A DOG ON THE INTERNET

These realizations—realizations more profound than those I discovered through my seminar paper project itself—came to me partly because of my involvement in TESL-L, an e-mail discussion list for professionals in the field of teaching English to speakers of other languages (TESOL). Through my participation in this list, I learned many things—including what it means to be a member of an academic field. This experience was especially important because I was working in relative isolation. Although Miami University had a community of graduate students in its strong master's and doctoral programs in composition and rhetoric, I was the only graduate student who was interested in contrastive rhetoric or second language writing. The fact that my first real interactions with people in my field were through an e-mail list rather than through print publications turned out to be very helpful, because the interactive nature of the list helped me become keenly aware of my audience and their expectations as well as my own construction of a discursive self in relation to them.

As I was typing away many of my postings—some of which were surprisingly well-informed for a first-year MA student, others of which were naive at best, if not totally wrong-headed—I sometimes thought of the legendary cartoon in *The New Yorker* that depicted a dog sitting at the computer, saying to another dog, "On the Internet, no one knows we are dogs." That's right. No one had to know I was "just a graduate student." I carefully crafted my postings so as not to give away the part of my "autobiographical self" (Ivanič, 1997, p. 23) as a young graduate student, although I am certain that it came through in my discursive voice from time to time. For example, my "signature" at the bottom of the screen simply read:

```
Paul Kei Matsuda
Miami University
pkmatsud@miavx1.muohio.edu
Perfection is not my goal; effectiveness is.
```

The signature included my name, institutional affiliation, and email address but nothing about my status as a graduate student. I had seen some graduate students identify themselves as "MA TESOL" or "PhD Candidate in Applied Linguistics," but I chose not to. I added the slogan at the end partly because that was the sum of what I tried to convey in many of my contributions in the discussion of writing and teaching, but I also used it as a way of deflecting some annoying flames that pointed out my "nonnative errors" in an attempt to discredit my arguments and possibly to undermine NNES professionals in general. For instance, someone made a big fuss about my misspelling of "pronunciation" as "pronounciation," which was what prompted me to use that slogan.

Instead of talking about my institutional "rank" as a graduate student, I learned to foreground my own background as an ESL writer as well as my work with other ESL writers as the main source of my ethos, which I continue to use in some of my publications. In other words, I learned to use discourse as a way of constructing my professional identity and of building my credibility as a writer (or of concealing the lack thereof). I was active, assertive, and authoritative. On the screen, my discursive voice must have painted the image of me as a competent scholar–teacher with many, many years of experience (whether people bought into it or not is another matter); at the computer desk in my one-bedroom apartment, however, I was an insecure MA student desperately trying to impress other people on the list, hoping that no one would find out I was actually a dog.

Insecure was I. One day, I found a personal e-mail message in my inbox. It was from another TESL-L member who found my postings "insightful" and wanted to collaborate with me on a research project. What did I do? I freaked out. How could I—a first-year MA student with no experience in research or publication—collaborate with a "professor" at another university? Not knowing how to respond without revealing my insecurity—or, worse yet, incompetence—I deleted the message without responding. (If you are reading this chapter, my profound apology.) Now that I think of it, I probably could have collaborated with him fruitfully, but I wasn't ready. I might have been talking like a professional, but I was still thinking like a graduate student.

DISCOVERING THE AUDIENCE

Partly because of my assertiveness in my TESL-L postings, I sometimes got myself into heated debates with other people who had strong feelings about certain topics—a mistake many novice listserv users make. One of the most intense and prolonged discussions I was engaged in through TESL-L was on the topic of contrastive rhetoric. After discussing my ideas with others on the list, I came to realize that there were strong, even emotional oppositions to the notion of contrastive rhetoric among ESL teachers and researchers.

Using my own personal experience as an ESL writer as well as my experience in working with other ESL writers in my arsenal, I tried to argue that *ki-shoo-ten-ketsu* was not just a fantasy created by ethnocentric native-English-speaking readers, as some people seemed to be arguing. In fact, I was explicitly taught to use it by one of my elementary school teachers, my parents, and some of the popular writing handbooks in Japan. This organizational scheme was also apparent, I thought, in some student texts that I encountered in my work as a tutor.

But some people just wouldn't let me have it. Any evidence I presented—from John Hinds's articles and quotes from Japanese writing handbooks to my own analyses of student essays and anecdotal sightings of *ki-shoo-ten-ketsu* in literary essays and cartoons—they denied without offering any counterevidence. I was frustrated because people seemed to accept negative arguments more readily than they were willing to consider positive arguments. Their argument, it seemed to me, was just this: It's been critiqued, therefore it's completely wrong. I was, according to them, just imagining it or imposing my expectation as a "researcher" on the texts that I analyzed.

What bothered me was that some people dismissed *ki-shoo-ten-ketsu* completely as if it did not exist. I did realize that it was not the only way Japanese writers organized their texts, nor was it a typical organization for academic texts. I was even aware of a popular writing handbook that denounced *ki-shoo-ten-ketsu* as a useful organization scheme for academic writing (Sawada, 1977). But I wanted them to acknowledge that it was one of the ways in which some Japanese ESL writers—especially inexperienced writers—might organize their texts because of their explicit or implicit exposure to it. (In fact, Sawada's denouncement seems to suggest that many novice academic writers do use *ki-shoo-ten-ketsu*.) It also bothered me that I seemed to be the only native Japanese speaker on TESL-L participating in the discussion.

My argument grew stronger as I received encouragement from contrastive rhetoric enthusiasts who sent personal e-mail messages asking me to "keep going." But no matter what I did, some people responded by saying "you are just imposing your expectations." I was so frustrated that I ended up arguing my case more strongly than I should have. In fact, John Hinds himself e-mailed me personally—which really took me by surprise—and said that I was "doing a disservice by making it seem more pervasive than it was."

He was right. I realized that I was succumbing to the vicious circle of dichotomous oppositions; the stronger my argument, the more resistance I felt, which led me to respond even more strenuously. As a result of this discussion, I became aware of the importance of seriously engaging with—not just acknowledging—various views and of forming a balanced perspective. I also felt the need to contextualize my claims more to reduce the risk of being misinterpreted. In addition, this experience helped me realize that authors and readers are living human beings and that I need to be fair and respectful when I represent them in my texts (this is not to say that I wasn't being respectful)—just as students deserve to be treated fairly and respectfully in the research literature.

By then, it was apparent to me that TESL-L was too restrictive for the kind of serious and extended discussion I wanted to have. The postings were supposed to be limited to two screens, and follow-up clarifications were discouraged in order not to clutter people's inboxes; what I thought were the unique advantages of e-mail lists—flexibility, spontaneity and interactivity—were no longer available. I needed to find another site of discursive practices where I would be able to write longer texts replete with all the supports and qualifications to present, justify, and defend my perspective. I needed to write journal articles.

READING, READING, AND READING TO WRITE

But my very first seminar paper was not it. After that TESL-L discussion, I decided not to send it out because I didn't feel I had developed the ability to judge my own work critically enough on this controversial topic. As I look back to this experience, I am glad I didn't send it out. I had heard some senior scholars warn younger members of the profession against rushing into print, and had I been successful in placing that article somewhere, it would have been a perfect example of what not to do. I still do think it was a strong material (yeah, of course), but it was not nuanced enough; I hadn't read widely enough on the topic to anticipate and re-spond to all the critiques that could have been raised.

In order to prepare myself for future publications (and especially to de-velop more nuanced arguments), I decided to read everything that had been published on the topic of contrastive rhetoric and second language writing. I went to the library and searched through the online catalog as well as indexes such as ERIC and MLA databases. I spent many hours in the periodicals stacks browsing through *College Composition and Com-munication*, *ELT Journal*, *Journal of Basic Writing*, *Language Learning*, *TESOL Quarterly*, *The Writing Instructor*, *Written Communication*, and many other journals that seemed relevant, looking for any article that had to do with contrastive rhetoric or second language writing.

After I collected the articles, I put each of them in a manila folder. Un-able to decide whether I should sort them by date, author, or title, I spent many a night shuffling through the growing pile of manila folders, rear-ranging them again and again. This seemed like a waste of time at first, but it helped me familiarize myself with the trends in the field and to see publi-cations in their historical contexts, which prepared me well for my histori-cal work. After going through this process so many times, I finally settled for alphabetical order by author. (I later discovered that Tony Silva, my dis-sertation advisor and collaborator on many projects, had gone through a similar process of acquiring everything in the field, although he had orga-nized his files chronologically.)

I devoted a small bookshelf just to books on L2 writing, arranged by publi-cation date, as well as other to-be-filed articles and documents on the sub-ject. I also replaced all the L2 writing books from the library with my own copies. When I found out about the *Journal of Second Language Writing* (*JSLW*) through an article in *College Composition and Communication* (Harris & Silva, 1993), I wrote Tony and asked for subscription information. When the subscription form arrived, I ordered the journal immediately and, once satisfied with the quality, bought all the back issues and put them on my L2 writing bookshelf. I had heard LuMing Mao, my MA thesis advisor, de-scribe the *Journal of Pragmatics* as his "home base"; I decided to make the *JSLW* my home base. Building a professional library turned out to be an im-portant part of my preparation for academic publishing. It made a world of difference when I had all the materials I needed within my reach.

Because I had accumulated so many books and articles on second language writing and contrastive rhetoric, I decided to write my mas-ter's thesis on the historical development of contrastive rhetoric (Matsuda, 1995), focusing on how it came to be appropriated as a re-search agenda rather than as a pedagogical theory, as Bob Kaplan origi-nally called for. In it, I traced the origin of the notion of contrastive rhetoric to its theoretical antecedents in both composition studies and applied linguistics and explained how it was a significant step away from the exclusive focus on sentence-level concerns in L2 writing instruction. I then discussed how contrastive rhetoric departed from the original pedagogical exigency to grow into a research agenda of its own, and argued the need for a pedagogical theory of contrastive rhetoric to bridge the gap between research and instruction.

I began my MA thesis project with the possibility of publication in mind, but I wasn't sure what kind of publication. When I told some of my committee members, however, they didn't seem enthusiastic. I was told that this goal would make my task more difficult because the demands of publishers and reviewers are often different from the expectations of the committee members. I didn't fully understand the significance of their concerns at the time, but I decided to do as I was told.

A GRADUATE STUDENT WRITING A THEORY

At my thesis defense, Paul Anderson, one of my committee members, asked me, "So, Paul, are you going to come up with a theory that you argue for in your thesis?" I smiled, hoping that he wouldn't ask me to do it before he signed the approval form. I didn't think I was up to the challenge. The thought of constructing a theory—theory not in the sense of empirical theory-building but discursive theorizing—frightened me. From my readings, I had the impression that theory and history were something that only older, more established scholars did. I thought I was daring enough to be doing a historical study. I couldn't possibly do theory when I was just a 24-year-old MA student. Even if I did, I was convinced that no one would take me seriously. After all, I was young and unpublished. I was just a graduate student.

For some reason, it didn't occur to me at the time that there were ways of establishing my credibility other than being old, widely published, or a professor. I didn't fully realize that I could establish my ethos by demonstrating my broad knowledge of the subject or by constructing arguments carefully and thoughtfully, anticipating and responding to various questions and critiques that might be raised by the readers—the kind of skills I had already developed to some extent through my participation in TESL-L. Still smiling, I replied to Paul, "Well, eventually," hoping that he wouldn't pursue the idea any further. I was rescued by the laughter of other committee members.

But Paul's question stuck with me. I ultimately did muster the courage to articulate a pedagogical theory in my project for Tony Silva's seminar on second language writing, which I took during my first semester of PhD coursework at Purdue in 1995. This project resulted in my first refereed journal article, "Contrastive Rhetoric in Context: A Dynamic Model of L2 Writing" (Matsuda, 1997), but my fear that a young graduate student is not in the position to construct a worthwhile theory crept into it. My goal in that article was to articulate two pedagogical theories of contrastive rhetoric—a static theory that seemed to inform existing attempts to apply insights from

contrastive rhetoric and a dynamic theory that would account for the negotiation of various linguistic, cultural, and educational backgrounds through
the process of writing. I used the term *theory* to describe the static theory,
which was not my own but a reconstruction of what seemed to underlie the
popular and somewhat uncritical attempt at applying contrastive rhetoric to
pedagogy. For the alternative pedagogical theory that I proposed, which incorporated various existing theories and research insights, I hesitated to use
the term *theory* and used *model* instead.

Even after it was published, it took me a while before I was able to admit
that it was my attempt at constructing a theory. Rereading Susan Miller's
essay, "Writing Theory : : Theory Writing," helped me understand my
sense of inadequacy and gave me some confidence:

> This stultifying thinking is legendary: "Theory" is written by the smart for the
> smart. "Theory" is too abstract and general to have much to do with actual
> writing practices that can be investigated with more concrete research
> methods, or with the act of teaching students to engage in and analyze these
> practices. A good theory must be a magnificent machine, a system applica-
> ble to explaining and predicting everything. "Theory" is written by (great,
> White) patriarchs, or their textual equivalents. "Theory" is, finally, simulta-
> neously too exciting and too boring to claim as our own. (Miller, 1992, p. 62)

I was further encouraged to find out that my first article was well received—several people have told me that they have used it in the graduate
courses they teach, and it has been cited in a few books and articles. When
Tony and I decided to include it in *Landmark Essays on ESL Writing* (Silva
& Matsuda, 2001), I was finally able to characterize it as an integrative theory of second language writing (Matsuda & Silva, 2001, pp. xx–xxi).

CHALLENGES TO THINKING LIKE A PROFESSIONAL

After the success of the first publication, I felt like a different person, but I
didn't know how to describe it at the time. I remember saying something
like "I feel as if I have just upgraded the operation system." Now I think of
that moment as a point when I was able to stop thinking like a graduate
student and to start thinking like a professional. I continued to write all my
seminar papers with the goal of publication in mind, but my motivation
had changed. My goal was no longer just to publish but to respond to the
conflicts, gaps, and discrepancies I perceived in the professional literature
by contributing my perspective, which is informed by my inquiry—be it
philosophical, historical, or empirical. I was no longer simply trying to express my ideas or to present the data I had collected but trying to engage in
conversations with people in the field through my writing. At conferences,
I tried to meet those people whose work I had read in order to gain a better
sense of who they were and where they were coming from. I also saw it as

a way of constantly reminding myself that they are real people who have not only interesting ideas and perspectives but also feelings—about issues in the field and about their own professional identity.

My status as a graduate student did not get in my way for the most part, but there still seems to be some resistance to the idea of graduate students as professionals. A few years ago, Tony and I were invited to lead a discussion session at TESOL. After a generic e-mail invitation was sent to all the discussion leaders and academic session presenters, someone objected to my being listed as one of the invited presenters because I was "still a graduate student." (I still wonder how this person managed to figure out that I was a graduate student without also finding out about my qualifications.) As a compromise, the Interest Section chair asked Tony if he would mind being listed as "Tony Silva with Paul Kei Matsuda," as if I were assisting him in the project I had initiated. Fortunately, Tony stood up for me and said he would not participate unless I was listed as the first presenter, and the chair supported our position.

Now that I have a tenure-track job, however, I have come to think of being a graduate student as a somewhat privileged status. At Purdue, I was only teaching three courses per year. I had no obligation to administer programs, serve on academic committees or mentor graduate students, although I did so voluntarily. Most important of all, I had more freedom in choosing which conversation to join and in which form, whereas I now feel some pressure to focus on certain types of publications, such as monographs and articles in prestigious journals. Some of my professional colleagues have also told me about the pressure they felt about the need to develop a coherent professional profile that was in sync with their teaching. My professional identity will no doubt be influenced by the ever-so-unclear requirements for tenure and promotion. But will I be able to continue thinking like a professional whose goal is to contribute to the field regardless of how it will be evaluated? Will I start thinking like a junior faculty member who will publish for tenure and promotion—for the sake of having published? Or will I be able to find a happy medium? The biggest challenge I faced as a graduate student continues to confront me.

REFERENCES

Connor, U., & Johns, A. M. (Eds.). (1990). *Coherence in writing: Research and pedagogical perspectives.* Alexandria, VA: TESOL.

Connor, U., & Kaplan, R. B. (Eds.). (1987). *Writing across languages: Analysis of L2 text.* Reading, MA: Addison-Wesley.

Gibaldi, J. (Ed.). (1992). *Introduction to scholarship in modern languages and literatures* (2nd ed.). New York: Modern Language Association of America.

Harris, M., & Silva, T. (1993). Tutoring ESL students: Issues and options. *College Composition and Communication, 44*(4), 525–537.

Hinds, J. (1983). Contrastive rhetoric: Japanese and English. *Text, 3,* 183–195.

Hinds, J. (1987). Reader–writer responsibility: A new typology. In U. Connor & R. B. Kaplan (Eds.), *Writing across languages: Analysis of L2 text* (pp. 141–152). Reading, MA: Addison-Wesley.

Hinds, J. (1990). Inductive, deductive, quasi-inductive: Expository writing in Japanese, Korean, Chinese, and Thai. In U. Connor & A. M. Johns (Eds.), *Coherence in writing: Research and pedagogical perspectives* (pp. 87–109). Alexandria, VA: TESOL.

Ivanič, R. (1997). *Writing and identity: The discoursal construction of identity in academic writing.* Amsterdam: John Benjamins.

Johnson, D. M., & Roen, D. H. (Eds.). (1989). *Richness in writing: Empowering ESL students.* New York: Longman.

Kaplan, R. B. (1966). Cultural thought patterns in inter-cultural education. *Language Learning, 16,* 1–20.

Kroll, B. (Ed.). (1990). *Second language writing: Research insights for the classroom.* New York: Cambridge University Press.

Lunsford, A. A. (1992). Rhetoric and composition. In J. Gibaldi (Ed.), *Introduction to scholarship in modern languages and literatures* (2nd ed., pp. 77–100). New York: Modern Language Association of America.

Matsuda, P. K. (1995). *Contrastive rhetorics: Toward a pedagogical theory of second language writing.* Unpublished master's thesis, Miami University, Oxford, OH.

Matsuda, P. K. (1997). Contrastive rhetoric in context: A dynamic model of L2 writing. *Journal of Second Language Writing, 6*(1), 45–60.

Matsuda, P. K., & Silva T. (2001). Introduction. In T. Silva & P. K. Matsuda (Eds.), *Landmark essays on ESL writing* (pp. xiii–xxv). Mahwah, NJ: Lawrence Erlbaum Associates.

Miller, S. (1992). Writing theory : : theory writing. In G. Kirsch & P. A. Sullivan (Eds.), *Methods and methodology in composition research* (pp. 62–83). Carbondale, IL: Southern Illinois University Press.

Purves, A. C. (Ed.). (1988). *Writing across languages and cultures: Issues in contrastive rhetoric.* Newbury Park, CA: Sage.

Raimes, A. (1986). Teaching ESL writing: Fitting what we do to what we know. *The Writing Instructor, 5,* 153–166.

Sawada, A. (1977). *Ronbun no kakikata* [How to write a thesis]. Tokyo: Kodansha.

Silva, T., & Matsuda, P. K. (Eds.). (2001). *Landmark essays on ESL writing.* Mahwah, NJ: Lawrence Erlbaum Associates.

Singer, M. R. (1987). *Intercultural communication: A perceptual approach.* Englewood Cliffs, NJ: Prentice-Hall.

Zamel, V. (1990). Through students' eyes: The experiences of three ESL writers. *Journal of Basic Writing, 9,* 83–98.

4

On Beginning to Write at 40

Stephanie Vandrick
University of San Francisco

I have always been an avid, even addicted, reader, and I have always been in love with words and language. I have always loved the academic world, the world of the university campus, of classes, of the library, of scholarly and intellectual discussions and pursuits. Thus although throughout high school and college I had little idea of what I wanted to do with my future, it gradually became clear that of course that future had to include books, ideas, and campuses. As a new graduate assistant in the English Department at the age of 21, I was assigned to teach English as a second language (ESL), and after my first day of teaching, I knew that teaching at the college level would be my career. I pursued that career and have taught ESL and other subjects (literature, Women's Studies) my whole adult life. But I didn't begin seriously writing for scholarly publication until I was forty. Before that, I wrote some short pieces, some newsletter articles, some reviews, but not a lot. I was in writing, as I have been in other parts of my life, a late-bloomer.

WHY DIDN'T I WRITE EARLIER?

A primary reason that I didn't write earlier was the difficult working conditions during my first 15 years of full-time teaching. Although I have been teaching ESL (and other areas) at the college level my whole adult life, my teaching situation during my first 15 years was one that did not encourage, and in fact actively discouraged, research and writing. I worked under very negative conditions at my institution, both at the department level and at the university level. ESL was considered a service field, and ESL instructors were expected to teach a heavier-than-normal load, attend many meetings, do quasi-administrative work, work on curricula, organize social events, and in general put in long hours. Efforts to do research were actively discouraged; for instance, teachers (including me, on at least two occasions) who asked to teach a certain class again in order to follow up on initiated research were purposely assigned to completely different classes. Although we were full-time faculty, and grateful for that status, we suffered many of the indignities that part-time faculty in our, and other, fields so often face: heavier teaching loads than other faculty had, desks in a large room rather than private offices, no individual telephones, no access to research or travel funds, low status. Even worse than the specifics of this negative situation was the hostile attitude of the administrators at the time; they not only did not attempt to improve working conditions, but thought that the conditions were perfectly appropriate for the faculty and believed that the faculty should be grateful for having their jobs and should not complain.

I can't begin to describe the pain that this difficult and hostile work situation caused my colleagues and me. It was difficult for me, as someone who had had a happy, secure childhood, to believe that people could behave in this way. I had been raised to think that if a person did her or his job well, she or he would be valued. I had always thought that people were basically good and generally treated each other decently. I honestly couldn't comprehend cruel, manipulative motivations and behavior, and was shocked to observe it and to be its target. Still worse was to observe it in people with power over my colleagues and me. Even today, when I have been in an infinitely better situation for many years, I sometimes realize how much that time in my life affected me. Just recently, when the subject happened to come up during a conversation with a new colleague at a professional conference, I found myself choking up and briefly unable to continue speaking.

Readers may wonder why I didn't simply leave this toxic situation; I am sure some of my friends wondered the same thing at the time. Perhaps I should have left then. Yet leaving a full-time university position in ESL, in a premier geographical location, especially knowing of the scarcity of such positions, made it very hard to leave. I also had family and roots in the area. After moving often during my childhood, I didn't want to keep moving as an adult. And perhaps I was just plain insecure about looking for a new job.

All of these conditions interacted with my own lack of confidence in myself as a scholar and researcher. Some of the reasons for this had to do with my own personality, and some had to do with gender. Some had to do with the internalization of others' regarding ESL as a second-class field. Although intellectually I did not and do not believe these belittling conceptions about my field, all the stereotypes insidiously seeped into my mind, as I know they do, unfortunately, for many teachers in our field: *ESL is only remedial; anyone who speaks English can teach English; you are "only" dealing with "foreigners;" ESL is not a real discipline.*

Other less personal factors that made me less likely to write were the fact that 25 years ago there were far fewer scholarly journals in the field of ESL and applied linguistics and far fewer faculty in full-time university positions in TESOL and applied linguistics; therefore, except for a few prominent scholars at a few institutions, there was not much of a culture of expectation of writing and publishing. In addition, most of the writing and publishing that was done was on topics related to linguistics and language learning. As a person who came to ESL through my interests in literature, language, and culture, my focus was more on literature and on sociopolitical issues than on, for example, second language acquisition research. I thought that in order to write, I would have to do quantitative research, use statistical analysis, and write about, for instance, how language learners acquired a certain grammatical competence.

Readers may also wonder whether I was and am just using the difficult situation at my institution as an excuse for why I didn't write. I myself have wondered this at times. Sometimes I thought, and think, that if I had only been more motivated, more disciplined, harder working, more confident, I could have and should have written anyway, despite the difficult work setting. Perhaps it is true that I could have and should have done more anyway. But I was not strong enough to surmount the difficulties. I need at least a bit of support and encouragement from my professional community, or at the very minimum a neutral setting rather than a destructive one, in order to write.

WHAT CHANGED?

What allowed me to start writing and publishing at 40? First, much of the unhappy situation at work changed quite radically. Our university's faculty union was instrumental in fighting for better working conditions. A new administration, and in particular a new dean, had a very supportive attitude and followed through with tangible support. For example, the ESL faculty's teaching load was reduced to the same as that of other college faculty, and in some cases, including mine, it was later further reduced to allow for research and writing time. For another example, I was finally assigned a private office, with my own telephone, computer, windows, and lock on the door. As Virginia Woolf famously said, people—and in particular women—need "a room of one's own" in order to think and write (Woolf, 1929/1959). In addition, a close colleague and friend became department chair, and she was tremendously encouraging and supportive of my writing.

I particularly remember a meeting that my colleagues and I had with our new dean, the supportive dean I mentioned earlier. He told us that he would immediately reduce our teaching load to the same load that all faculty at our university had. But, he said, we would then be expected to do the same kind and quantity of research as other faculty were expected to do. I remember experiencing a tiny moment of panic, and then a bracing rush of optimism and confidence. This was another moment of epiphany: I suddenly realized that this was the moment I had been waiting for. YES, I told my dean. Yes, of course I would do that research and writing. No problem. Where did that confidence come from? Apparently it had been lurking underneath the surface, waiting for the opportunity to come out. It was a moment of hope and joy for me.

Simultaneously, partly as a result of the increased respect for me and my profession shown by the university and the increased support the university gave me, I began to believe in myself as someone who could share her ideas with others by writing. Until then, on some level I had thought of writing and publishing as something that others did, others who somehow knew more, knew the magic inside information that allowed one to write and publish. Now a shift happened in me which allowed me to picture myself as, at least potentially, one of those people: a writer who publishes.

It is hard to know whether this shift was mostly a result of age, a result of the earlier-mentioned external factors, or some combination of the two, some alchemy brought about by their interaction. Perhaps, too, I was experiencing that burst of creativity that one often sees these days among women at midlife. Women in general tend to be "late-bloomers" compared with men; whether this is inherent in females, socially constructed (see, e.g., Rubin, 1979), or simply a matter of the logistics of managing a family life along with a career (see, e.g., Apter, 1993; Hochschild, 1997) are knotty questions that feminists and others have not yet resolved. In any case, I know many women writers, artists, actors, musicians, photographers, and others who didn't fully come to their creative work until their 40s or even later. Perhaps they were too busy with their jobs and families earlier; perhaps they lacked confidence and were not expected or encouraged to give themselves the time and opportunities to work on their art earlier. For whatever reason, I believe I am just one of many who are part of this phenomenon of late-blooming creative women.

Connected to this midlife "flowering" is the sense that most people, women or men, have: the sense that time is running short and is not as inexhaustible as one thought when one was 20 or even 30. I am someone who tends to put things off, thinking I will do a given project "someday." But I realized at 40 that my "somedays" were not unlimited, and I started to feel that if I were ever to write, it should be soon.

And although these other factors were all preparing the ground, so to speak, I did have a definite, sudden, and distinct epiphany one day: I suddenly realized that I did not have to force myself to become interested in a linguistic topic that I didn't really have knowledge about or interest in, but that I could write about the topics I was most interested in: sociopolitical issues such as gender, class and identity. Prior to that epiphany, I had thought of those topics as very important to me and to my teaching but never thought of them as topics to write about for presentation and publication in professional arenas.

With great excitement, I embarked on my first full-length article, one that took the position that it was important for teachers to act on their social and political beliefs and not try to keep them out of the classroom. This article was published (Vandrick, 1992), and I went on to write about gender and pedagogy, class and privilege, literature in the writing classroom, and other topics close to my heart.

A SENSE OF URGENCY

Another turning point for me, soon after I wrote and published that first full-length article in a refereed journal, came in the spring semester of 1994, when I had a sabbatical. I was determined to use the precious sabbatical time to move forward with my still very new writing career. I decided to write about critical pedagogy and ESL, a topic that was important to me. As I started reading and researching, I found myself drawn more particularly to feminist pedagogy. I knew I had found "my subject." After all, I had been a feminist since high school days, and I often taught women's issues in classes, gave lectures to international students and others on feminist issues, and considered my feminism an important part of my personal, political, and academic life. As with the first article, described earlier, I felt a great sense of excitement and "rightness" about this topic. With enthusiasm and dogged determination as well, I read every book and article I could find about feminist pedagogy and eventually wrote several pieces on various aspects of the topic.

During that 1994 sabbatical, I found that I could work best in my office at the university and that although there were distractions to avoid there, the distractions were fewer and less pressing than those at home. Besides, I had all my necessary materials around me in that office: my books, my files, my computer; the university library was nearby and convenient as well. I had the sense that time was very valuable, and that I wanted to use my one semester sabbatical well. After all, there was an increasing urgency now that I was 44 years old.

My resolve was badly tested that semester, as a series of events made it hard for me to move forward. Renovation was being done on our building, and twice I had to move out of my office temporarily. Throughout that semester, there was noise from jackhammers and from workers yelling to each other; dirt and dust invaded my office; I felt unsettled. But nothing could stop me at that point. I just kept right on working, though complaining loudly and often. Out of that sabbatical came several publications, most notably two publications on feminist pedagogy, that I felt pleased with and that were well received (Vandrick, 1994, 1995).

I write about these difficulties, and my overcoming them, in order to indicate the urgency I felt at that point in my writing life. I felt desperate about preserving my time and my forward momentum; I feared the time some-how being stolen from me or evaporating before I knew it, and I just could-n't let that happen. I also felt a great joy in writing, and that helped to keep me moving forward despite the moves and noise and dust. After all, such distractions and inconveniences were nothing compared with the psychic and logistical obstacles I had experienced for so many years in the past.

As I wrote and my articles began to be accepted for publication, and as I got some positive feedback from colleagues and readers, I became more confident about my right to speak, to write, to "join the conversa-tion." This sense of being part of the professional conversation was im-mensely joyful for me, and this confidence helped me, in turn, to continue writing and publishing.

Also of great help to me has been my writing group, consisting of two col-leagues and me; we have, for about 10 years, met regularly to talk about our writing. We have written several articles and a book together, and we read and respond to each other's individual writing as well. We encourage each other, support each other, and console each other when rejection letters ar-rive, and we celebrate together when invitations or acceptance letters arrive.

A HAPPY ENDING?

This is not a completely happy story for me. I still sometimes mourn the years in which I could have been and perhaps should have been writing. The experience of writing and publishing and being part of the profes-sional conversation is one that feels so right that I wish I had begun much earlier. I blame certain conditions and even certain people for holding me back. And sometimes I blame myself for not managing to write despite the obstacles. But, as a colleague said to me, I need to remind myself that all those years were not wasted regarding writing. All the reading, teaching, thinking, discussing, and experiencing I did during those years nourishes the writing I am doing now. Maybe I wasn't ready earlier. Maybe I didn't re-ally have a lot to say earlier. In any case, the past is the past, and it is useless and even destructive to waste energy bemoaning it.

And I have discovered that there are some advantages to coming to writing late. My life experiences and thinking certainly enrich my current writing. And because writing for publication came hard and late to me, I do not take for granted the conditions that allow me to write and the satis-faction and pleasure of writing and having other people read and re-spond to my ideas. Incidentally, my publications also helped me to get a promotion, which is certainly a result that I celebrate, but truly this happy result was almost beside the point compared with the gratification and fulfillment I have experienced since I began to be a writer. And an impor-tant by-product has been that as a writing teacher I finally feel that I am practicing what I preach to my students!

This is also not a completely happy story in terms of its implications for others in our field. I tell my personal story in the hope that it may be encouraging to others in our field who may feel that only "others" are qualified to write or who feel that because they haven't started yet, it is probably too late to start. When I first thought about writing this chapter, this was the major message that I wanted to convey. My narrative had a rather traditional arc, with the main character (me!) overcoming tremendous obstacles to triumph in the end. But on reflection I realize that the story and its implications are much more complex than that. I do not want this to be a naive story about how "anyone can do it," because I know that despite my earlier difficulties, I have been fortunate enough to have many factors in my life and professional setting which (eventually) gave me the luxury of writing: a full-time job, tenure, supportive administration and colleagues, reasonable teaching load, private office, computer and computer support, and funds for travel to conferences, among others. And many other teachers in our field, perhaps even most others, do not have these positive conditions.

So I am now conveying a very mixed, inconclusive message. On the one hand, I want to say that if writing and publishing is your dream, don't give up; it is never too late; you too can do it. But on the other hand, if what allowed me to write and publish, finally, was mainly a change in my academic situation, and in the time and support and status and facilities available to me, then what does this say to people in our field who do not have access to these resources? What about the many in our field who have part-time positions, or full-time positions with no or low rank or security, teach a heavy workload, do not have private offices or technological resources and support, do not have funds available to attend professional conferences, and do not have support from their administrators and institutions?

I realize that my originally intended message is in fact naive in that it suggests that one must overcome adversity on one's own in order to succeed. In fact, the obstacles that were at least partially responsible for my not writing for so many years were and are endemic to our profession; they are institutional and societal obstacles. They are closely tied to the low status of the field of ESL, as well as to the continuing low status of any field in which women practitioners predominate. The way that these obstacles have cut off many valuable voices is a real loss to our field, as well as to the individuals whose voices have been silenced.

What message, then, can I salvage from my story? One point that I can still legitimately and sincerely make is that age itself need not be a factor. In other words, because one has not written and published at a younger age does not mean one cannot do so at an older age. In that sense, at least, it really is never too late. I do believe that sharing one's ideas and expertise through writing is within the grasp of many people who may feel it is not, especially those who feel this way because they feel that they are too old, and that it is too late. I would like very much to encourage those people to take the leap of faith and begin.

And the other message I would like to convey is to women in our field who have been too intimidated to write for our field's journals and publishers. Although many women in our field do write and publish, they do not do so in proportion to the number of women who teach ESL; women are underrepresented in our publishing venues. The same situation can be found in other (also generally low-prestige) fields in which women dominate: composition, education, nursing, and so on. So I urge my colleagues, particularly female colleagues, in TESOL not to be intimidated, not to believe that only others have the necessary ability, knowledge, and connections to publish their work. I urge that my colleagues, however old they are, take heart and plunge in.

REFERENCES

Apter, T. (1993). *Working women don't have wives: Professional success in the 1990's.* New York: St. Martin's Press.

Hochschild, A. R. (1997). *The time bind: When work becomes home and home becomes work.* New York: Metropolitan Books.

Rubin, L. (1979). *Women of a certain age: The midlife search for self.* New York: Harper and Row.

Vandrick, S. (1992). Politics in the university ESL class. *CATESOL Journal 5*(2), 19–27.

Vandrick, S. (1994). Feminist pedagogy and ESL. *College ESL, 4*(2), 69–92.

Vandrick, S. (1995). Teaching and practicing feminism in the university ESL class. *TESOL Journal, 4*(3), 4–6.

Woolf, V. (1959). *A room of one's own.* London: Hogarth Press. (Original work published 1929)

5

Striving for Original Voice in Publication?: A Critical Reflection

Ryuko Kubota
University of North Carolina, Chapel Hill

As an Asian woman, I acquired academic writing skills in English as a second language (ESL) during adulthood and began actively participating in academic publishing communities in the United States in my late 30s, 5 years after finishing my PhD dissertation. My earliest attempt to publish an article in an American peer-reviewed journal was unsuccessful. In retrospect, I see that I was not experienced enough to write for publication from scratch without help, as opposed to publishing from a dissertation that had already been reviewed by experts. Furthermore, I had not established credibility as a researcher in the field. After receiving a rejection letter, I simply gave up on this publishing project.

When I moved to a major research university in 1995, I faced immediate pressure to publish. I was informed that in order to obtain tenure, I would need to publish 12 to 15 articles in peer-reviewed journals in 5 years! It seemed that the quickest way to publish was to revisit my PhD dissertation and turn it into several journal articles, as I sensed I would have a fairly good chance. Breaking a large study into independent papers was more difficult than I had anticipated. One unexpected obstacle was a reviewer's demand for a statistical reanalysis of data. Despite such an obstacle, I managed to complete the project within 2 years without any major difficulties. My papers were published in the *Canadian Modern Language Review*, *Journal of Second Language Writing*, and *Written Communication*.

My publishing experiences, however, did not always proceed as smoothly as these instances did. The largest challenge I felt in the process of negotiating meaning with reviewers, editors, and proofreaders was that of expressing my original voice or communicating what I wanted to say in the way I wanted to say it. The issue of original voice, which I have found to be a contentious notion as I engaged in critical self-reflection in the preparation of this chapter, seemed to have two dimensions: content and form. The content-related issue involved negotiation of academic discourse with gatekeepers, whereas the form-related challenge had to do with negotiation of linguistic appropriateness with copyeditors. Thus, it seemed to me that expressing original voice in terms of content meant being able to express my own views and arguments, whereas original voice in terms of form concerned my own use of particular vocabulary, expressions, and structures. While experiencing these challenges, the following questions came to mind: Am I able to negotiate the reviewers' demands without undermining my original voice? Am I able to find a copyeditor who respects and retains my original linguistic intentions?

In addressing these issues of voice, however, I have begun to critically review its concept. The way I had interpreted my own experience was perhaps influenced by the romantic notion of authentic voice, autonomy, and self-expression that became popular in composition studies in the 1960s and 70s (Bowden, 1999). However, another view situates writing in social and discursive contexts, in which writers both appropriate and are appropriated by available linguistic and discursive possibilities (Ivanič, 1998). This view regards writing practice not as authentic expression of individual voice or autonomous inner self but rather as intertextual reproduction based on the writer's previous encounters with texts and discourses (Prior, 2001). The latter part of this chapter presents a self-critique of the notion of original voice that I initially relied on in interpreting my experiences.

STRUGGLE FOR ORIGINAL VOICE

Negotiating Meaning With Reviewers

I experienced the first major obstacle when I submitted a manuscript to *TESOL Quarterly*. Initially, both of the reviewers recommended rejection. However, recognizing their comments that the paper deserved revision, the editor invited me to resubmit it. One of the reviewers, who wrote three pages of detailed comments, requested that I make a significant change in my conceptual approach. I struggled for several weeks to fully understand what the reviewer meant and to figure out how to respond to the critique. I then had a chance at a Teachers of English to Speakers of Other Languages (TESOL) conference to have long conversations with a friend who helped me understand the major points of the critique. This experience was a breakthrough—I then felt confident enough to revise the paper. I also felt fortunate to find a colleague in my department who helped me understand relevant theories and concepts and provided thorough editorial suggestions.

In the process of revising the paper, however, I increasingly felt as though I was writing my paper on behalf of the reviewer or for my colleague. My preoccupation to have the paper accepted compelled me to comply with every single suggestion given by the reviewer and my colleague. Although I tried to make my own arguments, I eventually felt that much of the content and language did not really belong to me; I felt I had lost the ownership of my ideas and words. This was a difficult dilemma. My second revision still did not completely satisfy the reviewer. The editor was extremely helpful when I telephoned her to seek advice regarding my subsequent revisions. The final revisions did not entirely meet the expectations of the reviewer, but the editor accepted the manuscript. The article was eventually published in 1999.

The challenge illustrated here suggests that trying to meet the demands of reviewers is worth the effort if the only goal is to publish the paper. However, this could leave the writer feeling that her or his authentic voice has been severely sacrificed. It could deprive the writer of the sense of ownership of her or his own text. In contrast, not responding to the reviewer's suggestions would decrease the chance of being published. This is indeed a tough dilemma. Nonetheless, as I discuss later, this dilemma might not actually manifest itself as a challenge to expressing voice—it could indicate that the concept of originality is an illusion and that newcomers to the publishing community wishing to gain membership simply need to be socialized into the already existing ideas and ways of using words.

In this example, my colleague also provided extensive guidance in content and language. Although this helped me polish the paper, it also reduced my sense of textual ownership. Over several years, however, I have learned that obtaining feedback from as many colleagues as possible before sending the manuscript for a review helps me gauge the legitimacy and persuasiveness of my arguments. The collegial feedback also encourages me and reduces the feeling that my writing has to be recognized and controlled by only a few gatekeepers.

Finding a Home for the Manuscript

In the previous example, my effort to negotiate meaning with reviewers eventually led to publication. Prior to this experience, I made a similar attempt to faithfully follow the reviewers' and editor's suggestions. However, that earlier experience resulted in failure. I submitted to *TESOL Quarterly* a manuscript arguing that second language professionals should broaden their perspectives on pedagogy by listening to voices from various minority perspectives in fields other than TESOL (viz., teaching L1 English to racial minorities, teaching foreign languages to English native speakers with learning disabilities, and teaching less commonly taught foreign languages) rather than promoting wholesale "communicative approaches" uncritically. The reviewers recommended that the paper be rejected, claiming that it did not convincingly argue why these minority perspectives were relevant to the field of TESOL. However, just as in the previous example, the editor encouraged me to revise and resubmit, suggesting that I present a more convincing reason why TESOL professionals should look to these fields. In my revisions, I made a drastic change by framing my arguments in the context of teacher education and referring to publications that proposed greater collaboration among professionals in ESL, bilingual, and foreign language education. Although these revisions still did not satisfy the editor, she gave me another chance and I revised the paper again. Despite these major revisions, the editor eventually rejected the paper because she thought that the major concern—that is, the relevance of my arguments to TESOL—was still not resolved.

Although this rejection was quite disappointing, I did not give up. I contacted the editor of the *Canadian Modern Language Review* and sent the same paper in its revised form for a review. Her initial response was negative. I asked her if she would read the original version of the paper—the very first version of the manuscript I had sent to *TESOL Quarterly*. I felt that this version best reflected my original voice and thus presented the most convincing argument. As I predicted, the editor's response was positive—she thought that the manuscript was stronger and made its point more clearly than the other version. The article (Kubota, 1998) was eventually published with very few revisions. In this case, I felt I was able to retain my original voice by finding an appropriate home for the paper.

I had two other experiences of being rejected by one journal but accepted by another. In one case, I had written a paper that introduced the concept of World Englishes in teaching social studies and sent it to a journal for social studies teachers. After receiving a rejection letter that contained no comments from reviewers, I simply sent the same version of the manuscript to another social studies journal. I made this decision because the editor who rejected my paper had not responded to my inquiries about the status of the manuscript for more than a year. I sensed that the editor was not interested in the topic and that he had not even bothered to have the manuscript reviewed. In contrast, an editor of the other journal was very helpful in brainstorming with me on the telephone in order to make the paper appeal to its readership. It was clear from that exchange that this editor was enthusiastic about my topic and wanted to see the paper published.

In the other case, one journal rejected my research paper that reported a case study on the effectiveness of distance education in a Japanese as a foreign language class in a high school compared with conventional teaching of the same language in another high school. The reviewers criticized my paper arguing that the two groups of students were incomparable on many dimensions and that the instruments I used to measure students' achievement were not adequate. The reviewers' comments convinced me that the study would have to be reported in a different way. At the same time, I believed that my research was still worth publishing. Thus I revised the manuscript extensively by focusing entirely on the group that received distance education and emphasizing pedagogical implications. I then sent it to another journal with a stronger focus on pedagogy than the other journal. The revised manuscript was accepted with minor revisions. These experiences suggest that a writer should make a sensible judgment about which criticism to respond to and how much to revise. At the same time, it is necessary to look for a journal that is a good fit for the manuscript.

CHALLENGES AS A SECOND LANGUAGE WRITER

An author's voice is conveyed through the surface structures of text in addition to the content. Expression of voice in this sense can be a major issue for second language writers. Whereas I believe that academic communities should broaden and diversify their rhetorical possibilities, I also think it is important for second language scholars to write clearly and convincingly to appeal to mainstream readers by following conventions of writing. If we do so, we can participate as legitimate members of the community, which then opens up possibilities of injecting alternative perspectives and expressions into the field. Conforming to existing conventions does not necessarily mean assimilation into the discourse of power; it can serve as a tool for transforming the status quo. It is therefore important to acknowledge the double-edged nature of language espoused by critical literacy; on the one hand, language can be used for domination and social control, but on the other it can be appropriated by the marginalized to resist power structures and to transform the norm (Canagarajah, 1999; Delpit, 1992, 1995; hooks, 1994). In my experience, the more the publishing community recognizes the credibility of my work, the more I feel empowered to explore alternative ways of expressing ideas. Thus, it is advisable for a writer to follow closely the conventions at least in the initial stages of writing for publication in order to gain the cultural capital that will facilitate her or his initiation into the academic community.

As a way to ensure linguistic and textual appropriateness, I always have my manuscript copyedited by someone before submitting it to an editor. I have worked with several people, including PhD candidates, graduate assistants, and professional copyeditors. In my experience, the most skilled copyeditor is the one who not only has expertise in editing for grammar, spelling, organization, and format (such as APA or MLA styles) but also respects a second language writer's original intentions. Some relatively inexperienced copyeditors I have worked with failed to make necessary corrections, making the manuscript sound less polished than expected. In contrast, some experienced copyeditors made quite a few editorial corrections, particularly stylistic ones. Excessive editing is not only intrusive but often inefficient, because I then have to spend extra time deciding whether I should accept the corrections. Sometimes I struggle to judge whether the correction indicates a stylistic option or a lexicogrammatical error. Too many corrections often undermine the expression of the author's original voice. For nonnative writers, editing is an extra step that strips them of their original voice. In my experience, the most skilled copyeditor retains an author's voice while making appropriate corrections so that the text appeals to mainstream readers. I feel fortunate to be able to work with an individual who has exceptional skills to meet my needs in this regard.

EXPRESSING ORIGINAL VOICE OR BEING POSITIONED IN EXISTING DISCOURSE?

So far I have described my challenges from a perspective of original voice. In negotiating meaning with reviewers, editors, and proofreaders, I have often felt that my original voice was undermined. As I began establishing my publishing career, however, I felt as though this negotiation was becoming easier, partly because I was becoming accustomed to the process of receiving criticisms and revising on the basis of suggestions without feeling too intimidated. In a way, I have developed a certain level of confidence in accomplishing my ultimate goal. But does this mean that I have developed my original voice? Am I becoming an autonomous writer who can express my real self? Is there really such a thing as original voice, or is it an illusion? Writing this chapter has raised these questions and provided me with an opportunity to reflect critically on the meaning of voice.

The notions of an individual writer's authentic voice, originality, and creativity have been a target of critical scrutiny in composition pedagogies since the 1990s. Although these notions imply the writer's potential to express her or his own unique ideas or selfhood, critics argue that these notions, which constituted the core of the popularized expressionist approach to writing in the 1960s and 70s, obscure the social nature of writing. More specifically, writing can be seen as a social activity constituted by repetition, reproduction, and reinvention of ideas and linguistic expressions that are already available in discursive fields (e.g., Bowden, 1999; Ivanič, 1998; Prior, 2001). From this perspective, a writer is not an autonomous self detached from social contexts but a social being learning to align him- or herself within available discourses as well as existing power relations. Texts manifest not the autonomous voice of an individual writer but intertexual reinvention or reproduction. Drawing on Fairclough (1992), Ivanič (1998) explained that intertexuality can be divided into two categories: *manifest intertexuality*, which is observed in a text in the forms of quotation, paraphrase, and copying, and *interdiscursivity*, an observable pattern of text or genre or a set of conventions for language use. This view suggests that authorship and text exist always in relation to other available discourses and texts. Intertexuality and the practice of borrowing others' words are also discussed in the field of TESOL in relation to plagiarism. For instance, Pennycook (1996) pointed out that the notion of textual ownership and originality is a modernist invention of the West, which contradicts the postmodern notion that "we are not speaking subjects but spoken subjects, we do not create language but are created by it" (p. 209). There is also a degree of hypocrisy in academic conventions that prohibit plagiarism on the one hand, while requiring writers to use a fixed canon of knowledge and terminology on the other.

These discussions suggest that what is conceived to be originality in academic writing is not the expression of autonomous self divorced from existing theories and discourses; rather it always involves, to a large extent, already legitimated thoughts within a certain theoretical or conceptual framework. Thus, if my argument deviates from any of the existing academic stances, whether it is a quantitative, qualitative, or critical approach to applied linguistics, the possibility of my being accepted for publication becomes slim. The target of conformity can be even more specific than an academic stance or theoretical framework—it can involve specific publication guidelines or the ethos of a particular journal. Conversely, if my arguments align with an acceptable discourse, the paper is more likely to be accepted. This applies to linguistic conventions as well. Adhering to linguistic conventions increases the chance of being published. Writers actually strive to gather and adopt acceptable ways of writing from available sources. Ivanič (1998) demonstrated that student writers pick up words, phrases, sentences, argumentative strategies, and structuring devices from reading and incorporate them later in their writing. I too pay attention to words, phrases, and other strategies while reading published works and try to use them in my own writing.

As I discussed earlier in this chapter, the challenges I have experienced appear to have stemmed from my inability to express my original voice. Once I had joined some publishing communities, however, I felt as though I became increasingly capable of expressing my original voice. But the earlier discussion indicates that in actuality I have been socialized into academic discourse communities and appropriated by academic discourses and that I have reinvented existing ways of thinking. Obtaining collegial feedback and incorporating the suggestions in revising my drafts also manifests the collective or shared rather than the purely individual nature of text. Here, the notion of original voice vanishes and is replaced by that of reinvention of discourses. This certainly does not imply that academic activities remain stagnant. Publishing communities constantly produce new ideas and approaches. However, a writer who innovates needs first to be recognized as a legitimate participant in the community (Lave & Wenger, 1991). With a legitimate status, the writer can transform the perspectives from within the field by introducing new thoughts. There exists here a dialectic relation of being subject to a discourse and being a creative subject of a discourse.

CONCLUSIONS AND SUGGESTIONS

As a nonnative scholar in the United States, I began developing my academic publishing career at a major research university. Through writing, revising, and seeking opportunities for publication, I have experienced what appears to be a struggle for original voice. However, a critical analysis of the concept of voice as well as a perspective of critical literacy indicates that this struggle is part of the process of being initiated into a publishing community, which requires aligning oneself with the acceptable linguistic and discursive possibilities of the community. This view, however, does not imply that the writer is a blind subject of the academic discourse. Positioning oneself in the acceptable discourse enables a writer to gain the status of a legitimate participant who can transform the discourse from within. As I gained more credibility as a member of a publishing community, I felt more empowered to express my views and use alternative styles.

Although my experiences and situation may not directly apply to the contexts of other scholars, they can provide the basics for some general suggestions, particularly for newcomers to writing for publication:

1. Seek feedback from one or more trusted colleagues during a draft stage. Incorporate their suggestions in your revisions before sending the paper to a journal.
2. Be open to criticisms from reviewers and editors. Receiving criticisms is often intimidating, but learning to accept them and aligning yourself with existing academic discourses are keys to professional success.
3. At the same time, do not try to adhere slavishly to the suggestions given by reviewers. Too much preoccupation with following their suggestions can spoil the focus and coherence of your paper. At a certain point, it may be wise to look for a better home for the paper than to keep trying to meet the demands of the reviewers or editors.
4. Never give up. If one journal rejects your paper, it does not necessarily mean that your manuscript is not worth publishing. If you think your manuscript presents legitimate arguments, send it to another journal.
5. Save your drafts, especially when you make significant changes in your framework and arguments. A different journal may prefer your earlier draft.
6. For second language writers, try to find a good copyeditor who not only has good linguistic skills but also has the ability to retain your

original intentions. Not all copyeditors or educated native speakers can accomplish this demanding task.

Publishing in professional journals is in no way an easy task, but determination and open-mindedness can enable one to become a member of the publishing community. Gaining legitimate membership in the community also requires accessibility of resources. I feel I am quite privileged to have access to excellent library and electronic resources as well as grant opportunities to cover editing costs. I realize that many nonnative writers of English who try to publish in major English language journals, including graduate students and those in smaller institutions or in non-English speaking countries, lack access to these resources. The field of applied linguistics faces an imminent need to increase participation of periphery scholars and practitioners (see Canagarajah, this volume; Sasaki, this volume) because its theories are produced mostly in the center, despite the fact that a large amount of pedagogical practice takes place in the periphery (cf. Canagarajah, 1996; Phillipson, 1992). As a nonnative scholar now serving increasingly as a reviewer of English language journals, I must remind myself of the challenges that these less privileged colleagues face.

REFERENCES

Bowden, D. (1999). *The mythology of voice*. Portsmouth, NH: Boynton/Cook.

Canagarajah, A. S. (1996). Non-discursive requirements in academic publishing, material resources of periphery scholars, and the politics of knowledge production. *Written Communication, 48*, 435–472.

Canagarajah, A. S. (1999). *Resisting linguistic imperialism in English teaching*. Oxford, England: Oxford University Press.

Delpit, L. (1992). Acquisition of literate discourse: Bowing before the master? *Theory Into Practice, 31*(4), 296–302.

Delpit, L. (1995). *Other people's children: Cultural conflict in the classroom*. New York: The New Press.

Fairclough, N. (1992). *Discourse and social change*. Cambridge, England: Polity Press.

Hooks, B. (1994). *Teaching to transgress: Education as the practice of freedom*. New York & London: Routledge.

Ivanič, R. (1998). *Writing and identity: The discoursal construction of identity in academic writing*. Amsterdam: John Benjamins.

Kubota, R. (1998). Voices from the margin: Second/foreign language teaching approaches from minority perspectives. *The Canadian Modern Language Review, 54*(3), 394–412.

Lave, J., & Wenger, E. (1991). *Situated learning: Legitimate peripheral participation*. Cambridge and New York: Cambridge University Press.

Pennycook, A. (1996). Borrowing others' words: Text, ownership, memory, and plagiarism. *TESOL Quarterly, 30*(2), 201–230.

Phillipson, R. (1992). *Linguistic imperialism*. Oxford, England: Oxford University Press.

Prior, P. (2001). Voices in text, mind, and society: Sociohistoric accounts of discourse acquisition and use. *Journal of Second Language Writing, 10*(1–2), 55–81.

II

Negotiating and Interacting

6

Negotiating the Gatekeepers: The Journey of an Academic Article

George Braine
The Chinese University of Hong Kong

The literature on academic writing has been enriched by publications that have explored academic writers and various aspects of the academic publishing process. For instance, Canagarajah (1997) described the nondiscursive challenges faced by academics such as himself in third-world countries, and Connor (1999) and Li (1999) narrated their apprenticeship to American academic discourse. Gosden (1995, 1996) and Flowerdew (1999a, 1999b, 2000) investigated the publishing process of nonnative scholars from Japan and Hong Kong. The increasing pressure on scholars worldwide to publish in Western (mainly Anglo-American) journals (see Braine, 2000, September) has added further impetus to explorations of the challenges of academic publications.

To my knowledge, however, it is rare to see a first-person account of a writer's own experiences and perspectives on academic publication through the description and analysis of the journey of an academic article—from conception, composition, selection of journals for submission, negotiations with editors and manuscript reviewers, decisions to revise or not, and finally, acceptance and publication. In this chapter, I narrate the process by which I nurtured an academic article from conception to publication. Within the narration, I reflect on the reasons for writing the article, the basis on which I selected journals for submission, and the nature of my negotiations with journal editors and reviewers. The latter concern receives the most attention because of the complex sociopolitical and psychological aspects of such negotiations, and also because the process was influenced by my experiences as editor of the *Asian Journal of English Language Teaching (AJELT)*.

BACKGROUND

In 1989, I was hired by the English Department of a public university in the southeast United States. Because the university aggressively recruits international students, about 800 such students were enrolled at the university during my 6 years there.

At this university, first year writing courses were sequenced as Composition I and Composition II. During the early 1990s, students were required to pass an exit test on completion of the Composition I course in order to enroll in Composition II. About 2,000 students took the exit test annually, most during the fall quarter. Beginning in the winter quarter of 1992, three sections of Composition I were reserved for English as a second language (ESL) students, and these students were given the choice of enrolling in either the regular or ESL sections; most ESL students chose to enroll in ESL sections. Another noteworthy event around this time was the hiring of a new director of freshman composition whose specialization was rhetoric and composition.

THE EXIT TEST

Although the exit test had been in place for some years, the following discussion is limited to its administration from the winter 1992 academic quarter, when separate ESL sections were first designated for Composition I, until winter 1994. This is also the period covered in the article that is the focus of this chapter.

During the winter and spring quarters of 1992, three prompts designed by the director of freshman writing with the help of the Freshman English Committee were given to the students a week before the exit test. A typical prompt given during this period is shown in Fig. 6.1. In most classes, students prepared for the test by writing responses to all the prompts, which were discussed and commented on by the teachers. Only one of the prompts would be given to them at the 2-hour exit test. About 2 weeks before the test, teachers in the English Department had participated in a calibration session. In preparation for this session, teachers read selected student papers from previous tests and rated the papers according to a rubric based on a holistic 1–6 scale, followed by a discussion. Immediately after the exit test, a few teachers read a sample of student papers, created a second rubric for evaluating the papers, and selected a set of range finders from the sample student papers that related to each level in the rubric. The new rubric and copies of the range finders were given to the teachers along with the student papers for evaluation. All student papers were read

---

The value of compromise: Many national and political problems are resolved by compromise; one side or another has to give up some of its demands. Compromise is part of our everyday lives, too. What stands out in your mind as one of your major compromises? Was it difficult to accept? How did you distinguish it from failure? From your personal experience, what would you say is the value of yourself? Which of your own cultural values do you value? Are there some you think should change?

FIG. 6.1. Typical prompt from Composition I exit test, winter and spring 1992.

twice, by different teachers. For a paper to pass, both readers had to assign a score of at least 4 on the rubric.

Partly as a result of the extra attention the students received in ESL sections, and also as a result of a strategy used by some of them (of writing responses to all three prompts given a week before the test, memorizing the responses, and copying the appropriate response at the test), their passing rates in the winter and spring quarters in 1992 were 84% and 60%, respectively.

In the beginning of the 1992–1993 academic year, the format of the exit test was changed to emphasize both reading and writing. The process that led to the test began with a screening of suitable reading passages by members of the Freshman English Committee. To be considered for the test, the readings had to be about 1,500 words long and judged accessible to all students irrespective of linguistic or cultural background. Three readings were selected, copied, and distributed to all students about a week before the test was administered. As in previous years, the readings were discussed extensively and analyzed in Composition I classes. In addition, all the teachers created hypothetical prompts based on the readings, and students wrote practice responses to these prompts, both in and out of class. The Freshman English Committee, with the guidance of the director of freshman writing, then developed prompts for each reading and selected one prompt on the basis of one of the readings to be administered at the test. The process of calibration, creation of a second rubric after the exit test, and the evaluation of student papers on the basis of the rubric remained unchanged.

Despite their inability to use the "memorize and copy" strategy, ESL students performed quite well in the exit test during the 1992–1993 academic year. The passing rates for ESL students in the fall, winter, and spring quarters were 56%, 39%, and 42%, respectively. (See Braine, 1996, for an analysis of the performance of ESL students in the exit test during the 1992–1993 academic year.) One of the prompts given in fall 1992, when the reading–writing format of the exit test was introduced, is shown in Fig. 6.2. This prompt was based on a reading titled "Comparing Work Ethics: Japan and America" (Ouchi, 1981).

By fall 1993, however, the passing rate for ESL students had dropped to 31%. The 80-word prompt from the fall 1993 test (shown in Fig. 6.3) was, in addition to being a complex writing prompt, also a reading task, which would be stressful to L2 students writing under time pressure. The prompt required the writers to explain the quotation, describe a special time for the student writer, discuss the special time, and relate the special time to the writer's review of White's essay.

The sloppy prompt design reached an even lower level by winter 1994. One of the readings for the exit test was a seven-page, 47-paragraph essay titled "Thinking as a Hobby" by William Golding (1966). In the essay, Golding classified thinking into three grades. Grade 3 thinking was described as feeling—thoughts full of prejudice, ignorance, and hypocrisy. Fully 29 of the 47 paragraphs were given to describing Grade 3 thinking with vivid anecdotes and examples. Grade 2 thinking was described as the detection of contradictions. Again, Golding illustrated Grade 2 thinking with anecdotes and examples in six lengthy paragraphs. However, Grade 1 thinking was described with one anecdote, Golding's meeting with Einstein, who is identified as an "undeniably grade one thinker." During the meeting, Golding and Einstein stand

---

In a well-written essay, discuss and analyze Ouchi's view of the Japanese work ethic ("collectivism"). Using examples from your experience, include a detailed and well-supported account of situations when either teamwork or individualism was more effective.

FIG. 6.2.   Prompt from Composition I exit test, fall 1992.

A special experience can provide a person with a rich source of understanding about one's self and about the time and place in which the experience occurred, as E.B. White demonstrates in his essay "Once More to the Lake." What does White mean when he writes that "those times and those summers had been infinitely precious and worth saving"? Describe and discuss a special time or season of your own and relate it to your review of White's essay.

FIG. 6.3.   Prompt from Composition I exit test, fall 1993.

side by side on a small bridge at Oxford University in near silence for about 10 minutes, watching the stream below. Finally, Einstein points to a fish in the stream, utters the word "Fish," and ambles off. No other anecdotes or examples are cited and the entire description takes only five short paragraphs. Yet, the prompt for the exit test required students to draw "a verbal portrait of the best 'grade one' thinker you have ever personally known" (see Fig. 6.4).

The passing rate for ESL students plummeted to 29%. When I examined some exit test papers written by ESL students, I could clearly see the students' desperation when confronted with this prompt. In fact, a number of students explicitly referred to the difficulty of the prompt in their exam answers. One student wrote:

> To tell something about my personal experience is really hard for me because I am not old enough to gather experience and it is almost out of my dreams to have a personal experience with a grade one thinker.

Other students were more creative, identifying fictitious characters hurriedly invented during the test.

I interviewed two teachers who taught ESL Composition I classes that quarter and asked for their reactions to the prompt. They were both surprised that Grade 1 thinking was the focus of the prompt, because the reading referred to such thinkers only briefly, and the only example given of a Grade 1 thinker was Einstein. Therefore, they had paid little attention to Grade 1 thinkers during class discussions of the Golding essay. They said that it was difficult to explain Einstein's genius without a sound knowledge of physics. Both teachers felt that their students were unfairly penalized by the prompt.

When I later interviewed a number of ESL students who had taken the exit test, they too said that they did not expect to be tested on Grade 1 thinkers. Since Grade 2 and Grade 3 thinkers were discussed in greater detail in the Golding essay, they could relate such thinkers to people they personally knew and could describe these people with anecdotes. The students stated that although they knew Einstein to be a genius, they did not know enough about Einstein to relate his thinking habits to someone

---

Draw a verbal portrait of the best "Grade 1" thinker you have ever personally known. Provide at least one anecdote about this person's thinking habits. The point of your essay is to describe and discuss first rate thinking as vividly and thoroughly as possible.

FIG. 6.4. Prompt from Composition I exit test, winter 1994.

they knew personally. In any case, they were unlikely to meet anyone of Einstein's caliber in their lifetime and admitted that when they saw the test prompt, they created a character that they could label as a Grade 1 thinker. But because the Golding essay did not clearly state what Grade 1 thinking was, they could not proceed beyond naming or physically describing these fictitious characters.

THE MANUSCRIPT

I was convinced that the confusion caused by different rubrics used in the calibration sessions and during the actual scoring of exit test papers may have been partially responsible for the rapid decline in the passing rate. On the basis of my analyses of test prompts and my interviews with teachers and students, I was convinced that carelessly designed test prompts may also have contributed to the dismal passing rate.

My move to Hong Kong at the beginning of the 1995–1996 academic year and the attendant obligations to other projects caused the data to be shelved. Two years later, I was compelled to take an extended period of leave due to illness, and the availability of all the data I needed gave me the opportunity to write at home. Strictly speaking, the data could be transformed into a case study of an exit test in one writing program. Although I would describe and analyze the failure of the test, I did not wish to contextualize it within a lengthy literature review or a comparison of other exit tests that did not fail. The reasons for this were threefold. First, I had little background in testing and did not wish to explore aspects of exit tests at length; my priorities were in other areas of composition research. Second, although I had been a member of the TOEFL Test of Written English (TWE) Committee,[1] I did not place much confidence in the ability of tests to measure writing proficiency. Third, I assumed that, because I had not only relied on textual analysis but also studied the problem from the viewpoint of students and teachers, I had a richly described, triangulated, self-contained case study, which did not have to be corroborated or supported with other studies.

I wrote the initial manuscript before choosing an appropriate journal for submission. In it, I provided detailed background information on the university, its international students, the Composition I course, the textbooks that were used, and the development and administration of the exit tests. I also described the calibration sessions and how the student papers were scored. In addition, I included a series of figures consisting of sample prompts from the exit tests in order to illustrate the increasing sloppiness in the design of test prompts. The figures included prompts

---

[1]The committee consisted of seven ESL composition specialists and designed, evaluated, pretested, and approved items for the TWE.

from the 1992 test (Fig. 6.1 in this article), the fall 1992 test (Fig. 6.2 in this article), the fall 1993 test (Fig. 6.3 in this article), and the winter 1994 test (Fig. 6.4 in this article). I also included a bar graph that vividly illustrated the plummeting passing rate for ESL students, from 84% in the Winter 1992 to 29% in Winter 1994. In two appendixes, I presented the rubrics used by students in Composition I classes and by teachers in the calibration sessions and a sample of the ad hoc rubric hastily created by teachers for evaluating each exit test. My list of references only contained eight items, and three of them were composition textbooks used in the Composition I course. The manuscript, inclusive of the appendixes, was 17 pages in length.

SUBMISSIONS UNDER "RESEARCH" TITLE

Initially, I was unsure how to frame the article. Should it be a straightforward report, sequencing the events that led to the plummeting passing rate, or would it be more acceptable if framed as a research article, a genre I was more familiar with? I eventually chose the latter option, especially because I could present it as a longitudinal study.

As I composed the article in the final months of 1997, I felt that it had to be addressed mainly to readers in L1 composition studies because I was describing a situation that, in my opinion, had been caused by a composition specialist (the director of freshman English) trained in an L1 composition program that may have paid little or no attention to the needs of L2 students enrolled in tertiary-level writing courses. I hoped that teachers of graduate programs in rhetoric and composition, administrators of freshman writing programs at the college level (who were for the most part L1 composition specialists), and heads of English departments would pay attention to the debacle at my former university and take steps to avoid it.

Accordingly, I chose to submit the article to a journal that addressed itself to administrators of writing programs at North American universities. I was aware that many heads of English departments in North America subscribed to this journal. According to its "Author's Guide," the journal was interested in publishing articles on, among other topics, the establishment and maintenance of composition programs and the training of writing teachers. Research articles were only acceptable if they had a relationship to the administration of composition program. The journal had recently published an article that dealt with the placement of ESL students in first-year writing classes, and I therefore hoped that my article would be read with interest by the journal's editor and reviewers.

The title, which I thought sounded suitably academic, was "A Longitudinal Study of the Performance of ESL Writers in an Exit Test." The abstract was as follows:

This article describes a longitudinal study of the performance of ESL students in the exit test of a first-year writing program at a U.S. university. The passing rate, which averaged 72% when the exit test was based solely on a prompt, declined sharply when the format was changed to a test based on a reading passage. This study is based on an analysis of test prompts, reading passages, student responses, and interviews with teachers and students. Results of the analyses show that a lack of consistency in the scoring of the exit test, inappropriate reading passages, and careless prompt design contributed to the decline in the passing rate.

The manuscript was mailed in October 1997. In early December, I received a response, not from the editor but from an editorial assistant. It stated that the manuscript had been read with interest but went on to claim that "unfortunately, we do not feel that it is suitable given the scope of the journal and the type of contribution we require."

Included below the opening paragraph was a general statement of the journal's policy, the writer stating that all the policies may not be relevant to my manuscript. According to the general statement, manuscripts should not ignore recent research and should have "something to offer researchers in the field." The letter went on to state that the journal was not interested in papers that focused on teaching and testing issues, "in other words, practically oriented studies."

This response, which was contradictory to the aims of the journal stated in its "Author's Guide," made me wonder whether the editor had even read my manuscript. I was tempted to send a rejoinder, pointing out that the editor may have sent me the response meant for another manuscript. But in previous jousting with another journal editor, where I had conclusive evidence that the editor had mixed up manuscripts, I had been the loser. The general opinion among colleagues and friends in academia was that editors were a stubborn breed, an opinion I felt was partly justified by my own behavior and attitudes as an editor towards authors and manuscripts that were submitted to *AJELT*. Further, reading between the lines of the editorial assistant's response, I felt that my manuscript would not be published in the journal anyway because it was critical of mainstream composition programs and would cause some embarrassment to such programs and L1 composition specialists.

Would an L2 journal, which I knew also had a readership among L1 composition specialists, accept the manuscript? The particular journal I had in mind had two editors, one based in the United Kingdom and the other in the United States. Without making any changes to the manuscript, I submitted it to this journal in December 1997. The response (a rejection) arrived in early March 1998. One of the editors wrote that the consensus among the reviewers was that "while the project may be of local interest, the paper itself is too narrow" for the readership of the journal. Unlike in the case of the first journal, three reviews were enclosed; two rejected the manuscript outright in the first sentence itself.

The first review, the longest at five paragraphs, stated that the manuscript contained no review of the literature and that it did not contextualize the study within the field of composition studies and testing and assessment. It pointed out that the manuscript reported "absolutely no research" and criticized me for not examining the reasons for the students' poor performance! In conclusion, the reviewer recommended that in order to discover the reasons for the students' performance, I should use research methodology that included "systematic analysis of the content and tasks of the exam questions, systematic textual analysis of the responses, systematic interviewing of the participants, and a systematic examination of the pedagogical context." The repetition of "systematic" stood out as if in scarlet letters.

The second review, which consisted only of two short paragraphs, was even more emphatic in rejecting the manuscript. The reviewer did not "think that the manuscript raised serious scholarly issues" and further stated that it offered "little that would generalize beyond the predicament of the program being discussed." Curiously, the reviewer took a somewhat subjective stance, cautioning that the "authors should rethink whether or not they want to hold up their program to ridicule in a public forum" and went on to suggest that "perhaps the program and the ESL students involved would be better served if the authors made gradual efforts to bring about change in the program."

The third reviewer, who only wrote one brief paragraph, was more complimentary, appearing to apologize for being unable to recommend the manuscript for publication despite it being "clearly written and easy to read." However, the criticisms of the previous reviewers were echoed in the statement that the manuscript made no attempt to place the study in the context of the broader areas of testing or writing assessment.

REFLECTION AND REVISION

The harsh rejections, as they usually do, stung. But at least I had some suggestions on how to revise. First, it began to sink in that the manuscript did not really report empirical research, the title was a misnomer, and the abstract was misleading. Try as I might, I would not be able to transform the manuscript into a research article. I would need a new title, a new abstract, and a new format.

Second, the study needed to be contextualized—within L2 composition studies, testing, or in some other relevant field. As I have pointed out earlier, I had no interest in conducting background research into testing, and there was hardly a chance of contextualizing the manuscript within L2 composition studies because nothing I had read in this field related to the detailed analysis and critique of an exit test. I was therefore fortunate to come across an article authored by Silva, Leki, and Carson (1997) in *Written Communication*, in which these well-known L2 composition specialists argued that mainstream composition studies in the United States had largely neglected ESL writing. They pointed out that such neglect would lead to problems at both theoretical and practical levels.

Here was the context I needed, and also support for my position that an L1 composition specialist, unaware of and untrained in ESL writing, contributed to the failure of the exit test I described. Thus, building on the argument posed by Silva, Leki, and Carson—who were addressing a mixed L1 and L2 readership in *Written Communication*—I could begin my article by stating that placing a new director, who was an L1 composition specialist in charge of composition programs that included a large number of ESL students was detrimental to these students.

As stated earlier, I also needed a new "non-research" sounding title. I settled on "When an Exit Test Fails" and decided to label the manuscript a "report." Accordingly, the abstract of the revised manuscript read as follows:

This report describes the performance of ESL students in the exit test of a first-year writing program. The passing rate, which was high when the exit test was based solely on a prompt, declined sharply when the format was changed to a reading–writing test. The report is based on the analyses of exit test prompts, exit exam transcripts, scoring guides used in writing classes and during the calibration sessions to evaluate exit exams, reading passages, and interviews with students and teachers of first-year writing courses. Results of the analysis show that a lack of consistency in the scoring of the exit test, the use of inappropriate reading passages, and careless prompt design contributed to the decline in the passing rate.

The new version required little revision. I felt that the new title, the report format, and the contextualization provided by references to Silva, Leki, and Carson (1997) would be sufficient to give the manuscript a new look. In any case I had no inclination to invest more time in a manuscript that dealt with composition studies in the United States. I was now settled in Hong Kong and involved in local research. I had moved on.

RESUBMISSION UNDER "REPORT" FORMAT

With confidence gained by the revision, I was ready to face an L1 audience again. While searching at the university's library for a suitable L1 journal, I came across one that called itself "the oldest independent scholarly journal in rhetoric and composition." The journal was published in the United States, and the call for papers stated that, among other topics, it published manuscripts on the teaching and administration of writing and rhetoric at the tertiary level and, most appropriately, "institutional issues of interest to the field's teacher-scholars." Here was my journal! I was confident of a more sympathetic review of my manuscript and the issues it raised.

In late March 1998, I submitted the revised manuscript, now 18 pages in length, to this journal. Three months later, in June, I received a one-page reply from the editor. The news wasn't good. The editor agreed with both reviewers that the results of the study were not "particularly revealing." (The reviews were not enclosed.) The editor went onto say that it was clear that the motivation for ESL classes was driven by a desire to provide better instruction for these students. According to him, although the manuscript seemed to imply that the exit test failed on the basis of L2 writing instruction, the causes of failure didn't apply to ESL students alone: "It doesn't seem like anyone would have a good chance of divining what a 'grade one' thinker is." The failure was a result of general incompetence, not just ESL-related incompetence. He suggested that a more compelling story could be about the fate of the ESL classes rather than the "ill-fated" test.

In the second paragraph of the letter, the editor continued that the claims I made about ESL in most composition programs "struck a chord with him." At his university (which he named), there were about five to six ESL students in each composition class, more than the national average of two mentioned in the manuscript for composition classes nationwide. Nevertheless, his university had "zero tenure-line" faculty with ESL credentials, a situation similar to the previous universities where he had taught. He admitted that the separation of ESL and composition as professional discourses and institutional entities was not helping the majority of teaching assistants and writing program administrators. The editor ended by inviting me to write a review essay on two ESL composition books, which he had received, from publishers. (I did not accept his invitation.)

I was back to square one. Neither L1 journal had sent me copies of the reviews, and the best guidance I had was from the L2 journal I had submitted to earlier. So I decided to go back to an L2 journal that was published in Europe and had a broad readership in the United States as well as in Asia. It has an impressive editorial board, which includes some of the best known names in applied linguistics and ELT. The aims and scope of the journal said that manuscripts relating problems associated with the study and teaching of ESL and EFL would be considered. Manuscripts needed to have a sound theoretical base with a practical application, which could be generalized. I knew I was at a disadvantage in two aspects: My manuscript was not based on theory, and the journal appeared to publish manuscripts that had a wider, international appeal. But, I decided to plunge in.

So in April 1999, without further changes, I submitted the manuscript to this journal. After a long delay, on October 22, the first review arrived via e-mail. Although he did not know me personally, the editor addressed me "Dear George" (a welcome change from the style of other editors who knew me quite well but would address me stiffly as "Professor Braine") and began by offering his "humblest apologies" for the "unconscionable delay" in reviewing my manuscript. Apparently, one reviewer of the manuscript had disappeared despite numerous reminders (a situation that I was quite familiar with as an editor of *AJELT*). He had managed to recruit two "fast-track reviewers" and sent me the first review he had received, which he said was largely favorable but required revisions in the manuscript.

I read the opening sentence with delight and relief. It said "publish but with revisions" and went onto say that the reviewer

> enjoyed this paper mainly because of the insight it gives into U.S. writing programs, the problems faced, and the kinds of decisions that need to be taken. It is valuable for the very practical insights that it offers, and I believe that it is appropriate to share these with a larger audience.

Exactly what I had in mind.

I had a suspicion that the reviewer was from Europe, first because of the British-style spelling in the review, second because of the admission that my manuscript provided insights into U.S. writing programs, and third because the reviewer was critical of my writing style, saying that "cohesion completely breaks down" at one point in the article. Although the "fast-track" review may have caused the confusion, this wasn't the first time that a European reader had found my American writing style somewhat irritating. Nevertheless, I felt comforted in that the reviewer would not be defensive of an U.S. writing program as a previous reviewer had been. This would be to my advantage.

The reviewer gave me nearly two pages of feedback, often with references to specific paragraphs and lines in the manuscript. However, as in the case of a reviewer of the previous L2 journal, this reviewer seemed to assume that I was responsible for the design and conduct of the exit test:

> The authors need to say somewhere what it is they THINK they wish to measure. The next question is HOW they are going to do this. And the third question is HOW MUCH of the writing ability the students need to undertake academic work in other disciplines. (emphasis in the original)

The reviewer went on to suggest that instead of abandoning the exit test, I (and others responsible for it) should have improved the test:

> If the sole reason for the failure of this test was the poor quality of the prompt and so on, then you just make it better next time. But that's not what the authors did. They abandoned the test completely.

Nevertheless, the reviewer concluded on a more positive tone, stating that the manuscript provided an interesting insight into the problems of a writing program at one university, and its strength lay in sharing those problems with the academic community and suggesting how and why these problems arose and could be solved in ways that are generalizable to other circumstances. The reviewer wanted a "much improved" version of the manuscript and said that he or she would "be more than willing to read a revised version."

At last, I had a sympathetic editor and a reviewer who appeared to sympathize with my reasons for writing the manuscript. Therefore, the second review, which arrived by e-mail on November 3, 1999, came as a rude disappointment. The editor prefaced the review by saying that the second review was "very negative" and that the two reviewers clearly disagreed fundamentally. He further stated that if I were to submit a revision, he would have to find new, independent reviewers for the manuscript. The review itself consisted of one paragraph of 10 lines, which began

> This [is] really not worth publishing. It consists of a simple description of a test and its results and the comments of some of those who took it, assessed it. There is absolutely no hard evidence provided other than this to show how and why [it] was unsuccessful.

The reviewer added that the manuscript read more like a "letter to a newspaper or journal than a serious article." It concluded with a highly subjective statement, similar to the ones I had seen in previous reviews: "I think it might even be dangerous to publish the article, as the institution in question could be easily identified if one really tried."

What could I do now? My manuscript clearly hung in the balance, and it was unlikely to survive the two independent reviewers the editor had in mind. On the other hand, I could relieve this kindly editor of the dilemma he faced as a result of the conflicting reviews by withdrawing my manuscript or by not responding at all. As an editor of *AJELT*, I always urged reviewers to be collegial in their comments on manuscripts. The second reviewer had not been collegial. Further, when conflicting reviews of *AJELT* manuscripts arrived, I would intervene in the process, evaluating the manuscripts in the light of *AJELT* submission guidelines in order to decide whether to accept or reject a manuscript or ask for a revision and resubmission. I therefore decided to not to give in but to negotiate more actively with the editor and the reviewers.

On the following day, November 4, 1999, I responded to the editor by e-mail. I began by saying that the second review came as a disappointment, especially because the first review had been mainly favorable. I wondered if the second reviewer had really read my article. I summarized my argument in the manuscript, that graduate programs in rhetoric and composition appear to ignore ESL writing instruction, and as a result, news of such programs could cause serious and irreparable damage to ESL writing students and courses. I said that I had presented a case study to justify my argument, showing through a detailed description and a clear graphic how the passing rate of ESL students in the exit test fell dramatically within a 2-year period. I said that in four pages under the Discussion section and elsewhere in the manuscript, I had attempted to show where the test may have gone wrong (in the selection of reading material, preparation of test prompts, and evaluation of the tests). I emphasized that this was not a letter to a newspaper, but a plea to graduate programs in rhetoric and composition and administrators of first-year writing programs as well as a caution to ESL specialists so that such catastrophes could possibly be avoided. What I argued for was more sensitivity towards ESL students in required writing courses. I said that I was intrigued by the possible "danger" of the article, as the reviewer had cautioned. I asked if we shouldn't be concerned about the ethics of testing and of not helping ESL students who were failing as a result of incompetent program administrators. I said that in my view, this November review was unprofessional. Nevertheless, I explained that I did not wish to place the editor in a dilemma. This manuscript had already been sent to three reviewers (although one had never replied), so I asked him to decide if it was worthwhile to resubmit the manuscript.

His reply arrived forthwith, advising me to revise the manuscript according to the recommendations of the first reviewer, who the editor claimed was one of the journal's most reliable reviewers, and, if possible, also to counter the objections of the second reviewer. He invited me to resubmit the manuscript, which would be sent to the first reviewer and another. The editor admitted that his reviewers were not usually so "diametrically opposed."

It became clear to me that the fate of my manuscript lay with the first reviewer, who, as I pointed out earlier, appeared to have misunderstood my role in the Composition I course, the exit test, and related matters that I described. A few years earlier, an author who submitted a manuscript to *AJELT* and who met with resistance by a stubborn reviewer had resorted to the strategy of addressing the reviewer directly. As the editor, I was surprised to receive a letter addressed to the reviewer (although not by name, since *AJELT* is refereed, and reviewers and authors are not identified) but had forwarded the letter to the reviewer. And the reviewer had acquiesced. Hence, I decided to address this reviewer directly (see Appendix at the end of this chapter for the letter I wrote). In the letter, I made it clear why I was unable to respond to some of the queries by stating clearly that I was not responsible for selecting the reading passages, the design of test prompts and rubrics, or the cancellation of the test. This letter was enclosed with the slightly revised manuscript which I resubmitted 2 months later, on June 7, 2000.

It worked. The reply from the editor, which arrived only a week later, contained the first reviewer's response:

There's just something about [the manuscript] that's nagging my head. It's one of those that's really right on the edge, and I just want to sit on the fence. But I guess I can't do that. So, here goes. I'll recommend publication IF the author(s) can …

The reviewer suggested that the abstract be revised to indicate the general relevance of the paper so that others could learn from this specific example. According to the reviewer, this was clear in the text, but not in the abstract. Second, the reviewer suggested that the distinction between the new holders and the tasks and prompts in the writing test be clarified because he or she was "not sure whether the new holders ARE RESPONSI-BLE FOR WRITING the tasks and prompts, or whether someone else does this and they end up suffering in some unspecified way" (emphasis in the original). According to the reviewer, the latter "confusion" was the source of his or her "nagging doubt."

The suggestions, especially regarding the abstract, were reasonable. Accordingly, I added the following sentences to the abstract, at the beginning and at the end.

Within the context of recent concerns that mainstream composition studies in the United States have largely neglected ESL writing, this report describes the performance of ESL students in the exit test of a first year writing program at a U.S. institution.… The report suggests that the employment of new teachers, who have had little exposure to ESL theory and practice, as directors of Fresh-man Writing may be detrimental to programs that enroll large numbers of ESL students. The report concludes with a suggestion for the inclusion of some course work in ESL writing in rhetoric and composition programs.

The revision was acceptable to the editor, and after a few minor changes were made, the manuscript was published in early 2001.

CONCLUSION

Did I achieve what I had set out to do, to address readers in L1 composition studies because the debacle of the exit test had been caused by a composition specialist trained in a L1 composition program? Probably not. But I did have the whole sorry saga on record, and at least ESL specialists in English departments would now be warned and could take adequate precautions to prevent such debacles. Although the manuscript was published 7 years after the exit test was canceled in 1994, the events are still valid and applicable for the same reasons.

Was I stubborn in resisting that criticism and advice of reviewers who pointed out that the manuscript did not have a sound theoretical basis or a review of the literature, and that the study was not carried out systematically? As a nonnative speaker of English who acquired academic literacy in a non-American environment, I have occasionally questioned the American (Western?) scholarly style of reporting research. My resistance was due partly to these doubts and also because I did not wish to be deeply involved in areas that I had no long-term interest in (testing of writing, ethics of testing, etc.).

Did a sympathetic, broad-minded editor play a role in the eventual publication of the manuscript? Undoubtedly. But, although a rarity, I am confident that this editor is not unique in being willing to accept an unconventional manuscript. On occasion, I too have encouraged such submissions to *AJELT.*

What would I say to a novice author who must publish or perish in the academic milieu? The world of academic publications is often baffling and frustrating. Its inhabitants include unsympathetic and authoritarian editors, and reviewers who can be crass and infuriatingly demanding. They will sometimes request the impossible—that the research design be changed, that more subjects be added, or that the scope be extended—from an article written well after the research had been completed. Prestigious journals sometimes publish poorly written articles, much to the chagrin of authors who may feel that their own (rejected) manuscripts were far superior. A glance at some of the journals in applied linguistics will show that they have published a few authors repeatedly, naturally at the expense of others.

Nevertheless, the prospects for novice authors have never been better. Consider the proliferation of academic journals. The TESOL organization's web site lists more than 50 journals in applied linguistics that display a variety of specializations within the discipline and represent most geographical regions. In Hong Kong alone, with a mere seven universities, the past 5 years have seen the emergence of three refereed journals in applied linguistics. In fact, the appearance of new journals seems directly linked to the pressure to publish, a phenomenon first observed in the United States but which has since spread to the United Kingdom, Australia, Hong Kong, and other countries as well. Authors now have a wide choice of journals to choose from, depending on how soon they wish to see their articles in print, what readers they wish to reach, and in which part of the world they wish to publish.

REFERENCES

Braine, G. (1996). ESL students in first-year writing courses: ESL versus mainstream classes. *Journal of Second Language Writing, 5,* 91–107.

Braine, G. (2000, September). *Overcoming barriers to academic publication: Hong Kong's success story.* Paper presented at the Symposium on Second Language Writing, Purdue University, West Lafayette, IN.

Canagarajah, A. S. (1997). "Nondiscursive" requirements in academic publishing, material resources of periphery scholars, and the politics of knowledge production. *Written Communication, 13,* 435–472.

Connor, U. (1999). Learning to write academic prose in a second language: A literacy autobiography. In G. Braine (Ed.), *Non-native educators in English language teaching* (pp. 29–42). Mahwah, NJ: Lawrence Erlbaum Associates.

Flowerdew, J. (1999a). Writing for academic publication: The case of Hong Kong. *Journal of Second Language Writing, 8,* 123–145.

Flowerdew, J. (1999b). Problems in writing for scholarly publication in English: The case of Hong Kong. *Journal of Second Language Writing, 8,* 243–264.

Flowerdew, J. (2000). Discourse community, legitimate peripheral participation, and the non-native English speaking scholar. *TESOL Quarterly, 34,* 127–150.

Golding, W. (1966). *Thinking as a hobby.* In C. Muscatine & M. Griffith (Eds.), *The Borzoi Reader* (pp. 5–11). New York: Knopf.

Gosden, H. (1995). Success in research article writing and revision: A social-constructionist perspective. *English for SpecificPpurposes, 16,* 37–57.

Gosden, H. (1996). Verbal reports of Japanese novices research writing practices in English. *Journal of Second Language Writing, 5,* 109–128.

Li, X. M. (1999). Writing from the vantage point of an outsider/insider. In G. Braine (Ed.), *Non-native educators in English language teaching* (pp. 43–55). Mahwah, NJ: Lawrence Erlbaum Associates.

Ouchi, W. (1981). *Theory Z.: How American business can meet the Japanese challenge* (pp. 47–51, 64–66). Reading, MA: Addison–Wesley.

Silva, T., Leki, I., & Carson, J. (1997). Broadening the perspective of mainstream composition studies. *Written Communication, 14,* 398–428.

APPENDIX

A note to the first reviewer:

Thank you for your detailed comments and suggestions and for expressing a willingness to read my revised manuscript.

In the report, my argument is that graduate programs in rhetoric and composition appear to ignore ESL writing instruction, and as a result, new PhDs of such programs could cause serious and irreparable damage to ESL students and writing courses. I presented a case study to justify my argument, showing through a description and clear figures how the passing rate of ESL students in the exit test fell dramatically within a 2-year period. In the Discussion section and elsewhere, I attempted to show where the test may have gone wrong (in the selection of reading material, preparation of test prompts, and evaluation of the test). This report is a plea to graduate programs in rhetoric and composition and administrators of first-year writing programs, and a caution to ESL specialists so that such catastrophes might possibly be avoided. What I argue for is more sensitivity towards ESL students in required writing courses.

In the revision, I have addressed many of the issues that you raised, including the lack of cohesion. However, I am unable to respond to some of your queries, such as how the cut score of 4 for passing the exit test was arrived at. The reading passages were not selected by me, nor did I have a hand in the design of test prompts or of the scoring guides. These tasks were the responsibilities of the Freshman English Committee under the direction of the director of freshman writing. In fact, I had no hand in the eventual abolishment of the test either. The director's refusal to address these problems with the exit test, when the writing was clearly on the wall, eventually led to this debacle.

Thank you again for reading my manuscript.

7

Reflections on Being a Gatekeeper

Sandra Lee McKay
San Francisco State University

This is my 23rd draft and the fourth time I have seriously considered e-mailing Chris and Stephanie to tell them I will be unable to submit a chapter for this book. I have been mulling over why this paper has been so difficult to write and decided that one of the main problems has been trying to establish an author's voice that is appropriate for this paper. Why has this been difficult?

I think there are several reasons. First, I framed the paper with the working title, "Being the Gatekeeper," as if my position as editor were somehow a solitary role in which I made decisions. This, of course, is far from true. My role as editor of a major journal in the field of teaching English to speakers of other languages (the *TESOL Quarterly*), as I imagine is true for most editors, was far from individual. Rather it was affected by a range of factors, some involving other individuals, some policies, and some traditions. Hence, my initial idea to approach a description of my role as editor as an individual gatekeeper was, I think, a mistake.

Second, in earlier drafts when I started to write about the various factors that influenced my role as editor, I found that a sense of confidentiality got in the way. Authors, reviewers, production staff, all, I felt, were depending on me to maintain a degree of confidentiality in our relationships even now, long after the fact. Because of this, on many occasions when I started to write about a particular incident I felt that if I discussed it in great detail I would be violating the trust of other individuals involved in the process of publication, even if no names were mentioned. As a result, I resorted to very analytic descriptions of what occurred. How can I resolve this dilemma? I have decided to try another approach, namely to show you what

I have written and then to comment as honestly as I can on what I said and why. What the reader will find is the result of many drafts with a reflection on my final draft both as an author and as an editor. For clarity, my added commentaries are indented. The reader will note that most of my reflections occur early in the paper when I had the greatest problem in establishing an appropriate voice.

The Gatekeeper

God greeted two newcomers to heaven. One was a preacher, the other a lawyer. He ushered the preacher to a small shack and settled him in to his austere quarters; then he led the lawyer to a huge, luxuriously appointed mansion.

"I don't understand," the lawyer puzzled. "That man was a preacher, and you gave him a shack. And yet, you've said I am to live in this luxurious mansion. Why?"

"Sir," said God, "We've had lots and lots of preachers here. But you, sir, are our very first lawyer."

We've all heard countless gatekeeper jokes in which some poor soul receives his or her just due from an all-powerful authority. In many ways, this story contrasts sharply with those of real-world gatekeepers in which gatekeepers are typically surrounded by a good deal of bureaucracy that masks the idea of an individual making a decision. Personnel departments in corporations, administrative offices in universities, and health insurance companies are just a few of countless organizations that have been established to make and administer decisions that significantly affect an individual's life. What such organizations do is suggest that a gatekeeping decision was made not by an individual or individuals but rather by a faceless bureaucratic organization. The larger the organization, the more pronounced this suggestion. In many ways this situation protects those individuals who are making the decisions from being held individually accountable.

Such protection, however, is frequently not afforded to those making gatekeeping decisions regarding publication because in the view of many contributors to journals, publication decisions are made solely by one individual, namely, the editor. Even though my experience as editor of the *TESOL Quarterly* clearly demonstrated to me that this is not the case, as editor I realize I was often perceived as the sole arbiter in making a publication decision. One of my goals in this essay is to illustrate the complexity of the role of an editor. Whereas editors, like all individuals who manage gatekeeping organizations, have a good deal of power and discretion given to them, there are nonetheless many internal constraints that reduce the power of an editor.

To begin, I would like to explore what I see as the some of the central roles I played as editor of the *TESOL Quarterly* from 1994 to 1999: the gatekeeper as policy maker, decision maker, and politician. I then reflect on my personal reactions to playing these roles. In closing my commentary, I elaborate on how what I experienced as editor might be of benefit to those who are seeking to participate in the publication process of writing for scholarly publications.

> In my initial beginning, I recognized quite early that I needed to make the point that as an editor and gatekeeper I was not acting alone. My mistake perhaps was then to proceed with a framework that was essentially describing my individual role rather than to describe how this role was affected by and, at the same time, exerted influence on a variety of other publication parameters.

THE GATEKEEPER AS POLICY MAKER

One of the key functions of a gatekeeper is to enforce existing policies. Often the formulating of such policies is undertaken by some official body. The *TESOL Quarterly*, as with most journals, has an editorial board. (Later I explain some of the dilemmas editors face in selecting board members.) Typically board members are chosen by the editor to serve for a specified time. Most major policy decisions regarding the *Quarterly* are made by this body at the annual meeting held at the TESOL national convention.

Several of the policy decisions made while I was editor demonstrate the kinds of issues that must be dealt with in the publication process. One issue, for example, was the question of how many times an individual author could publish an article in the *Quarterly* within a specified time period. On the one hand, some board members believed that there should be a limit as to how many articles were accepted by one author so that many voices were heard in the journal. On the other hand, other board members believed that if we were to have blind reviews in which articles were judged solely by the merit of the work, then if more than one article from an author were accepted in the process of blind reviews, there was no reason why it should not be published. After a good deal of discussion, the board accepted a policy that no more than one article could be published by one author within one volume of the journal. If an author had more than one article accepted in a year, then, although they both would eventually be published, one of the articles would have to wait for publication. The formulating of such policies demonstrates that in many cases policies represent a compromise of competing views of the publication process. In addition, the crafting of such policies is not made by the editor; rather it is a matter of compromise among board members.

> What was not mentioned in this paragraph, but what was one of the important factors that was driving this discussion, was a larger issue of the image of the journal. Some members believed that the *Quarterly* already tended to publish too many articles by the same individuals, often individ-

uals who were presently on or who had served on the editorial board. In the view of some members of the board this perception led some readers to feel that the journal was an "old boys' club," closed to those who were not members of the club. The policy decision in some ways then was a debate over how to make the publication process both appear and, in fact, be more open.

The fact that policy making is a shared process is often not recognized by contributors to a journal, who often believe that it is the editor who has sole discretion in all matters of the publication process. From an editor's perspective, however, I found that having policies formulated by the board were essential as they provided a basis for fairness in the publication process. They were also important to me as editor because I did not then have the sole responsibility for making significant decisions but was sharing these decisions with respected peers.

Another policy issue that arose while I was editor addressed what the maximum length of manuscripts should be. When I began as editor, more and more qualitative research articles were being submitted, with the result that the existing policy of a 20-page limit, formulated with the idea of quantitative research reporting, was not appropriate. Whereas most board members agreed that the maximum length needed to be increased, some felt that by doing this we would reduce the number of articles that could be published in a year. Furthermore, some board members were reluctant to encourage prospective authors to submit qualitative research. Whereas I personally was in favor of encouraging the consideration of qualitative research studies, I saw one of my roles as editor as providing a forum for the board members to share their opinions on issues and to then formulate a policy as a board. In short, I did not see my role as a decision maker in reference to policy development.

> Again my initial rather objective account of this issue masked one of the real agendas behind this discussion. When I became editor there was great hesitancy among many in our profession regarding the wisdom of including qualitative studies in a journal that for a long time had published mainly quantitative studies. Some viewed qualitative research as a subjective method that lacked the rigor of quantitative research methods; others viewed it as a valuable approach for gaining further insight into language acquisition and pedagogy. And although my initial draft suggested that I was unbiased, that my role was merely to provide a forum for board members, in fact I did support the publication of rigorous qualitative research. In order to convince others of this, I encouraged the publication of a special-topic issue on qualitative research methods. In this way, I cannot honestly say that I did not try to play an active role in policy formation. Several of my goals, such as making the journal a truly international journal with contributors from all over the globe and ensuring that the journal was rigorous but readable, led me to play an advocate role in a variety of policy decisions.

THE GATEKEEPER AS DECISION MAKER

Questions such as exactly who will review a manuscript, when an accepted manuscript will be published in the journal and where it will appear in relation to other articles, who will serve on the editorial board, and who will be the editor of various sections of the journal are just a few of the decisions editors make that significantly affect the publication process. In what follows I highlight some of the decisions I faced as editor.

Perhaps one of the most stressful decisions I faced was who to invite to serve on the editorial board. The difficulties I faced in making this decision arose from what I saw as the dual purpose of an editorial board. On the one hand, the status of a journal is frequently measured by the prestige of the members of the editorial board. Often potential contributors look at who is on the editorial board as one indication of the quality of the journal. On the other hand, it is the members of the board who review manuscripts, judge their overall quality, and provide contributors with substantive feedback as to the rationale for their assessment of the paper.

The kind of feedback contributors receive from reviewers plays a key role in the quality of articles that are published in a journal. In my experience as editor, almost all authors who published in the *Quarterly* were asked to revise their paper at least one time. How successful authors were in this revision process was closely related to the kind of response they received from their reviewers. Those authors who received lengthy and substantive feedback were often able to submit revised papers that were greatly improved and frequently ready for publication. The problem I faced as editor was that some individuals who had published widely in the field and thus achieved a good deal of prestige in the field were at times not the most helpful reviewers, often because their dedication to their own writing sometimes took precedence over their commitment to providing thoughtful and elaborate feedback.

> My comments here reflect my frustration from occasionally receiving reviews from widely published board members that were inadequate. Often they were very brief, unhelpful commentaries that essentially said to publish or not publish a manuscript with no reasons offered for the decision. What I then had to decide was whether to send the review to the author or to get another review. If I took the latter course, I often had to burden reviewers who always did thorough reviews with additional work and to delay feedback to the author. In the long run I found that I tended to send manuscripts to board members who typically did thorough reviews so that authors could benefit from constructive feedback. What bothered me, however, was that this course of action did not result in a fair distribution of work in reviewing manuscripts.

In general, the policy I followed in selecting reviewers for a particular submission was to send manuscripts to board members who had published or who had expertise in the particular subject area of the manuscript. Several factors, however, made it difficult to follow this policy all the time. In some cases, those that had expertise in a particular area were already reviewing a manuscript, and hence I did not want to send them another manuscript in the interest of equally distributing the review work of board members. In other cases, there was no one on the board who had expertise in a particular area, which led me to ask individuals who were not board members to review a manuscript. In this way, finding a competent reviewer for a particular topic was frequently a difficult task. It was equally challenging at times to select a reviewer who would not be biased in their reading of a manuscript as a result of their particular values regarding research and pedagogy.

> My last point reflects a complex problem. At times reviewers had a clear philosophical stance toward particular language-learning and teaching theories and were not receptive to articles that espoused alternate theories. At other times, manuscripts had critical comments on the work or stance of a potential reviewer; therefore I was concerned that if I sent the manuscript to this individual, it might be more difficult for the reviewer to write an objective review. And occasionally even though a manuscript was submitted with all references to the author deleted, the reference list, which contained many references to the author, made it clear who had written the article. If I knew the author and potential reviewer were critical of each other's work, I felt it was best to avoid the selection of this reviewer for the manuscript. Hence, the selection of a reviewer is clearly a value-laden decision.

A final challenging decision I faced as editor was determining which articles to include and how to order them. Having an article published as the first or lead article of an issue carries prestige. In this way, editors can influence how an article is received by deciding the order of the articles. Although ideally one could argue that the most important criterion in determining the choice of a lead article should be the standards of research exemplified in the paper as well as the quality of writing, judgments regarding these two factors can, of course, vary widely.

In fact the excellence of the work is not the only factor that an editor may consider in selecting a lead article. In some cases an editor may want to make a statement regarding the direction of the journal. In addition to the overall quality of the manuscript, two other factors influenced my selection of lead articles. First, I firmly believed that equal status should be afforded to sound qualitative and quantitative research. Second, I believed that it was important to recognize the unique contributions that bilingual speakers of English can make to our field. Like all editors I hoped to be impartial in my decision-making, even though there is no question that the decisions I made were influenced by my beliefs and values.

The preceding paragraph does not emphasize sufficiently my belief that the profession of teaching English to speakers of other languages (TESOL) and the *Quarterly* needed to reflect a more international authorship. I was convinced that as a profession we needed to challenge the myth of the native speaker of English as the target for language pedagogy and research. Hence, I was anxious to see quality work, done by bilingual speakers of English, as the lead article of an issue. Nonetheless few articles by bilingual speakers of English were published while I was editor, some of this due to the small number of submissions I received from such contributors. My international work convinced me that one of the major reasons for this fact is that unfortunately many bilingual researchers outside of the United States believe they are in some sense inadequate because they are not native speakers. One of my goals was to convince such individuals of the strengths they have in being bilingual and bicultural, particularly in the TESOL profession.

THE GATEKEEPER AS POLITICIAN

Although the term *politician* can have negative connotations, I use it in a neutral sense. In my view editors act as politicians in providing contributors and readers with clear rationales regarding their decisions. Typically editors are accountable to three main groups: the editorial board members, contributors to the journal, and the body that funds and oversees the journal. In general I found that I most frequently had to provide a clear rationale for my decisions when I was interacting with contributors. In some cases, authors felt that their manuscripts had not been given the kind of treatment they should have been given. In these instances, some authors argued that on the basis of the reviews they had received, their manuscript should have been published, or at the very minimum they should have been given further chances to revise it. My role then was to listen to their arguments, make a decision, and then provide a rationale for my decision. It is important to note, however, that the *Quarterly*, like most journals, does have a procedure for contributors to challenge an editor's decision. In the context of the *Quarterly*, authors can present their grievances to the TESOL executive board.

My comments here arise from an unpleasant experience I had as editor when an author questioned the decision made not to accept his or her article for publication. In this case the author submitted a very strongly written letter regarding the decision and my role in this decision and sent it to the president of TESOL and the executive board. The board then asked me to respond to the author's criticisms. My letter convinced the board to support my initial assessment of the manuscript. However, the entire experience was, of course, stressful. I felt I had received public and widespread criticism before I had had an opportunity to justify my decision to the author. In recounting this experience, I do not mean to suggest that authors should not question a decision that is made regarding their manuscript. Rather, authors should initially write to the editor directly to register their complaint, and then, if they still believe they have not been treated fairly, they should contact other officials in the publication process.

My function as a politician also entailed encouraging potential authors to submit their work to the journal. In some cases, authors had various possibilities as to where to submit their work, and thus if I believed their work—described in a conference presentation or unpublished paper—appeared to be of significance and quality, I would encourage them to submit their manuscript to the journal. In some instances, authors were hesitant to submit a paper to the journal, believing they could not meet the high standards of the *Quarterly*. I therefore felt one of my roles was to encourage these individuals to participate in the publication process, without leading them to believe that their manuscript would necessarily be published.

In other cases my role as politician involved my relation with the TESOL executive board and those individuals who were designated to oversee the workings of the journal. In my tenure as editor, I found the executive board extremely supportive of the journal. There were, however, instances when I needed to provide board members with a rationale for editorial decisions. For example, the length of a particular issue plays a significant role in the cost of producing an issue. Therefore, when an issue was particularly long, as occurred in some cases with special-topic issues, I needed to demonstrate why the length was necessary in terms of meeting the interests of the readers of the *Quarterly*. I also needed to provide a rationale for an operating budget that I believed was necessary for clerical help, postal expenses, and phone calls.

My workings with the editorial board of the *Quarterly* also demanded tactfulness. The lengthy meetings of the editorial board at the national conventions were often tiring, resulting in some friction among board members that needed to be addressed. In general, however, I found my work with the editorial board to be very rewarding, with members typically supporting and respecting other board members even when they differed significantly in their opinions and values.

PERSONAL REACTIONS TO PLAYING A GATEKEEPER ROLE

Being involved in policy and decision making, as well as working with the various stakeholders in the publication process, was a taxing endeavor. Perhaps the most challenging experience was seeing the first issue through the publication process. I questioned myself on every decision I had as editor, from selecting and ordering the contents of the issue to editing all of the copy. My primary initial concern was obtaining a sufficient number of manuscripts to complete an issue. As a new editor, I had not been involved in the process of acquiring manuscripts for a long enough period to have a backlog of manuscripts that had been accepted for publication. I therefore was concerned that I would not have enough copy to make a substantive issue.

Another major concern I faced was editing the copy. Although I had a support staff member to help me in this aspect of the process, I carefully reviewed all of the copy, making sure that it was clear and conformed to American Psychological Association (APA) guidelines. This was a tedious job that took countless hours because I found myself worrying that perhaps I had missed something, particularly an element that did not conform to APA guidelines. By the time the first issue was in production, I began to dread taking on the whole process once again. Luckily the process did get much easier as I found ways to manage all of the demands of compiling an issue.

> The comments above perhaps do not demonstrate sufficiently the worries I had during my initial year as editor. Like many beginning editors I was overwhelmed by the details involved in the job. I found myself spending many hours on the journal and in the process becoming tired and stressed by the job. There were occasions during the first year when I felt that I would not last another 4 years as editor. This was especially true when I had spent a long day involved in the tedious but necessary work of editing a manuscript that needed a good deal of sentence-level editing.

One of the most daunting aspects of being an editor is the number of details that are entailed in the job. While I was editor, the *Quarterly* received over 130 manuscripts per year. I needed to read each of these manuscripts to determine whether the topic was appropriate to the goals of the *Quarterly* and, in addition, whether it met the standards of quality listed in the Information to Contributors. In some instances I suggested that authors submit their manuscript to another journal, one more appropriate to their topic. In other cases, manuscripts did not meet the standards for submission outlined in the contributors' guidelines. In over half of the cases, however, the submissions did go out for review. When this occurred I had to decide which two reviewers to ask to review the manuscript, which as I mentioned earlier could be a difficult decision. Reviewers had 6 weeks to complete their review. When manuscripts were not returned within this general time frame, I had to remind reviewers to submit their reviews. Approximately 10% of submitted articles were eventually published. Although this may be a discouraging statistic for contributors, it is important to note that almost half of the submissions were not at all appropriate for the journal to begin with.

After both reviews were received, I read the reviews and wrote to the authors, indicating in general that their paper either had not been accepted for publication or that their paper needed to be revised before it could be considered for publication. Once a paper had been accepted, then the time-consuming task of editing the article for publication began. In short, each submission to the journal entailed a variety of steps from the initial reading of the manuscript through the review process and finally the revision and editing process. The entire process then of acquiring manuscripts, reviewing them, and eventually editing some for publication is a demanding process.

Although there are clearly many challenges and frustrations to being an editor, there are many rewards. One of the most enjoyable aspects of the job for me was the people I worked with, including editorial board members, contributors, and TESOL central office staff members. Many individuals that I had known previously only through their publications and conference presentations became close colleagues and friends. Another rewarding aspect of being editor was the breadth of information I acquired from reviewing incoming manuscripts. As editor, I read manuscripts dealing with areas of the field that I had not been familiar with. I became aware of key issues and publications in various areas of specialization. Finally, of course, being the editor of a major publication in the field is empowering. Though like most editors I strove to make sure that all authors were treated equally and that existing journal policies were followed, I had—like all editors—biases regarding my areas of interest, approach to knowledge, and view of the publication process.

> Empowering is currently such a popular word that it warrants my elaborating on what I mean by this term. Making decisions regarding what would be published and what direction the journal would take was empowering in the sense that I felt I had personal power over a complex publication process. At the same time, I realized that deciding who would be on the board, what would be the lead article in an issue, and who would review a particular manuscript affected not only the overall effectiveness of the journal but also personal lives. In this way, the empowerment was quite humbling. I also am aware that the fact I was an editor of a widely circulated journal had prestige. Certainly it was flattering for individuals to seek out my advice because of my position as editor. Finally, I was empowered by the new areas of knowledge that I was exposed to. I felt I was aware of the latest research in various areas and knew the issues that surrounded controversial topics.

GATEKEEPERS AND CONTRIBUTORS

In light of the insight I have gained from my experience as editor, let me offer a few suggestions to journal contributors. To begin, authors, of course, cannot hope to gain entry to the publication process unless they meet particular standards. Most journals clearly specify the standards contributors must meet. These standards relate primarily to the quality of the research undertaken, the clarity of writing and, in the case of the *Quarterly*, the explicit links that are made between theory and pedagogy.

In addition to meeting these standards, authors need to adhere to the etiquette of the publication process. In the case of journal submissions, authors should submit their work to only one journal at a time. Occasionally individuals who have not published before do not realize that this is standard policy. Hence, they submit their work to two or more journals at the same time. However, almost all editors look with disfavor on such an approach and will likely reject any manuscript that they learn is being considered by another journal at the same time.

This problem occurred a few times while I was editor. In several cases, the authors could not understand why such a policy existed. One of the main reasons for this policy is to protect the reviewers and editors. Because reviewers volunteer their time to contribute to the publication process, it is unfair if reviewers offer their time and expertise to provide authors with feedback only to learn that an author has decided to publish his or her article in another journal.

It is also extremely important to recognize that contributors to journals have rights. They have a right to receive a timely review and substantive feedback on their manuscript. If this does not occur, an author should withdraw his or her manuscript from consideration and submit it to another journal. Also in reference to the feedback that authors receive from reviewers, authors are under no obligation to follow all of the suggestions made by reviewers. As editor I encouraged authors when they were not pleased with aspects of a review they had received to specify in a letter which suggestions contained in the review they did not agree with and why.

Having been many times in the role of a potential contributor to a journal, I know the feeling of anger that can occur when an individual receives a negative review. What I learned as a writer was to try to consider the feedback as objectively as I could, separating what I saw as a valid criticism or suggestion from those I considered ungrounded and unwarranted. As an editor, I now realize how many factors can influence a particular review. As I mentioned earlier, reviewers occasionally and unfortunately do not take their role seriously and do not read a manuscript with the care they should or write the kind of substantive feedback that authors deserve.

> Because it is likely that many readers, like me, have had the experience of receiving a negative review, let me clarify some factors that can lead to such a review. First, there is the possibility that parts or most of the review are warranted in that an author has not done the necessary groundwork for the article. I recall one rejection I had that in retrospect was quite justified. I was a young author and had done a good deal of reading on a topic but had not clarified my own purpose in writing the article other than to add a publication to my resume. As I look back, the negative review I received was fully justified and perhaps even gentler than it might have been. However, there are other reasons that can lead to a negative review. A reviewer may have personal and professional biases against the positions taken in the article and not write the kind of objective review that should be written. Reviewers may also be under personal and professional stress and not write the balanced and thorough re-

views they normally do. And finally, there are some individuals who are by nature highly critical and phrase their criticisms very directly.

Like reviewers, editors bring to their job particular biases and values and are influenced by other pressures and responsibilities they may face. As editor, I needed to juggle my responsibilities as editor with my teaching responsibilities, my own research and writing interests, and most importantly my family and friends. At times, these factors kept me from doing the kind of job I would ideally have liked to do. In short, having experienced the publication process from both the editor's and author's perspective, I realize that it is important to recognize the human aspect of the process.

As I reflect on my initial closing advice to contributors, I realize there are two main points I hoped to make to potential contributors. First I wanted contributors to recognize that they have responsibilities and rights in participating in the publication process. At the same time I wanted them to realize that that the publication process is a human endeavor and that human biases, values, and priorities play a significant role in the outcome of journal decisions, so there will be occasions when such decisions are not the fair and objective decisions that contributors and editors both want to see.

8

Tangled Webs: Complexities of Professional Writing

Ilona Leki
University of Tennessee

Anyone involved with professional writing in any capacity probably has dozens of stories to tell—often painful ones, ones that in one way or another constitute a threat to "face." To some degree that is what each of the authors in this book is writing about, at least partly in an attempt to reassure other authors with the pleasant(?) news that these assaults on personal dignity are not exclusively reserved for certain groups (though some groups clearly experience them more than others) but oddly enough seem to be part of the communal experience in professional writing. This communal experience is undergirded by a tangle of social relationships between and among authors, editors, reviewers of manuscripts, and readers. In this chapter I reflect on the tangle of social relationships that accompany being a journal editor and, at the same time, an author in the same discipline, and I explore different angles of the conflicted subject positions occasioned by the requirement to write professionally. My goal here is to clarify some of the circumstances I think editors find themselves in, on one hand, and, on the other, to document the difficulty and sometimes the pain associated with writing for academic publications, even for experienced authors.

THE DOOR(WO)MAN'S LIFE

"I don't believe you."

—Bob Dylan in answer to someone in a crowd calling him a Judas for going electric

As a journal editor of the *Journal of Second Language Writing*[1] (*JSLW*), I often feel myself at the nexus of the web of these social relationships, where one of my jobs seems to be to negotiate between authors and reviewers, between readers and authors, and between reviewers and readers.[2] Each coupling has its claims to forward, and although the demands are often mutually supportive, that is not always the case, with one or another of the web inhabitants claiming infringement of their rights or needs or moral–ethical sense. Personally I feel very sensitive to the question of by what right I presume as an editor to arbitrate these positions, but there is no reason for any of the other subjectivities in the web to be aware of the particulars of my insider's view or of my discomfort as arbitrator. So I should not be surprised to be seen as a gatekeeper (as uncomfortable as that feels to me), with each of the inhabitants in the web urging me to open or close the gate on someone, though I myself feel much more like a door (wo)man than a gatekeeper. And yet we rarely have the luxury of controlling our own identities, of fully defining to others who we are.

In the many sessions on publishing held at the American Association of Applied Linguistics (AAAL) and Teachers of English to Speakers of Other Languages (TESOL) conferences, the point has often (though not always) been made that nearly all editors of professional journals edit these journals on their own time (i.e., in my case, without released time from regular university work of teaching, doing research, serving on committees, advising, etc.) and without pay. The realization that many editors (though not all) work for no pay but for a commercial publisher highlights the weird economic relationship that holds between publishers and academic authors and editors. While book authors can at least hope to receive royalties on their creative production, journal authors, reviewers, and editors create a product that makes money only for the publisher (and such ancillary entities as printers, courier services, and purveyors of office supplies and machinery like photocopiers). In return for their work, academic editors are perceived to be compensated with, as one publisher told my coeditor and me, glory. These circumstances might make it understandable that editors may become impatient with certain misunderstandings (aka, criticisms) of what editors do. Dissatisfaction of the kind that potentially threatens social relations and that I have experienced in my editorial work has come from three sources: readers, reviewers, and, most obviously, authors.

---

[1]Tony Silva and I coedit the *JSLW*. As coeditors, Tony and I have shared much of what I describe here, but in this article I will refer only to myself, not wanting to presume to speak for him.

[2]There are other relations, of course, for example, with the printer and the publisher, but while these may be variously aggravating and gratifying, they are not fraught in the same way as are relationships with other colleagues, so I pass over them here without further comment.

ACCOMMODATING READERS

It has not been my experience that readers often voice grievances with the *JSLW* to me, but because I do hear complaints about other journals from readers, I can only wonder what comments escape me. It is possible that readers assume editors have more power than they actually do to shape journal content. My experience has been that I feel much less in control than readers might assume. For example, there are certain topics within L2 writing that have probably been overdone in a North American context but that have perhaps been less explored in EFL or other international settings or topics that I for one find unproductive. So we might find ourselves as editors torn between, for example, a commitment to publishing work done outside a North American context and boredom with the topic itself, or we might be not especially enthusiastic about a piece of research that is clearly well done and well reported but simply not a feature of L2 writing that intrigues us personally. And there is the obvious observation that we cannot publish manuscripts that are not sent to us, so that even if there are topic areas I would very much like the journal to publish, even my own preferences are accommodated only to a limited extent.

On the other hand, readers have expressed dissatisfaction with articles that have been characterized as leading the profession astray by expressing a point of view that the readers don't share, articles that are not ideologically correct. A most striking example of such dissatisfaction, though not directed at the *JSLW*, appeared in an article in which the author complained that the particular journal's editor should have in effect censored a certain point of view because it was so clearly wrong. The author also claimed that some in the profession have "wondered openly how individuals who were in some cases quite unknown and untrained as SLA [second language acquisition] researchers themselves obtained access to supposedly scholarly journals." At the *JSLW* when we have been lucky, readers have sent us a publishable response to an article they object to, airing their objections publicly and allowing the authors to respond. When we're unlucky, we hear these criticisms through the professional grapevine and sigh.

Oddly enough, readers' complaints are the easiest to accommodate psychologically because they usually involve only the reader and the editor. More difficult to negotiate are relationships with reviewers because these involve authors as well.

NEGOTIATING WITH REVIEWERS

Like so many aspects of academic life, being asked to review manuscripts as an outside reviewer or as part of an editorial board sometimes looks better on a CV than it feels in practice. Furthermore, in many ways reviewers are the real arbiters of a manuscript's success because editors may simply not be knowledgeable enough about a particular subfield of the discipline to fully evaluate the quality of a submission. Like editors, journal reviewers are not paid for their time, and often they remain unknown to the author and so cannot even be properly acknowledged, let alone compensated, for the time they spend on reviewing a manuscript and the help they give an author through their feedback. And for the same reasons, although reviewers are given deadline dates by which they are asked to produce their reviews, editors nag reviewers at the risk of losing them as reviewers and even, perhaps, at the risk of impairing the relationship between editor and reviewer, whether personal or strictly professional. For those like me who react to deadlines somewhat anxiously, needing to remind a reviewer that a review is 2 weeks, 4 weeks, even 2 months overdue feels extremely awkward and frustrating. Who am I to tell reviewers that what I need from them should come before other tasks they have? Yet because most reviewers are authors themselves who, like the authors of the manuscripts they review, eagerly await the verdict on the manuscripts they have submitted somewhere, one would think this shared position would inspire reviewers to do everything they could to review manuscripts sent to them expeditiously, doing unto others as they would have ...etc. But sometimes life gets in the way. Then in addition to already feeling discomfited about pushing reviewers to hurry, the editor suffers the further indignity of seeming incompetent or disorganized, or the journal develops a reputation for being slow.[3] At a minimum it is the editor who has to respond to irritated reminders from authors that they haven't heard anything about their manuscript submission in 5 months. During such stall periods, it hard to know what to say to either the late reviewer or annoyed author when one runs into them at conferences.

Another problem editors face in negotiating between reviewers and authors is the tone of the review. Most reviewers know that their remarks will be passed on verbatim (i.e., uncensored) to authors and that professional courtesy is expected, and yet apparently one reviewer's courtesy is another author's insult. I once heard a conference presentation in which the speaker strongly criticized reviewers who did not maintain professional courtesy, yet I personally knew this speaker's reviews to be particularly harsh and harshly worded, though she must not have seen

---

[3]*The Chronicle of Higher Education* once published a painfully hilarious series of exchanges between an author and the engineering journal to which this author had submitted an article whose fate he was waiting to learn. The correspondence lasted 10 years (though with several long stretches of silence) with the author pleading that he needed a speedy decision on the publication of his article to aid his tenure bid. Then his promotion bid. Finally, in the last letter from the journal to the author dated 10 years after the correspondence first began, the journal editor informed the author that his article was rejected because the research reported was outdated!

them this way.[4] What reviewers themselves are shielded from (by editors) is the occasional irate author response to a review. There is little point in passing on to a reviewer remarks such as one author's accusation that the reviewers of his manuscript were more interested in showing off what they knew themselves than in offering constructive feedback on the article submitted.

AUTHORS' WOES

But it is, of course, authors who have the most at stake emotionally, much more than readers and reviewers, and therefore more reason to voice their emotions, both positive and negative. Negative comments come mostly from authors who are not personal acquaintances and whose articles have been rejected (usually as directed by reviewers). I have been accused of rejecting a manuscript because I was obviously unfamiliar with qualitative research paradigms, because I was obviously ignorant about the subject area, because I obviously failed to appreciate how difficult it is to reduce a 390-page dissertation to 30 pages; I have also been blamed for failing to provide clear-cut, specific guidelines for revising a rejected manuscript. These experiences are unpleasant but of course part of the package. More unpleasant is running into rejected authors at a conference.

An experience that many authors share, including me and including student writers, is receiving conflicting feedback from multiple responders, such as the very common occurrence of getting advice from one reviewer to expand a section so that it becomes more comprehensible and from another reviewer to cut that same section because it seems irrelevant. Experienced writers are perhaps not surprised by such contradictions but the fact that some authors are surprised and frustrated by them seems to betray a belief that underlying each textual instantiation of thought is the pure thought itself that could be expressed if only the Ideal Text could be found to translate that thought. In other words, the notion seems to be that because there must be one right way to express or report certain ideas, the fact that two readers' evaluations of a text conflict must mean that one of the readers is wrong. Nevertheless, negotiating conflicting reviews, or even deciding which reviewers' suggestions can and should be accommodated and which not, is probably difficult for all authors, as I believe it sometimes is for editors to decide whether reviewers' suggestions have been sufficiently attended to in revisions. In fact some reviewers have complained to see the published version of an article they re-

---

[4]I have purposely confused gender references throughout this text, partly to protect anonymity and partly because I do not want to bring up the vexed issue of gender politics that these pronouns would inevitably raise. Gender politics would add more additional layers of complication than I have room for here.

viewed that did not reflect all the revisions they had suggested. Yet another instance of the editor being at the fulcrum of a disagreement.

Exactly how much to intervene as an editor is an ongoing decision process. In one article the *JSLW* eventually published, the authors had argued that writers, particularly L2 writers, can and should claim the authority to violate conventions. I found the argument convincing, but when it came to all the conventions the authors themselves violated in their manuscript, faced with the reality of what those violations looked like, I could not bring myself to accept them. Similarly, our policy as *JSLW* editors has been to let people take responsibility for what they say and how they say it; we feel we have favored a relatively hands-off approach to contributors' writing over a policy that would do more to standardize or homogenize writing. Yet at times when bilingual writers have used English in an unusual way or in a World English variety, how to respond becomes less clear. Some authors may want their writing to sound entirely transparent to monolingual English readers; others may want to embrace another variety of English. Similarly, I have sometimes felt that certain authors may be presenting themselves through their writing in a way they may not want to be seen (arrogant, e.g., or disrespectful of student writing) and it is sometimes difficult to convey this sense tactfully.

As the push to publish increases (Braine, 2000), even for academics in institutions that have not traditionally required publication, potential authors and researchers seek out subjects to write about. This has had the effect, it seems to me, of occasionally creating situations where authors jump on the latest fad in order to get ahead of the crowd in publishing about that topic or else take a topic that has been (sometimes extensively) researched elsewhere and apply it to their own context merely because that context is available but without much thought about how that research contributes to the extension of knowledge in the field. The result is sometimes a submission that is undertheorized and underanalyzed, one that seems to follow the adage "have data, will publish," as a colleague once put it. But then obviously the notion of "extending knowledge in the field" begs the question of whose knowledge about what. To look at a great deal of publishing on L2 writing, for example, it would appear that the field might best be called not L2 writing but North American college students' L2 writing.

In each of the cases described earlier of what might be termed author–editor tension, the negative feelings flow from the author toward the editor, but there are instances as well when I have felt abused by authors by being placed, as I perceive it, in the role not just of doorwoman but of textual maid or housekeeper. In such cases, I get the impression that somewhere authors of such submissions have picked up the notion that they are the "think-people" in the publishing enterprise and need not bother themselves with such pedestrian concerns as verifying references, conforming to APA format, or even spell-checking because that is the editor's job, to clean up after the thinking has taken place. These attitudes have seemed abusive to me and toward me, but I cannot help wondering if I may have even shared them at one time, though that would have certainly been before becoming a journal editor. In all, as a journal editor, I experience social, ethical, and disciplinary burdens, but there is no escaping the interpersonal implications of this work either, sometimes generating warmth and support and other times hostility flowing in all the several directions that radiate out from the editor's position and then back.

EDITING INSULTS

Given the personal investment and exposure that writing for publication entails, it is hardly surprising that authors respond energetically and defensively to reviewers' or editors' remarks that the authors may perceive as insulting. The energy of an author's emotional response appears to vary, perhaps predictably, with publishing experience, possibly irrespective of the comments themselves. After all, an experienced author may feel confident that a text rejected by one journal may be accepted even without revision by another; a less experienced author may not have that sense of self-confidence or confidence in his or her work. Or a less experienced author may simply not have received much collegial feedback. For example, long ago at a professional conference a speaker who happened to also be an editor and who was attempting to illustrate appropriate feedback responses to L2 student writing, in an amazing gesture of self-assurance, invited anyone in the audience who had ever received feedback from him to tell the audience what that feedback had been like. I had. And despite the editor's characterization of his feedback as gentle, engaged, questioning, and suggesting rather than criticizing/demanding, to me, at that early stage in my career, the response had seemed perhaps condescending and had certainly made me feel much more like a student or an underling of some kind receiving feedback from a teacher or an overlord than like a professional getting constructive suggestions from a colleague. But I am at least partly convinced that the difference in how that feedback played to that editor and to me might have been as much a function of my own inexperience not only in the field but even in getting feedback on writing at all. During my college years professors didn't give feedback; they gave grades, and there were no second drafts, no peer commentary. It just wasn't done, didn't exist.

THE CURSE OF PROFESSIONAL WRITING

Despite understanding some of the problems and complications that reviewers and editors experience in dealing with and responding to manuscript submissions, as a disciplinary reader, reviewer, and author myself, I see the web from each of these angles as well, sometimes experiencing the same sense of infringement that can accompany each of them. As a reader I too have wondered why an editor may have published a given article. For example, I recently read an article reporting research on L2 writing in an L1 publication and felt proprietary, gatekeeping hackles rise in annoyance, knowing, or at least believing, that this article would not have been published in an L2 journal because it violated disciplinary norms by failing to take into account what I felt was already well established in the discipline. As a reviewer I too have fallen behind schedule or struggled with framing a negative review in a collegial, helpful way. But it is as an author that the whole publishing enterprise feels most abusive (and I suppose most satisfying). How, I have wondered, can my article be so completely rejected when after all these years I *know* that I know very well what has to go into a publishable article? How can it be that a reviewer instructs me to familiarize myself with Leki (19something) and then resubmit a revision? Or most disconcerting, how can it be that some manuscript I wrote that I thought reported on such important new findings is so old hat to the reviewer ("Don't insult us," said one review)?

When Tony Silva, my coeditor at the *JSLW*, and I first discussed the possibility of creating a professional journal dedicated to publishing work on L2 writing, our intent was specifically to develop an outlet for what seemed to us growing interest in the area and limited arenas to publish. *TESOL Quarterly*, for example, having to accommodate all the interests of TESOL members, could only devote a small portion of its space to L2 writing. In what soon began to seem to me to be the perfect irony, becoming editors of a journal focused on our own research interests meant being ourselves excluded from publishing in that very journal, the one that was intended to open the way for researchers just like us, but not us, everyone but us.

And intensifying the irony for me has been the fact that I would rather *not* write at all publicly. I enjoy doing the data gathering, the search through the literature, the thinking about what my findings mean, even the bursts of written reflection that constitute a kind of downloading of thoughts, links, and insights that occur to me in doing research. But not writing all this up. Public writing is a struggle for me. I watch with envy as my English department colleagues manage to talk off the top of their heads, informally, in the hallways, with more fluency, more grace, and certainly more vocabulary than I can muster after multiple returns to a written text. I'd rather do my income taxes than face the nightmare of writing a letter or sending holiday greetings; I prefer to avoid even addressing envelopes. And yet being in the professional conversation means writing—and publishing that writing. Professional voices in this discipline are heard best through writing; there is no escaping writing. So I read with some envy Suresh Canagarajah's (2002) description of the *oral* intellectual exchanges of his former academic colleagues in Jaffna, sitting around with graduate students and colleagues in a variety of disciplinary areas drinking tea and discussing their readings of Foucault. How unlike my own experiences with professional communication, sitting only with a computer and refusing to answer the phone for fear that some human might want to chat. What a pleasure to think that not all academics are forced to publish (yet). At the same time, it is ludicrous to romanticize the situation there; Sri Lanka suffers from civil war and from hegemonic domination by the West. Some might well even argue that it is public writing that will, would, or could help Sri Lanka break out of these twin oppressions. Again, there is no escaping writing.

And except for possibly a few particularly talented colleagues, perhaps there is no escaping the bruises that accompany writing either. Some time ago I submitted an article to a journal and eventually received back reasonably positive reviews that requested a fairly large number of revisions, some relatively easy to deal with, others that would have necessitated work that I felt was not essential. The editor's cover letter to me had two salient points, as far as I was concerned. First, the manuscript was accepted pending appropriate revisions, and second, the revised version needed to be completed with quite a quick turnaround time. Because it was the end of the semester, finding time to do the revisions in the amount of time allotted was a struggle, but (anxiously eyeing the deadline) I sent them off in time. Shortly after sending the revision, I received another communication from the editor. The revisions were not acceptable; the manuscript was rejected. I felt cheated, as though I had undergone some kind of surreptitious test that I hadn't realized was a test. And I had failed that test. Yet, as far as I was concerned, psychologically, that manuscript was by then part of the past in my own mind; I had achieved closure. The revisions satisfied *me*. But not the editor, and the article was not published, although the editor kindly offered to treat a further more extensive revision as a new submission, should I choose to revise, and to send it out again for reviews. What to do? Like any self-respecting person who feels she's been robbed or cheated, I had no intention of dealing with that journal again, despite realizing that this journal was probably the most likely placement for this article. Instead I immediately, without further revisions at all, sent the manuscript out to another journal. And then another. And I believe a third. In each case the article never even made it out to reviewers, the editors of each of these journals feeling that the manuscript simply was not appropriate for them (even though I thought it would be). Back at the drawing board, I reconsidered the original reviewers' suggestions, took my time revising, and sent the new revision back to the original journal. It went out again for review, again I revised according to a new set of reviewers' suggestions, and the manuscript was eventually published. In writing this now, I can only sympathize with the journal editor and the tangling of webs that my manuscript no doubt created for him.

Professional writing is a minefield (as it was for Dwight Atkinson, this volume), a roller coaster ride (as it was for Linda Blanton, this volume), or at least an obstacle course, one strewn with a variety of difficulties for each of those involved in any of the several roles that tie people together in what is finally a necessarily collective enterprise. It may be gratifying at times and at times bruising, but I do not know another way to stay in the professional conversation with the same intensity, effect, and pertinence. Issues of power, privilege, and control are inherent in the enterprise, but as Foucault has helped us see, that power circulates, as one or another of those involved twangs her or his strand of the web.

REFERENCES

Braine, G. (2000, October). *Overcoming barriers to academic publications: Hong Kong's success story.* Paper presented at Second Symposium on Second Language Writing, Purdue University, West Lafayette, IN.

Canagarajah, S. (2002). *A geopolitics of academic writing.* Pittsburgh, PA: University of Pittsburgh Press.

9

Reflections on Coauthorship and the Professional Dialogue: Risks and Rewards

John Hedgcock
Monterey Institute of International Studies

In a recent conversation with a close friend and colleague, I was struck by a simple parallel to coauthorship that offered some insight into the complexities of professional collaboration. As we chatted, my friend praised me for my work habits and productivity. I sincerely appreciated the compliment but felt that I did not genuinely deserve the approbation. While thanking her for the kind words, I light-heartedly pointed out that she had overlooked some of my well-known character flaws. "If you think I have good work habits," I said, "then maybe you don't really know me very well." My friend quickly shot back, "Of course, I know you, John! We've traveled together!"

Indeed, setting off on a travel adventure with a casual acquaintance or an intimate friend necessarily involves exposing our true selves as well as observing others' personalities and behaviors in unanticipated situations. Casual friends may decide to take a weekend backpacking trip; college classmates may plot out an extended adventure in a foreign land with youthful insouciance. The results can range from deeply enriching to downright disastrous, depending on how travel partners conduct themselves and on how much (or little) of their true selves they expose while on the road. When rated for the enjoyment and pleasant memories they generate, most travel adventures shared among friends probably fall somewhere between the extremes of catastrophic and

sublime. Over the years, I have traveled on four continents with a handful of friends. I haven't lost any friends yet, and I would like to think that
the bits of wisdom that I have accumulated so far will prevent unhappy
moments in the future.

In the discussion that follows, I explore the often delicate politics of academic coauthorship through the lens of my own experiences. As I perused
a list of my academic products (including books, refereed articles, and
conference presentations), I discovered that coauthored projects out-
number single-authored works by about two to one. I also realized that I
have collaborated with close to a dozen colleagues over the years. Most of
my experiences have yielded fruitful outcomes, although a few have
made me cautious. By exploring a sampling of my efforts as a coauthor, I
suggest that an appreciation of the complexities of collaboration can enable academic writers to anticipate common pitfalls of the process while
reaping its short- and long-term rewards. Because the two enterprises rely
on relationships that involve a certain kind of intimacy, traveling with a
friend and scholarly collaboration both offer occasions for self-disclosure,
with all of the risks and rewards that self-disclosure entails. Like setting off
on a foreign adventure, the journey of collaboration sets up for participants
an inherently interpersonal situation where values, beliefs, egos, and even
professional reputations may be at stake.

Considering the intellectual and emotional capital that professional
collaboration can exact, however, it is a little surprising that academic
writers do not give more thoughtful and systematic consideration to the
responsibilities and consequences of the process before they embark
on a journey that may be inherently fraught with interpersonal perils.
This lack of attention is even more perplexing given the measurable rise
in the number of coauthored and coedited publications over the past
decade or two, particularly in the social sciences (Hafernik,
Messerschmitt, & Vandrick, 1997). Not only are the factors underlying
this trend worth examining, the public and private dynamics of the collaborative process should perhaps be exposed and made transparent
to current and future generations of academic writers. After all, successful cooperation and coauthorship necessitate more than mechani-
cally following a conventionalized procedure. In fact, collaboration
engages participants in a sometimes risky process of identity negotiation (or reconstruction) that can both fortify and threaten professional
and personal self-images (Berkenkotter & Huckin, 1995; Delpit, 1998;
Ervin & Fox, 1994). Joint research and writing in academe can therefore
never be purely objective or dispassionate despite our best efforts to
suppress our egos, insecurities, and personal agendas. Coauthorship,
in particular, is inevitably political in that the process entails the transac-
tion of social goods—principally in the form of publication and, by extension, potential for professional stature.

WHY COLLABORATE?

As a graduate student in applied linguistics, and subsequently as a newly hired junior faculty member, I found myself almost continuously engaged in one or more joint research projects. Then, as now, I was occasionally troubled by the choice between working single-handedly on projects of my own design and collaborating on larger-scale efforts. As a solo researcher and writer, I could develop and pursue my own specific interests, plan and conduct my research without external input or intervention, and ultimately see my products judged on their merits alone. I was uncomfortably aware that both the strengths and weaknesses of my research and writing would be scrutinized by my professors, peers, prospective employers, and ultimately by influential gatekeepers in the field. I alone would be held accountable for the inaccuracies, oversights, and errors of judgment reflected in my work. As a novice, I thought it wise to pursue individual research and publications, not only to gain acceptance among established members of the profession but also to prove to myself that I was, indeed, capable of holding my own as a researcher and writer in the field. Passing qualifying exams and writing a doctoral dissertation, after all, were solitary endeavors where no collaboration was allowed. A corollary advantage of working as a solo author was that I could develop and claim my own authorial voice and style, carving a niche from which I could slowly construct a record of my own scholarly publication.

At the same time, the advantages and rewards of collaboration always appealed to me. In fact, they continue to attract me, though I take a more critical view of the frequently vaunted benefits of cooperation and collaboration in academic work than I once did. A widely cited benefit of collaborative work, grounded largely in constructivist arguments, is reflected in this simple maxim: "Two heads are better than one" (Bruffee, 1993; Kagan, 1989; Matthews, Cooper, Davidson, & Hawkes, 1995). Certainly, joint projects put us in league with other, like-minded professionals whose expertise ideally complements our own. Not only does collaboration allow us to share often onerous workloads, it allies us with people who may be more well-read in certain domains and who may have greater proven expertise in certain fields of knowledge. For example, I have found myself drawn to working with colleagues who are experienced designers of research plans and confident users of sophisticated statistical tools because I do not feel secure enough about my skills in these areas to work alone. I have gladly relied on collaborators and coauthors to offer their special expertise while eagerly making contributions that represent what I feel I do best, namely, collecting data, interpreting results, writing, editing, and so on.

When participants cooperate effectively, a significant by-product of collaboration is a form of peer teaching whereby each contributor shares his or her knowledge and expertise with fellow contributors. In this process, the peer teacher shares knowledge with her or his fellow collaborators and thus experiences the enjoyment and gratification of teaching others. When successful, collaboration intellectually stimulates researchers and writers, thereby promoting their individual and collective creativity—and, theoretically, diminishing competitive impulses (Kessler, 1992; Nyikos & Hashimoto, 1997; Oxford, 1997; Seaman, Sweeny, Meadows, & Sweeny, 1997; Wilhelm, 1997). An incident from a recent collaboration shows how collegial exchange can produce instructive dialogue, peer teaching, and tangible results. As a colleague and I set ourselves to planning a conference presentation one day, she almost off-handedly suggested that we look at some of her own data that might strengthen the ideas we had explicated in our conference proposal. Her idea, introduced in a stream of many options during a brainstorming session over coffee, quickly generated mutual enthusiasm and eventually evolved into the core material featured in our talk. Although our original plans had not included a focus on her data, our unplanned coconstruction of the project led not only to lively collaboration on our conference presentation but also to a subsequently coauthored manuscript. This experience brought home to me how two or more people, working toward a shared objective, can successfully coconstruct a means of accomplishing it.

In addition to collegiality and mutual enrichment, it is the sense of security associated with collaboration that has nearly always compensated for what I have surrendered in terms of pursuing my individual agenda, my "personal style," and my own "narcissistic gratification" (Bernays & Kaplan, 1997, p. 31). I believe that the esprit de corps entailed in collaboration serves as a primary motivating force for many professionals in language studies. That is, when I engage in cooperative research and collaborative writing, I find myself to be less vulnerable because I am not alone when faced with potentially adversarial forces. The blows associated with negative criticism and rejection, for example, are somehow softened when they are directed not at me as an individual but at a group. Egos can still suffer damage, to be sure, but the sting is less severe and lasting when I can respond to setbacks (or assaults) as a member of a collective enterprise with a set of common goals and responsibilities. On receiving a negative review of a jointly submitted journal article not long ago, I was understandably disappointed. Had I been the paper's sole author, however, I might not have rebounded as quickly or as effectively as I did. After I forwarded the evaluation to my coauthor, we took some time to understand and digest the feedback on our own. Then we debriefed: We agreed that some of the criticism was not well justified—some comments were even overtly mean-spirited. Venting, expressing indignation about the nasty remarks, and jointly lamenting our defeat strengthened our solidarity, which consequently bolstered our resolve to work quickly toward revising and resubmitting the paper. We paid careful attention to the reviewers' criticisms and suggestions, which focused on shortcomings for which we might have been blamed individually but for which we actually assumed joint responsibility. Our shared commitment to pursuing the paper's publication as well as our sense of mutual accountability led us to meaningful problem solving and brainstorming, rather than to counterproductive "blamestorming." Within several weeks, we had extensively revised and resubmitted our manuscript, which was eventually accepted for publication.

PERSONALITIES, POLITICS, AND PROFESSIONALISM

In thinking retrospectively about my professional collaborations and assessing how they stack up relative to one another, I have found myself returning to the parallel of traveling with a friend. With each joint project, as with each shared travel adventure, I have become better acquainted with my collaborator(s). Through this process, I have also become more aware of my own personal agendas, character traits, and idiosyncrasies. Given the potential for conflict in working and writing with a peer or group of peers, it is perhaps worthwhile to consider how diverse personalities and priorities converge on a set of goals, to say nothing of a common means of achieving them.

The reasons for which academics choose to collaborate may seem obvious: I elect to work with like-minded counterparts because I share common intellectual interests with them. Nevertheless, a common interest or background in a particular vein of research is by no means a guarantee of successful collaboration. Even when two or more people agree to initiate a project leading to publication, their underlying agendas may not necessarily converge, potentially precipitating subtle and not-so-subtle tensions. One such instance from early in my career demonstrates how overtly compatible goals do not necessarily coincide with the implicit expectations that individuals bring to the situation. In one of my early group projects, two colleagues and I had collected and analyzed a large corpus of data, which we struggled to interpret as we drafted a manuscript. One member of the group dropped out during this process, leaving two of us to decide how to proceed. We jointly decided on the journal to which we would send our manuscript as soon as we completed it. Before arriving at the submission stage, however, we realized that we were, in fact, at an impasse. I had envisioned finalizing our paper and submitting it within a few weeks: My objective was to pursue publication as soon as possible. At the time, I was anxious to list the paper as a work in progress on my upcoming faculty activity report. For me, our joint paper was part of my fast-track publication agenda. My colleague, meanwhile, had actually intended to work through another round of analysis, solicit more feedback from an outside reader, and perhaps even revise the paper an additional time before submitting it to an editor.

We fortunately avoided serious conflict, but arriving at a reasonable compromise required some painful negotiation. Through this process, I learned that, although we shared the same overt goal of completing our project and getting our paper published, some of our private goals actually diverged. Moreover, I came to understand that my colleague's wish to take more time in crafting our paper reflected a sincere desire to perform a thorough analysis before subjecting our work to external scrutiny, a quality that I came to appreciate only after we came dangerously close to overt conflict. Finally, I was forced to confront the uncomfortable realization that my own work habits at the time were driven primarily by the motivation to publish; my desire to strengthen and polish our manuscript was of secondary importance.

This experience revealed the crucial need for me to understand the vision, expectations, and work habits of my future collaborators. It also drove home the necessity to consider much more mindfully the terms of future working agreements. The nature of our collaboration and writing required close interaction and transparency on both sides. To overcome differences of opinion that might have compromised our chances of completing the project, we were at times forced to express our true aspirations and expectations to each other, much as traveling companions are forced to do when things don't go as planned—when the air has to be cleared. Such self-disclosure engenders a kind of intimacy between coauthors, who are given access to each other's private reflections, idiosyncrasies, insecurities, and personal faults. Just as travelers should reflect on their readiness to communicate openly before setting off on a trip with a companion, potential coauthors should be prepared for the honest interaction, self-disclosure, and trust that successful collaboration often requires.

Another key dimension of effective, nonconfrontational communication involves a clear delineation of each participant's roles, responsibilities, and contributions before the project takes off and while it progresses. I have already suggested that one of the chief benefits of collaboration entails combining the efforts of individuals whose talents, skills, and experience come together in a complementary, symbiotic way. To make effective use of such complementarity, collaborators must carefully consider the division of labor and the allocation of tasks as a project unfolds, though I would emphatically recommend considerable flexibility. When preparing for a trip with a friend, for example, I eagerly take on tasks such as finding air travel and car rental deals, making reservations, organizing logistics, and keeping track of money along the way. I gladly leave to my traveling companion tasks such as booking accommodations, organizing sightseeing activities, devising itineraries, and collecting provisions. Of course, these roles seldom remain fixed: Circumstances often require travelers to take on novel tasks and responsibilities for which they may feel ill-suited.

In a similar manner, collaborators and coauthors can facilitate the achievement of their collective goals by negotiating each participant's respective roles and responsibilities for each stage of a project's development. Specifying roles in advance equips each participant with an indispensable accountability tool. When each contributor has a job description of some sort, the work of measuring one's own and others' relative contributions becomes much easier than when no explicit responsibilities or boundaries have been established at the outset. As Hafernik et al. (1997) remarked, constructing a plan or program "intensifies motivation to get things done" (p. 34). For example, one of my colleagues and I got down to the brass tacks of task allocation before undertaking the writing of a book. Although we jointly drafted our prospectus, we agreed that each of us would compose an equal number of chapters. Each chapter would cover a topic that appropriately matched our respective areas of expertise. To ensure that we would meet the publisher's draft, review, and production deadlines, we devised a mutually acceptable calendar of our own. That calendar specified how and when each of us would review and comment on the other's sample chapters as well as which aspects of the manuscript development process we would handle individually. By that time we had already signed a contract with the publisher. It was our own, mutually negotiated contract, however, that actually provided the working framework that successfully guided our progress over the next 2 years. Talking about how we would work together and formalizing our plans made our task not only efficient but also pleasurable. Having established mutual trust and respect, we knew in advance what to expect from each other and thus had a straightforward guideline for fulfilling our individual and collective expectations for the project.

Coauthoring that book was enjoyable and rewarding because the work progressed smoothly and according to plan and because of the learning and personal growth that our collaboration generated. The process of drafting material, eliciting feedback, and providing commentary solidified our trust in each other's commitment to the project, thereby enhancing our confidence and diminishing personal barriers to accepting constructive criticism. As I suggested earlier, working jointly with a colleague whose work complements one's own can create a relationship in which genuine peer teaching and learning can take place. Not unlike the closeness that develops when people travel together, the intimacy of collaboration promotes instructive interaction and offers opportunities for exchanging insightful, incisive feedback. Unlike a disinterested colleague not involved in a joint effort, a fellow collaborator has a professional, if not personal, investment in the enterprise and is therefore likely to offer genuinely useful feedback. In my experience, colleagues who are not coauthors but who agree to review my work sometimes provide feedback that avoids critical commentary and criticism—partly, I'm sure, for fear of alienating or offending me. On the other end of the spectrum, anonymous reviewers, who have little or no stake in my work and who have nothing to lose by telling me what they really think, may provide commentary that is so thoroughly critical that it actually lacks much constructive content.

In contrast, a collaborator on a joint project has everything to gain from offering directed guidance and critical insights to his or her partner, especially when joint publications are at stake. Not long ago, a colleague and I decided to coauthor an article based on a conference presentation that met with a favorable reception. While exchanging comments and suggestions on coauthored drafts of a manuscript version of our presentation, my coauthor noted candidly but collegially that some of the passages that I had composed seemed to rely excessively on a broad swath of published research. My coauthor expressed the well-supported view that, in some respects, my account of the topical literature actually eclipsed the research findings that we had sought to feature in our paper. Because of my respect for my colleague's insights and my awareness that the feedback was aimed at improving our joint work, I carefully considered her recommendations and realized that I had to concur with her assessment. Although perhaps momentarily uncomfortable, the revelation was reminiscent of an incident where one of my travel partners once discreetly pointed out that I had the persistent habit of emerging from the men's room with suspicious-looking damp spots on the front of my hiking shorts, the result of enthusiastic hand-washing. Far from feeling offended, I genuinely appreciated the clue, which no doubt spared me future embarrassment. In both instances, I came to value each person's frankness, as well as their willingness to point out an undesirable but correctable behavioral tendency.

I have attempted to demonstrate that professional collaboration necessarily implicates personalities and interpersonal politics. That both cooperation and coauthorship are inherently political endeavors should not deter anyone from committing to collaborative projects. Indeed, I have gained valuable insights into my own professional capabilities and academic writing skills that working individually would not have provided. My joint research and publication efforts have, in fact, transformed me into a relatively enthusiastic proponent of collaboration. At the same time, I would like to think that my formative development as a collaborator has equipped me with an awareness that participation in joint efforts requires realistic expectations regarding what I can effectively offer as well as what I might gain.

CAUTIONS AND CAVEATS FOR COLLABORATORS

When offered an invitation to collaborate on a project, I now find myself weighing the decision as a function of what I have learned from my prior coauthorship experiences. The enterprise of professional collaboration is, after all, somewhat paradoxical. That is, I often enter into a collaborative relationship expecting to share ideas, insight, and hard work. I likewise anticipate that my partners will supply me with guidance, instruction, and moral support. However, I may be unprepared for the "substantive conflict" that is, in so many cases, quite normal (Burnett & Ewald, 1994, p. 22). I may also be surprised by what a joint project might unexpectedly reveal about me, about my fellow collaborators, and about our respective intentions and agendas.

What considerations have influenced my decision to engage in a joint conference paper, article, or book? One of the fundamental factors to consider with great care relates to the nature and goals of the project itself. Just as I would be wise to ask myself if I really want to spend time in that exotic place that a friend wants me to visit with him or her, I need to ask if a prospective joint project holds appeal and merit, irrespective of who is involved. On several occasions, professional acquaintances and colleagues have enthusiastically recruited me to collaborate on projects that were, in fact, peripheral to my primary research interests and priorities. A few of these projects have focused on issues that were very distant from realms of expertise in which I felt comfortable or credible. After completing a successful in-service workshop, for example, a one-time copresenter asked me to coauthor a prospectus for a multiple-authored book on simulation activities in teacher education—an area that I hardly knew anything about, let alone felt qualified to write a book on. In this case, I was spared the discomfort of declining the invitation because the project's inspiration apparently evaporated (I never heard anything more about it after our first couple of meetings). Had my colleague persevered, however, I would have been at a loss to account for my discomfort and to extricate myself from further involvement.

I can only speculate as to why I was approached for the project in the first place. Naturally, I would like to assume that I have some demonstrable knowledge about a topic, prior experience with similar projects, or a talent that someone else wants to tap into. It can be flattering and seductive to be invited to participate in a project when my prospective contribution is deemed valuable or even indispensable. However, it is prudent to examine what truly draws me to a project before committing to a collaborative effort that may require extended involvement. More than once I have found myself backpedaling in circumstances where I was initially compelled to accept an invitation from a well-liked, renowned, or highly respected colleague, but where I soon came to feel uneasy with the "fit." Serious reflection at the time led me to realize that my interest had been ignited less by the merits of the project itself than by the prospect of collaboration or coauthorship with a particular person. At other times, I discovered that my self-perceived range of skill was perhaps not suitably matched to the scope or magnitude of the project. In franker terms, I felt that I would be in over my head and consequently opted not to become involved.

Arriving at such a decision can be difficult and even painful because the process inevitably involves recognizing personal limitations. Nonetheless, approaching prospective joint projects from a critical, even guarded, point of view can certainly reduce the chances of confronting unpleasant surprises, disappointment, and wounded egos after a considerable investment of time and effort has been made. Clearly, it is essential to reflect carefully on commonsense factors such as our compatibility with fellow collaborators as well as the ways in which individual styles and work habits coincide. At the same time, I suspect that many, if not most, professional collaborations begin because participants are intuitively drawn to one another by their shared affinities for similar personality types, intellectual interests, and academic aspirations. In other words, selecting collaborators and coauthors may be as much a matter of experience and instinct as it is a matter of systematic decision making.

However, writers should not lose sight of the possibility that in the sometimes fraught evolution of a collaborative project, behaviors and relationships can change. As I have already suggested, the intimacy of collaboration—especially coauthorship—can facilitate productive, collegial interaction, yet it can also precipitate undesirable emotions and conduct that might not surface under less strained circumstances. Given the frequently intense nature of the writing process and the high stakes involved in getting an article or book into print, coauthors cannot always be counted on to be on their best behavior. Confronted with the stress of coauthorship, I occasionally find that my state of mind and coping mechanisms are at odds with those of fellow collaborators. Likewise, I may discover in myself latent predispositions that I had previously overlooked, ignored, or actively suppressed. For example, a succession of joint projects early in my career revealed my own tendency to become a somewhat panicky "control freak" when a leadership void unexpectedly opened up during the planning or writing of a paper, despite my best efforts to restrain this unattractive personality trait. Alas, I cannot honestly report that I have managed to master this impulsive demon, but I am at least alert to the possibility that undesirable emotions can surface when a collaboration seems to be in danger of unraveling.

Similarly startling revelations can occur during the major and minor emergencies that present themselves during joint travel ventures: Writing and traveling with another person entail comparable moments of stress and perceived crisis. I vividly recall the time I witnessed a friend temporarily lose composure after a series of disconcerting mishaps on a long-distance journey in Africa. We had made plans to meet up with our host and guide in a remote area, but when we arrived at the rendezvous point, he was nowhere to be found. With no means of contacting him, we waited an entire day with no sign from him and no idea what to do next. This unforeseen setback put us over a day behind on a carefully programmed itinerary that would theoretically take us to our departure city, from which we were booked on one of the very infrequent outbound flights. Meanwhile, my friend had developed an infection after suffering a nasty cut, and I had been immobilized by a virulent tropical fever. Typically a remarkably even-tempered person, my friend experienced a meltdown of sorts. Though I was nearly delirious, I was perceptive enough to be shocked and alarmed by this reaction. The circumstances, which seemed unquestionably dire at the time, activated a rare and wholly unanticipated response from my friend. This episode (which concluded happily, incidentally) taught me to be alert to the possibility of unpredictable reactions on the part of others and myself in the face of stress-inducing situations that can emerge in the course of a joint venture.

Now cognizant of some of my own impulses, I routinely endeavor to control them. I also avoid situations in which irrational behavior might compromise a project. Consequently, I have also become more sensitive to the possibility that my potential collaborators may also struggle with similar impulses, which can interfere with successfully completing joint writing projects. My individual predispositions, expectations, and styles of work can turn out to be incompatible with those of people whose interests and objectives I think I share at the beginning of a joint effort. I learned this lesson at a critical juncture during a collaboration that began quite casually. A colleague asked me for feedback on a major paper reporting a large-scale empirical study. Following my suggestion to submit a proposal for a presentation at a prestigious conference, my colleague subsequently invited me to coauthor the proposal. We would present the paper together, with my colleague taking lead author–presenter position. After the proposal was accepted, we cooperated simultaneously on both the presentation and a manuscript version of the same presentation. My involvement intensified as I reworked and edited the manuscript, incorporated my own bibliographic research into the paper's framework, proposed key methodological revisions, and performed several additional data analyses.

After copresenting the paper and before finalizing the manuscript version for its first submission, we discussed the attribution issue. As our coauthorship process had been productive and amicable, name order was of secondary, if not minor, importance to me: My overriding objective at that point was publication. Noting my role in analyzing the data and writing up the findings, my colleague and I informally but explicitly agreed that we would submit the manuscript with me listed as lead author. I felt that the proposed name order would appropriately reflect our respective contributions: My role in developing the manuscript seemed to strike a suitable balance with my colleague's role in developing the conference paper. Soon thereafter, I submitted the manuscript. The paper was initially rejected, revised, submitted to a different journal, and then returned with a recommendation to revise and resubmit. After the second resubmission, the paper was accepted for publication. My colleague provided suggestions and approval as we worked through each of these iterations; by implicit mutual consent, I had assumed primary responsibility for manuscript revisions.

We had not discussed attribution or name order since before the initial submission, but after I had proofread and forwarded the galley proofs to my coauthor, my unfortunate oversight precipitated an acrimonious (and probably unnecessary) altercation. On receiving the galleys, my colleague threatened to withdraw our submission altogether if I did not reverse the name order on the article. Positively stunned and deeply offended by the implied allegation that I had underhandedly attempted to claim undue credit, I summarized the name ordering agreement we had reached after our conference presentation, pointing out that I had been given no reason to suspect that our arrangement had changed. I further noted that my name had been listed first in all of our submissions and correspondence with editors. I was shocked that my colleague had not seized the opportunity to revisit the name-order issue much earlier, when we might have amicably negotiated our respective contributions. At the galley stage, I feared that the 11th-hour timing of this distressing confrontation had perhaps been calculated to coerce me—indeed, blackmail me—into accepting second author status, a position that seemed terribly unfair at the time, given my measurable efforts to get our paper published.[1]

My purpose in relating this incident is not to cast blame on my collaborator but rather to expose the insights gained from the experience. The incident highlights the need to discern a coauthor's underlying intentions in addition to his or her potential for displaying unexpected behaviors. I am still perplexed about the motives of my colleague, with whom my working relationship had been very collegial. Reflection on this less-than-perfect collaboration has nonetheless led me to accept responsibility for assuming too much about my partner's intentions and for not discussing the terms of our agreement as the project evolved. I have resolved to establish, explicitly and unequivocally, the terms by which my future collaborators and I will abide. Part of this process involves verifying, at various junctures, that my collaborators completely understand the terms to which we have ostensibly agreed. To echo one of my earlier recommendations, these terms should formally specify each participant's respective contributions, responsibilities, and privileges, including details such as name order, which can become a source of tension if not addressed at a suitable time (Burnett & Ewald, 1994). Although by no means a guarantee against conflict or misunderstanding, a working agreement can at least provide collaborators with a reference point and a potential tool for negotiation and conflict resolution.

---

[1]Because reporting the final outcome of this incident might offer clues about the identity of the other parties involved, I have deliberately elected not to indicate whether the paper was published.

NAVIGATING THE (CO)AUTHORIAL LANDSCAPE: PRECEPTS FOR EFFECTIVE COLLABORATION

A number of academic disciplines appear to be increasingly receptive to collaborative research and writing (Hafernik et al., 1997). If this trend continues, researchers will have much to gain from establishing cooperative relationships within and across disciplines. Often overlooked as a topic of scholarly inquiry, professional collaboration merits more extensive and systematic scrutiny. As I have argued, the dynamics of collaboration are complex, and the risks should be weighed carefully as one contemplates the obvious benefits. Like taking a long trip with a friend, successful coauthorship necessitates understanding among participants, efficient communication, as well as sensitivity and interpersonal skills.

In interpreting the episodes I have retold in this essay, I have attempted to examine the conscious and unconscious lessons I have learned along the way. The following self-directed questions, constructed as practical tools for pondering the pluses and minuses of embarking on joint academic endeavors and publications, are products of that exercise. The checklist following the questions presents practical precepts directed at readers who have chosen to collaborate and who wish both to facilitate the collaborative process and to avoid common pitfalls.

Reflection Questions for Prospective Collaborators and Coauthors

- Am I a suitable candidate for collaboration? On the basis of intuition or past experience, will I work effectively with my prospective collaborator(s)?
- Are my goals for the project fully compatible with those of my prospective collaborator(s)?
- Does the project itself appeal to me, and am I truly interested in the work itself?
- Will I feel at ease establishing my own and others' roles and responsibilities—and having a collaborator do the same for me?
- Will I be able to cope effectively with misunderstandings and conflicts?
- How will I negotiate the distribution of credit (or blame) as the project evolves?

General Precepts for Productive Collaboration

- Know your own strengths and limitations so that you can realistically offer your talents while leaving your collaborator(s) room to make their contributions.

- Familiarize yourself with the strengths, limitations, time constraints, and professional objectives of your collaborator(s).
- Because many professional collaborations require time-intensive, one-on-one communication, select collaborators and coauthors whom you like and respect.
- Be forthright and honest early on about your expectations and the conditions under which you will work as collaborator(s). Consider drafting an agreement specifying the division of labor, deadlines, terms for sharing credit, and so forth.
- Prenegotiate a mutually agreeable, flexible plan of action that accommodates each individual's availability, time constraints, and work styles.
- Devise an accountability system for evaluating individual and collective progress at suitable intervals. Prevent misunderstanding and conflict by communicating freely and regularly so that participants can give and receive useful feedback.
- Develop a means of keeping your writing and your collaborative relationship in perspective. Clearly, maintaining a good sense of humor goes a long way toward seeing a project through to completion!

My recollections and reflections on travel and professional collaboration do not represent a comprehensive cross-section of authentic experiences. Indeed, these events and my interpretation of them inevitably reflect my personal biases and shortcomings as a writer, coauthor, traveler, and friend. Nonetheless, I hope that my impressions and recommendations will encourage thoughtful discussion and meaningful investigations of the scholarly collaboration, which can be a highly rewarding process if approached with awareness and realistic expectations, as well as a degree of caution. A conscientious author should always remember that a colleague's and one's own academic and professional standing are intimately intertwined.

REFERENCES

Berkenkotter, C., & Huckin, T. (1995). *Genre knowledge in disciplinary communities.* Hillsdale, NJ: Lawrence Erlbaum Associates.

Bernays, A., & Kaplan, J. (1997, January 5). Can this collaboration be saved? *New York Times Book Review, 31.*

Bruffee, K. A. (1993). *Collaborative learning: Higher education, interdependence, and the authority of knowledge.* Baltimore: Johns Hopkins University Press.

Burnett, R. E., & Ewald, H. R. (1994). Rabbit trails, ephemera, and other stories: Feminist methodology and collaborative research. *JAC: A Journal of Advanced Composition, 14,* 21–51.

Delpit, L. (1998). The politics of teaching literate discourse. In V. Zamel & R. Spack, R. (Eds.), *Negotiating academic literacies: Teaching and learning across lan-*

guages and cultures (pp. 207–218). Mahwah, NJ: Lawrence Erlbaum Associates. [Originally published in T. Perry & J. W. Fraser (Eds.), *Freedom's plow: Teaching in the multicultural classroom.* London: Routledge.]

Ervin, E., & Fox, D. (1994). Collaboration as political action. *JAC: A Journal of Advanced Composition, 14,* 53–71.

Hafernik, J. J., Messerschmitt, D. S., & Vandrick, S. (1997). Collaborative research: Why and how? *Educational Researcher, 26*(9), 31–35.

Kagan, S. (1989). *Cooperative learning resources for teachers.* San Juan Capistrano, CA: Resources for Teachers.

Kessler, C. (Ed.). (1992). *Cooperative learning: A teacher's resource book.* Englewood Cliffs, NJ: Prentice Hall.

Matthews, R. S., Cooper, J. L., Davidson, N., & Hawkes, P. (1995). Building bridges between cooperative and collaborative learning. *Change, 27,* 35–40.

Nyikos, M., & Hashimoto, R. (1997). Constructivist theory applied to collaborative learning in teacher education: In search of ZPD. *Modern Language Journal, 81,* 506–517.

Oxford, R. L. (1997). Cooperative learning, collaborative learning, and interaction: Three communicative strands in the language classroom. *Modern Language Journal, 81,* 443–456.

Seaman, A., Sweeny, B., Meadows, P., & Sweeny, M. (1997). Collaboration, reflection, and professional growth: A mentoring program for adult ESL teachers. *TESOL Journal, 7*(1), 31–34.

Wilhelm, K. H. (1997). Sometimes kicking and screaming: Language teachers-in-training react to a collaborative learning model. *Modern Language Journal, 81,* 527–543.

III

Identity Construction

Narrative Braiding: Constructing a Multistrand Portrayal of Self as Writer

Christine Pearson Casanave
Teachers College, Columbia University, Tokyo, Japan

In this essay I wrestle with how to represent myself in my published writing and indeed with how to think about myself as an academic writer. Usually these struggles do not find their way into print because they tend to be private, and they tend as well, I believe, to be quite ordinary, and in academia, some people think we should not write about the ordinary. I think that by writing about ordinary matters I can potentially help readers who are themselves trying to find their way into print understand the normality of their own struggles. Part of the struggle involves figuring out what I want my relationship to a field to be (and understanding that this relationship probably changes over time, and in my case at least that it is fraught with ambivalence). Another major part of this struggle involves developing a persona through writing that will not come back to haunt me in the future. I would like my discoursal self to be authoritative but not arrogant, humble but not groveling, optimistic but not Pollyannish, critical but not complaining, and committed to a field without seeming either enslaved to it or blind to "real life." Constructing such a self can be tricky because I rarely see myself as, or feel, unified, and the result is that my portrayals never quite ring true to me. Perhaps most people who write find, like me, that the "discoursal selves" (Ivanič, 1998) they portray in different writings, with or without the use of first-person pronouns, sometimes don't feel genuine, authoritative, or whole.

One indication for me that I am not the only one whose discoursal self represents me only partially is that sometimes when I think I "know" a published writer in print, then meet that person, I feel as though I have met two different people. I am certain that I am not unusual in having read the published work of someone in my field, developed a sense of that person's identity (often knowledgeable, confident, authoritative, etc.), then having later met the author and been surprised at how different the person seemed. Not that authors I have met no longer seemed knowledgeable, confident, and authoritative. Rather I sensed that so much of this person's identity was missing in the article that I felt misled as to who the author was. I have the feeling that in recent years others have experienced the same jarring phenomenon with me, now that I have published some of my writing. My confessions of insecurity always seem to induce surprise and disbelief.

I recall a visit Dwight Atkinson made to our campus after he came to Japan to take a job at Temple University. I did not know him well at the time but had developed a certain sense of who he was through his often controversial writing. He may have also developed a sense of who I was through my writing. I don't know if he was surprised at seeing other identities in me, but he commented at a later date over lunch that he could not understand why so many accomplished women he knew seemed plagued by periodic self-doubt. In the case of my impression of him, getting to know him in person both surprised and pleased me in that I saw facets not recoverable from his published writing (some of which, to be honest, I had heavily marked in the margins with angry comments followed by exclamation points, stars, and capital letters). Similarly, when I approached Stephanie Vandrick to see if she was interested in collaborating on this book, she seemed both honored and delighted. When I revealed to her the low-confidence side of my professional identity as one of the motivating inspirations for this book, she reacted with surprise but also with understanding. A latecomer to publishing (see her essay in this book), she seemed pleased that her coeditor-to-be was not so different from herself, had entered the field rather late, and had also experienced periods of uncertainty and self-doubt.

This experience, repeated many times in my life, inspired this chapter, which has to do with the complexity of the identity issues that have surrounded my professional life. Even though I and others have written about the impossibility of constructing an essentialized and unitary identity in an academic writing life (Casanave, 2002; Ivanič, 1998), I think that I have always been seeking such a core. The search being fruitless, I have changed my strategy and present my current response to this dilemma in my contribution to this book. My solution requires that I tell at least three different stories and somehow convince myself and readers that all are true.

In this chapter, therefore, I construct three narratives of myself as an academic writer that differ in the ways I talk about participating in my communities of academic practice. In the first narrative, I portray myself as a card-toting Community Member. In the second narrative, I portray myself as a Boundary Pusher. In the third narrative, I might be labeled the Cynic at the Sidelines. (None of these portrayals, by the way, deals with still other selves, such as the Fluctuating Confidence Self, or the Healthy Living Enthusiast, or the Impatient-With-Telemarketers Self that flourish alongside the ones I focus on here.) Each of these narrative strands is true in the sense that each represents lived experiences, beliefs, and sensations and reflects roles I have taken. But each is also false in a postmodern sense: The selves in each narrative are constructed through discourse for different purposes, effects, and audiences, and each represents me only partially. Even the labels I impose on myself are misleading in that they suggest clear boundaries between selves and between communities. The narratives, then, are not intended to portray truth. Rather, taken together, braided as it were, the portrayals show how the single activity of writing for publication stems from sometimes conflicting motivations and experiences, and results in different interweavable–interwoven representations of self, both across and within pieces of writing. The braid metaphor allows me to envision the flexibility with which narrative strands can be combined and changed to represent a self in writing. This metaphorical self, though changed at each rebraiding, creates a sense of wholeness that satisfies me in spite of the separateness of the strands.

STRAND 1: COMMUNITY MEMBER

The place of narrative in the construction of knowledge and identity has been well-argued (Bruner, 1991; Clandinin & Connelly, 2000; Conle, 1999; Giddens, 1991; Linde, 1993; Polkinghorne, 1991). Academic writing as well has been depicted as constructing identities of authors (Ivanič, 1994, 1998). Nevertheless, as tightly constructed as our narratives of self, others, and events may be, including the narratives from which scientific knowledge is constructed, our knowledge remains partial, constructed through discourse, rather than through revelation and recording of facts (Haraway, 1988). Such knowledge may be true insofar as it is credible, critically evaluated, and accepted by members of a "community of practice" (Wenger, 1998). But (first-person) narratives can usefully be seen as tools for making meaning rather than for representing truth. For example, they allow us to restory the same event in multiple ways (Bell, 1997) or change our depictions and interpretations of our professional lives in an effort to make sense of change (Linde, 1993). As such, they can be revised throughout our lives as a way to provide us with biographical coherence and meaning in otherwise potentially fragmented lives (Giddens, 1991). Shared with others, they can forge connections that further stimulate reflection and meaning-making.

The previous paragraph depicts quite conventionally where my work on academic writing and professional identity might be situated. It also demonstrates that my own professional identity is constructed in great part through the voices of others (Bakhtin, 1981). I consider this goal of situating my work in relation to what others have said to be the singlemost challenging and important aspect of learning to write for publication. It is a goal that I believe novice writers understand differently from more experienced writers. The former write for grades from a teacher no matter how authentic the writing activity, the latter in order to communicate with a community of scholars. By recognizing this difference we can explain why new graduate students may have trouble figuring out who to cite even if they know how (i.e., the mechanics of citation practices) and why the tone and style of inexperienced writers often seems inappropriate, inconsistent, and mimetic.

From my earliest experiences at reading academic literature as part of learning to write in my MA program, it became clear that those who exuded authority relied heavily on the voices and authority of previously published scholars. Throughout my MA and PhD experiences, this perception was rarely challenged by me or my classmates. We saw that the sources of much of our own knowledge and our ideas for discussion, critique, and debate came from published sources, whose own authority came from other published sources in the form of literature reviews. We learned that being a scholar in academic settings in general and writing for publication in particular means situating our work, and our identities, within bodies of literature. I learned that even though the authors I cite are rarely people I have met in person, they are people with whom I need to have "conversations" if I wish to contribute my own voice to my field.

I did not understand this notion of academic conversations via publications for much of my graduate school time. I recall wanting my graduate school papers and early attempts at publication to look scholarly. I did not know what it meant to be scholarly, but I knew I had to refer to work that had already been published and that the "authorities" had to be cited somewhere early in the paper. There also had to be enough citations to give readers a sense that I knew something. I used to count the number of references in the reference list as I drafted my papers, hoping that I could find enough to impress readers. I felt satisfied if I could reach the arbitrary number of 15.

It was a shock, therefore, when a professor in my PhD program returned a paper I had done on the subject of reading with a comment that one of the citations I made did not fit and should be removed. I then noticed that in none of her work had I seen that author, nor several others, cited. This was my first realization that different camps in reading research competed and that they represented different philosophical and methodological approaches to reading. I had simply looked for any references on reading I could find and cited them all. I realized with some discomfort that if I wanted to write acceptable papers in graduate school and later for publication I could not simply select authors at random who had written in my general area of interest. I had to know who was who and what the current debates were. I had to select carefully whom to cite and know how that author was cited by others. I had to select a camp to align myself with.

At about the same time in my graduate program I was preparing my first major publication on a topic in second language reading. In the version I submitted to a well-known refereed journal I cited a well-known reading researcher quite critically, in the way that I had learned to do in my graduate seminars. When I received the reviews for this manuscript, I was somewhat taken aback at the suggestion that I had spoken too harshly of someone so well known in the field. This was my first encounter with the politics of publishing, an experience that paralleled in some ways my experience with my professor in reading research. In this case I was allowed to discuss this researcher (she was central in the field), but I would need to speak more politely about my elders in order to get published. With some reluctance I changed the tone of my comments and the article went to press. It was not until much later that I read the work of scholars such as Greg Myers (1989) and Ken Hyland (1996), both of whom investigated politeness strategies in scholarly writing, such as the softening of critical commentary and strong assertions that can be accomplished through hedging. However, it was not just the knowledge of linguistic devices for hedging that I needed then, but the awareness that I had to situate my work in relation to other work (i.e., other much more established scholars) in the field.

I see these experiences now as essential lessons in learning to write for publication in academic settings. But I also think I could not have avoided my mistakes at the time because I simply had not built enough background knowledge in the field through reading. I had to resort to mimicry of an authoritative voice and style until years later when I had actually read enough in my community of practice (which I broadly refer to now as academic literacy in higher education) to know who was who and to understand their relations with each other. But don't get me wrong: My early writing in graduate school and the first writing I targeted for publication were aimed at real readers, but ones whom I conceptualized as professors in the school setting (will I get an A??) and as people like me (graduate students, teachers) in the case of publications. I did not understand that my readers were also, and perhaps most importantly, the authors that I had cited and the scholars who themselves cited these authors in their own work. If I wished to contribute to knowledge in my field, I needed to see my published writing as part of ongoing conversations with other published writers, in addition to offering food for thought to graduate students and practitioners. I needed to situate my work in relation to other published voices, and to do this I needed to read everything I could about my area of interest (see Paul Matsuda and Aneta Pavlenko's essays in this volume). I needed further to write about the ideas of others, not just my own, in a way that was tactful and polite so that I would not insult them or their followers. Not to do so would be to lose readers and hence lose my voice and my message. This assumed I could get published in the first place, which was doubtful if I could not demonstrate that I knew how to play the game. In short, I was and am an accommodationist because I see accommodationist practices as the only way I can get my tiny voice into the conversation.

STRAND 2: BOUNDARY PUSHER

As someone who decided in my late 30s to get a PhD and forge a career in university level second language education, I was surrounded in graduate school by explicit and tacit assumptions about what it is that university professors do. They teach, of course, but that seemed to be the least of a professor's duties where I was studying. They also get grants, do research, write, publish, and present papers at conferences. I didn't want to spend the rest of my career teaching ESL 100% of the time and looked forward to expanding my horizons by learning some of these additional practices. I also knew at some level that having some publications would help me get a job later, just as I believed that my first early published writings helped me get into the PhD program in the first place.

However, I also had some goals that were more closely tied to my teaching and to my desire to help others write for professional purposes. In the midst of my PhD program, for example, I wrote and published three small sequentially related ESL reading textbooks, designed to fill what I saw as gaps in the field at the time. Additionally, during my PhD program and continuing into my later work at a Japanese university, I helped bring students and colleagues together to share research in language forums and to write articles for in-house edited collections of their work. Later I also coedited a book for publication that embodied a personally important issue, namely, the value of personal reflection in the professional development of language educators (Casanave & Schecter, 1997, discussed more later). These activities brought me great personal satisfaction, but contributed nothing to my career in the eyes of some. I was told by people in my PhD program that "textbooks didn't count" and later at the university in Japan where I worked for 12 years, as one of the explanations for why my first promotion application was rejected, that edited books, personal essays, and my language forums didn't count. I didn't even ask about textbooks.

Even though I sensed these pursuits did not fit the conventional descriptions of what a scholar is supposed to be doing, all of these professionally questionable activities suited both my personality and my desire to help shift the applied linguistics field in certain directions, even if in very small ways. In fact, I believe that I cannot contribute to my field without pushing at the boundaries, because maintaining the status quo does not constitute enough of a contribution. Moreover, working at the boundaries is the only way I know how to truly contribute, since purely conventional work cannot express my visions, dissatisfactions, beliefs, or multiple selves.

As I reflect back in time, I think I had two main choices (not mutually exclusive ones) as I made my way into my career. One was to work far enough outside the boundaries of conventional scholarship to remain immune to the influence of traditional conventions and expectations. I witnessed in my years in a Japanese university setting how some professors got their voices heard in ways that avoided conventional academic constraints. They published opinion pieces in newspapers and magazines, made TV appearances, or published in unvetted university publications. In the field of second language education there are newsletters, local publications, and local conferences where people can contribute in ways that require less jumping through hoops than is required to contribute through major book and article publications. For people who don't mind staring at a computer screen, Internet discussions and online publications provide another outlet. How each of these participatory activities is valued by others depends on the community one wishes to participate in: Teachers often scorn researchers, for example, and researchers tend to limit the value they ascribe to nonrefereed publications. But within communities of teachers, the prestige of a refereed journal means little. The point is that outside the rather narrowly circumscribed context of refereed publications all of us can find ways to participate in professional conversations.

My second choice in writing for publication, my clear favorite, was to push at the conventional boundaries themselves, from the inside (see Kubota, this volume). To fight the good fight against the stereotypical turgid prose of academic publications (Blanton, 1999; Williams, 1997); to help expand the range of accepted research methods; to speak out against cultural stereotyping; to shift some of the discussions of academic literacy from the conventional focus on texts to the less conventional focus on people who write texts; and to encourage a very student-writer-oriented field to recognize that studies of teachers and scholars who write need to be included under the umbrella of writing research. An accommodator can't contribute in these ways. I needed to actively try to do some things differently, but under the umbrella of academic scholarship.

I remember when an idea first descended on me for an edited collection of narratives by educators in first and second language education about their career trajectories (eventually published as Casanave and Schecter, 1997). I was standing in the location where I get many of my ideas (the shower, if you must know), and the vision for this book descended on me whole and intact. It did not emerge out of a void, of course. I had been reading some narratives and some work about narratives in the educational literature. In this respect, my idea grew (conventionally) out of my reading. But in the field of second language education I had not yet seen any inspiring collections of first-person narratives by teachers. On the contrary, the field has been characterized by its strong support of systematic and science-like research in language education and its growing support for certain kinds of qualitative studies. Narrative and first-person accounts by and about authors themselves, although present in growing numbers in first language composition studies and education (e.g., Roen, Brown, & Enos, 1999; Trimmer, 1997; Witherell & Noddings, 1991), had yet to make much impact in the second language education field. More importantly, I sensed that people in first and second (foreign, bilingual) language fields didn't read each other's publications. My vision was for a crossover book, one that brought together scholars from different communities of academic practice. My eventual coeditor, Sandra Schecter, liked the idea, and we immediately started brainstorming ideas for whom to invite to write essays.

Because we wanted our collection of essays published by a good academic publisher so that it would reach our intended audience, we faced the challenge of persuading someone to take a chance with us (two relatively unknown educators) and with a project that was reaching out to a mixed market—always a problem in the profit-motivated publishing world. This meant not just convincing an acquisitions editor that we had a good idea, but writing a book prospectus that would convince the reviewers selected by the editor that we had a good idea and, moreover, that we could pull it off. We selected several publishers whose lists included books that seemed compatible with ours, and began preparing our prospectus according to their guidelines. Somewhat paradoxically, we were obligated by the guidelines to prepare several versions (each publisher's guidelines differed slightly) of what turned out to be a very conventional prospectus. We followed each publisher's guidelines meticulously, not only showing that we could follow the formal conventions of the guidelines but also that we had done our homework: We wanted to show that we knew what was going in the field in terms of narrative research and pedagogy, and that we had persuasive theoretical and pedagogical reasons for believing that a book of first-person narratives by language educators would contribute to the broad field of language education. In other words, we had to follow some very conventional rules in order to be able to shift the rules.

We struggled with this book prospectus for a long time. Months and months and then more months, providing a theoretical rationale, citing appropriate literature, locating and describing possible competition, refining each sentence. Once the main prospectus was done, it was easy to adjust it to fit the formal guidelines for specific publishers. We sent the prospectus to five publishers, and managed to interest only one (although many months after this publisher had offered us a contract, another publisher that had never responded contacted us expressing strong interest). We were delighted that Naomi Silverman, the editor for the book you are now reading as well, liked ideas that were a bit different, liked our goal of push-ing at the boundaries of our field in terms of style, content, and market, and liked our commitment to high quality writing (not a characteristic of all ed-ited collections). She convinced Mr. Erlbaum to give us a contract.

Compared with what followed, the prospectus work was a piece of cake. We had gathered a wonderful group of language educators, all of whom we were convinced had insightful stories to tell of eventful times in their careers that would connect well with readers. A few authors sailed through our request that they write an unconventional essay, one that did not need to be situated amidst the voices of others but that fronted their own identities using (gulp!) first-person singular pronouns. I've discussed elsewhere some of the challenges I faced as both editor and author in pull-ing off this really very modest coup (Casanave, 2002), so I won't belabor the details here. Let me just say it was harder work than I had ever imag-ined it would be. In addition to the difficulties of just getting authors to draft essays that suited our goals (some authors had not written before in the ways we were asking them to), I was faced with the big question in this boundary-pushing project of what I meant by academic writing, why I thought that changes were needed, and what effect I thought these changes would have on writing, writers, and writing instruction in our field. Help! I had started out wanting to make one small change (I thought), but the reverberations were growing in ways I had not predicted. I felt (and feel) pressured to think critically and analytically and theoreti-cally about this work, all of which are conventional academic ways to eval-uate published writing. However, I wanted this work to be evaluated as well by criteria of grace, style, emotional impact on readers, and depth of insight. And I did not want readers to say, "This is a great collection of sto-ries but they are not academic." It turns out that opinions vary on this mat-ter and that sometimes I myself don't know what I mean by "academic."

I am still at the boundaries, and I am still struggling with some of the ques-tions that this first boundary-pushing project raised for me. I continue to want to work from the inside out and continue to want to bend some of the rules. Before writers experiment with their writing do they need the security of tenure (Bridwell-Bowles, 1992)? Or can I encourage my students and other newcomers to the field of writing for publication that they too can push at the boundaries? How much influence can I, or any writer, have on what is allowed to be said in our fields' publications? I won't know till I try.

STRAND 3: CYNIC AT THE SIDELINES

I have no idea why I persist in playing the absurd games that characterize the professional writing life in my field. Some of what I read is incompre-hensible, and other publications seem trivial and designed only to add an item to an author's CV. Why theorize and complicate a commonsense or intuitively obvious teaching–learning issue just to get one's name in print? The pressure to publish (for tenure, promotion, or even hiring for a part-time position) feels to me to be an endemic disease, corrupting the possibility that scholars might try something different, risky, or visionary. I feel this pressure and despise it, partly because I cannot escape it. I myself have pondered many times how I might be able to turn what seems to me to be a thoroughly commonsense teaching–learning experience into an "interesting" article for publication just so that I can demonstrate continuity and professional involvement on my CV.

I had this experience not long ago. Having worked for about 2 years on a major single-authored book project (my first and it felt at the time like the last), I was periodically beset by self-imposed pressure to get at least one article out. I can hear myself saying, "It's been a year since I've published anything." Then, "It's been 2 years since I published anything." Then, "How can I turn my current teaching experiences into any kind of article for publication?" I struggled to find something interesting or important to say and woke up on some days believing I had found it, and on other days I knew that I was going to have to create an aura of importance about something that was routine, already well-researched, or simply boring.

With a slight roll of my eyes, I decided that during a semester-long academic writing class for graduate students at my Japanese university I would write along with students, modeling my writing processes, describing my decision-making processes, and demonstrating the centrality of revision when one writes for publication. I could thus kill two birds with one stone. I could use my own writing as a teaching device and at the same time prepare something for publication within the short time span of a semester. I would select a refereed journal, but one with a teaching orientation so that I could write about the very class that I was currently teaching. It would be a journal that preferred short articles without a lot of theorizing and with a minimal literature review. I found what I thought was such a journal, and studied the guidelines carefully. I told my students that starting with such guidelines, rather than starting with a finished draft and then trying to figure out where it might be submitted, made practical sense if they wanted to increase their chances of getting published. I reviewed these guidelines with my students, commenting with as little outward sign of cynicism as possible that many of the stipulations in the guidelines seemed arbitrary, such as the stylistic requirements for citing and referencing, that others seemed designed to prescribe in suffocating detail what kinds of submissions would be considered appropriate and how many references (exactly) were allowed, and that still others were practical constraints having to do with features such as length. The articles, I was relieved, should be only about 3000 words. I told the students that I had not published anything for a long time, and that I wanted to do everything possible in my first submission to this journal to enhance my prospects for success. Because some of them needed to publish as part of their graduate studies, I felt this advice would be eminently practical.

The paper grew bit by bit each week, until finally I had a version that I was ready to share with a colleague. I let students know that nothing is quite so helpful as a good writing partner, someone who knows something about your field and someone you trust. I am lucky that I have a couple of colleagues who fit this bill, and in this case I gave the paper to a colleague who was teaching a parallel section of the same writing course. This was hard for me to do, because the cynic in me said there was no substance to this paper. I had chosen to write about one aspect of my teaching, give a rationale for it and a few examples, and that was it. I followed guidelines meticulously, some of which I thought were absurd, just because I wanted this paper to get published quickly. I had to explain some of these requirements for the paper to my colleague, thinking he might suggest that I expand this or that (sorry, no room because of length considerations), discuss the issues more theoretically (sorry, only a tiny bit of theory allowed), or revise some of the redundant reference formatting (sorry, this is the way they want it). I did so apologetically and once again tried to resist a knee-jerk (eye-jerk?) eyeball-roll. He liked the paper, but it may have been that because I was talking about very familiar territory, the issues and descriptions rang true. At any rate, I revised a few more times, found that at least half the time I was satisfied with the paper, and finally sent the article in by e-mail, expecting a quick response.

Why on earth did I care about getting something published at this time anyway? The book project I had been working on was rewarding; I had tenure and had been promoted to full professor; I was participating in conferences so it was not as if I was out of the loop; and I was busy at my Japanese university and at the American university in Tokyo where I (glutton for punishment) had a part-time job on some weekends. Driven by the absurd expectations in my field ("scholars publish several articles a year …"), I submitted a paper that on some days felt interesting and important to me and on other days felt like fluff. And I did not get a quick turnaround in spite of the e-mail system of this journal and the modest length of this small paper. Four months later an e-mail message came saying that the reviews were in, and would I consider revising and resubmitting according to the suggestions, including a suggestion by the editor to revise my reference list to fit the new style (see our web page) and to cut one reference because I had gone over the required limit.

I scrolled down the screen to where I thought the reviews would be, and found only one short paragraph, with one comment, which was to provide a concrete example of what I was discussing. (I thought I had.). I e-mailed back the editor of the journal saying I thought there had been a mistake, that his e-mail had referred to reviews, plural, but I found only this one short paragraph. Several weeks later an e-mail response came back saying that this was a summary of the reviews. I was surprised, given that full copies of reviews are usually forwarded to authors who submit articles to refereed journals, but I shrugged, and within a day had made the minimal changes that were requested and resubmitted the paper by e-mail with an explanation of what I had done, also as requested. My e-mail also included a question about the new reference list format on the journal's web page, which seemed to me to contain several obvious mistakes. Many weeks later, an e-mail came in from an editorial assistant requesting that I send an e-mail explaining why I had not responded to the reviewers comments or sent the required cover letter. My patience was running out, my cynicism running high, and I returned a response immediately asking what was going on and stating that I had in fact done all that had been requested. Many days later, a response came saying that this matter would be forwarded to the editor when he returned to town. Several weeks after this (I had by now given up the idea of getting an article published quickly, or even getting one published at all), the editor wrote back, not referring to this mix-up at all, but thanking me for resubmitting my article, and urging me to have patience while it was once again given to reviewers. This process takes a while, he reminded me. I knew now that "a while" meant 3 to 4 months, even for a 10-page paper when everything was done by e-mail. As a reviewer for a couple of major journals, I knew that reviewers are encouraged to return their comments within about 4 weeks. I was annoyed, to put it mildly. At the final drafting of my chapter for this book, I was still waiting to see the article in print. If it makes it at all, it will be 3 years at the earliest from the date of my first submission.

I was angry at the practices of this journal, and have told myself I will not submit anything there again. But I guess I was mainly angry at myself for having fallen into the "you-have-to-publish-every-year" trap and for not recognizing that the "quick-and-dirty" approach is both unrealistic and unprofessional. I am angry at the fact that unrealistic expectations dominate scholarly work in academia and run the lives of young scholars in particular, who may indeed have something to lose if they don't toe the line. But why me? Why do I feel I have to contribute to an enterprise that makes newcomers and oldtimers alike jump through hoops like this? I am angry for having internalized some of the values in my field that at some level I despise. At this stage in my career in particular, I should be thinking about writing for publication only when I have something to say that I believe is important, not because I have not published for a while. And sometimes I just don't feel as if I have anything to say (although this seems to vary with mood, energy level, and contextual influences). At those times I wonder if it is time to bail and get on to the serious and less pretentious things in life, such as reconnecting with old friends, gardening, and watching the movies I rarely have time to see.

BRAIDING

Lately when I work on a piece of writing for publication for a community of applied linguists who share my interests in academic literacy, I have not been aware that the three strands that I described work against each other in any counterproductive way. It may be that I have been in the field long enough to have accumulated the background knowledge and familiarity with key figures that I need to feel like a participating community member. At times, however, the strands still conflict to the point where I begin to feel distracted by self-doubt. Although not all scholars experience the self-doubt that has plagued me much of my career, I do not think that I am unusual in having a number of different selves that all converge in my academic life. Probably everyone has something of the Accommodator, the Boundary Pusher, and the Cynic in them. Nor do I think I am unusual in feeling that these selves do not describe different people, even though it is true that on some days I feel more like a conventional community member and others time more like a cynic on the sidelines. When I plan and execute a piece of writing, often over the many months or even years it takes to bring something to print, I am all of these selves. My Boundary-Pusher self keeps me excited about and engaged in projects I truly believe in and helps control the Cynic in me. The Cynic helps me keep off the bandwagon of fads and resist the hero worship that sometimes blinds us to other ways of seeing. The Accommodating Community Member self helps me move a piece of writing into print because I am clear about which constraints I probably should adhere to and which I can negotiate.

The metaphor of narrative braiding, as well as the act of constructing the narrative strands, has helped me appreciate rather than dismiss as abnormal the strands of narratives that portray my many academic selves. As is no doubt the case for most writers, these strands form a whole of sorts while the strands remain separate and changeable, if I as braider wish, at every rebraiding. And I am not sure about this, but I suspect that with each new piece of writing that writers begin, the braiding process begins anew or at the very least shifts as writers mature and their purposes change. Seeing myself as a braider of narratives, whether or not the narratives themselves appear in print, has also helped me understand that I am not a victim of disciplinary discourses, but an active agent in choosing how to represent myself in writing. This is not to say that choices are always easy or that they are only about choices of language. They are not. Constructing an identity in a professional life through writing is a social and political act (Clark & Ivanič, 1997; Ivanič, 1998) as well as a personal and linguistic one. These acts have consequences: They influence how writers position themselves as more or less powerful and authoritative relative to a particular community of practice and as how likely they are to be published in different venues. Narrative braiders can use the stories that represent their professional identities to help sort out their relationships and goals within their communities of practice and increase the chances that the complexities of these relationships and goals work in their favor.

It has taken many years for me to begin to understand how the different strands of my own narratives all represent me and how I can weave them together, or not, to suit my specific goals. I am not sure that I could have shortened the process, but I would have liked knowing earlier than I did the extent to which the narrative braiding in the construction of professional identity does not happen in isolation. In the construction of this essay, as well as in my other writings, others have always helped me figure out what each braid will look like in print and hence helped me understand my relationship with a community of practice in richer ways than would have otherwise been possible.

REFERENCES

Bakhtin, M. M. (1981). *The dialogic imagination: Four essays.* (C. Emerson & M. Holquist, Trans.; M. Holquist, Ed.). Austin, TX: University of Texas Press.

Bell, J. (1997). Shifting frames, shifting stories. In C. P. Casanave & S. R. Schecter (Eds.), *On becoming a language educator: Personal essays on professional development* (pp. 133–143). Mahwah, NJ: Lawrence Erlbaum Associates.

Blanton, L. L. (1999). Classroom instruction and language minority students: On teaching to "smarter" readers and writers. In L. Harklau, K. M. Losey, & M. Siegal (Eds.), *Generation 1.5 meets college composition: Issues in the teaching of writing to U.S.-educated learners of ESL* (pp. 119–142). Mahwah, NJ: Lawrence Erlbaum Associates.

Bridwell-Bowles, L. (1992). Discourse and diversity: Experimental writing within the academy. *College Composition and Communication, 43,* 349–368.

Bruner, J. (1991). The narrative construction of reality. *Critical Inquiry, 18,* 1–21.

Casanave, C. P. (2002). *Writing games: Multicultural case studies of academic literacy practices in higher education.* Mahwah, NJ: Lawrence Erlbaum Associates.

Casanave, C. P., & Schecter, S. R. (Eds.). (1997). *On becoming a language educator: Personal essays on professional development.* Mahwah, NJ: Lawrence Erlbaum Associates.

Clandinin, D. J., & Connelly, F. M. (2000). *Narrative inquiry: Experience and story in qualitative research.* San Francisco: Jossey-Bass.

Clark, R., & Ivanič, R. (1997). *The politics of writing.* London: Routledge.

Conle, C. (1999). Why narrative? Which narrative? Struggling with time and place in life and research. *Curriculum Inquiry, 29*(1), 7–31.

Giddens, A. (1991). *Modernity and self-identity: Self and society in the late modern age.* Stanford, CA: Stanford University Press.

Haraway, D. (1988). Situated knowledges: The science question in feminism as a site of discourse on the privilege of partial perspective. *Feminist Studies, 14,* 575–600.

Hyland, K. (1996). Talking to the academy: Forms of hedging in science research articles. *Written Communication, 13,* 251–281.

Ivanič, R. (1994). I is for interpersonal: Discoursal construction of writer identities and the teaching of writing. *Linguistics and Education, 6,* 3–15.

Ivanič, R. (1998). *Writing and identity: The discoursal construction of identity in academic writing.* Philadelphia: John Benjamins.

Linde, C. (1993). *Life stories: The creation of coherence.* New York: Oxford University Press.

Myers, G. (1989). The pragmatics of politeness in scientific articles. *Applied Linguistics, 10*(1), 1–35.

Polkinghorne, D. E. (1991). Narrative and self-concept. *Journal of Narrative and Life History, 12*(2–3), 135–153.

Roen, D. H., Brown, S. C., & Enos, T. (Eds.). (1999). *Living rhetoric and composition: Stories of the discipline.* Mahwah, NJ: Lawrence Erlbaum Associates.

Trimmer, J. F. (Ed.). (1997). *Narration as knowledge: Tales of the teaching life.* Portsmouth, NH: Boynton/Cook.

Wenger, E. (1998). *Communities of practice: Learning, meaning, and identity.* Cambridge, England: Cambridge University Press.

Williams, J. M. (1997). *Style: Ten lessons in clarity and grace* (5th edition). New York: Addison-Wesley.

Witherell, C., & Noddings., N. (Eds.). (1991). *Stories lives tell: Narrative and dialogue in education.* New York: Teachers College Press.

11

Narrating One's Self:
Public–Personal Dichotomies
and a (Public) Writing Life

Linda Lonon Blanton
University of New Orleans

> The narrative form of shaping the self, others and events, often with highly elaborated and specific detail, appears to be universal, though with highly varied genre characteristics and attribution of mental states across cultures.
>
> —Heath, 2000, p. 125

I vividly remember years ago reading an article by Jim Corder, a professor at Texas Christian University. Corder was then a person of considerable repute in L1 writing, and I'd heard him speak numerous times at national and regional conferences. Whenever I came across his name on a program or in a book, I sought him out because I liked his reflective manner, his humor, his discourse style, and the way he left me with ideas to mull over. To me, he spoke and wrote as if he were communicating with someone he'd known for a long time, someone he valued and respected.

That particular article, as I recall, began with a walk through the Texas hill country on a visit to his elderly mother. As Corder spoke, I could smell the pines and hear the crunch of needles and pebbles under his boots while he shared what was on his mind. I remember relishing his freedom to express himself so openly, so genuinely, and I also felt envious of his unabashed, unapologetic authority to communicate so directly and personally to his readers—to let them walk with him in the cool, crisp, morning air. Although deeply engaged by Corder's writing, I was at the same time taken aback by the directness of his style and the intimacy he created with his readers. Imagine, here was this college professor, this published academic writer, referring to his mother … and in a national journal.[1] I remember wondering how he could "get away with it." And that's exactly how I saw it—that he was getting away with something.

I reasoned this way: (a) He was after all Jim Corder, a person of renown; (b) he was male; and (c) he was Texan (and Texans, especially Texas men, never seem to lack confidence). Because I was neither a person of renown, male, nor Texan, I figured I couldn't get away with it, nor did I have the courage to try. I longed, though, to write publicly the way Corder did, not simply because it was a readable and engaging style—that's how it struck me—but also because it was a way of writing that was not at odds with who I was, who I am.

You see, I come from a mountain culture—from the Ozark Mountains of northern Arkansas—where public and private discourse is often carried out through stories, usually through short story vignettes. These vignettes, which most often take the form of telling about lived experience, are replete with metaphorical language and use details of everyday life to moralize, explain, highlight, analyze, and instruct. Even short explanations embed this vivid mode of communicating, as when an old chair maker, known for his split-oak rockers, informed me about a recent thunderstorm, and impressed me with the strength of the wind by telling me that the metal electric pole in his alfalfa field was "bent over like a chicken pickin' up corn."

In this mode of communicating, interpretations and applications are not the overt responsibility of the storyteller. It's more or less "if the shoe fits, wear it," which, if the shoe in fact does fit, allows a listener to save face. In this way, you see, admonishment and correction need not be direct. Still, woe be to the listener who doesn't get the message, especially if the message can and should be analogized to the person's own comportment in the community. And everyone's comportment is everyone's business, especially the business of the elder women. Rather than operating individually, members of the community are socially situated within family units and represent the family in how they conduct their lives, in who they are. (Or they don't represent the family, as in the black sheep, which to a degree lets the family off the hook, although the black sheep is still perceived as a family burden.) So, someone is a Johnson, or a Briggs, or a whoever. And that person's people are industrious, or sneaky (*lyin' 'n cheatin'*), or lazy, and so on. My people, the Lonons, were known in the community as

---

[1]The article was, I'm quite sure, in *College English* (early 1980s), but, try as I might, I can't locate it. My point remains the same regardless. See the articles (Corder, 1986; Corder & Baumlin, 1987) included in the reference list for the same sense of Corder's style. His mother also plays a role in the 1986 article.

smart but stubborn. (My mother and husband—not Lonons, of course—attest at least to stubbornness.)

A social value of communicating through stories is that tellers do not need to put themselves above their listeners—as if "I know more than you"—because instruction takes the form of "here's something I did, something that happened to me." Even more so, tellers are expected to deprecate themselves—as in "Here's something I did, the fool that I am." Given that listeners supply the connections and applications, what each takes away is individualized and arrived at through reflection and analogy. Maybe this is largely why I found Corder's writing so instructive.

I don't remember at the time going through any inner dialogue—Could I, could I not, write like Jim Corder? Dare I, dare I not, try?—because it never occurred to me that I had his choices. Corder was Corder. That was that. So I struggled to write like I thought I was supposed to—well into my professional life—assuming that dense and detached expression would mark me as someone who was appropriately part of academic culture. Although I didn't at the time see it this way, I felt, in fact, a lot of pressure to prove my academic worth—to be part of "the club"—particularly because I had grown up outside mainstream urban culture. So I taught myself to write sentences like these:

> A sensitivity to the levels of importance of notional units within a text has also been demonstrated to affect recall of those units, both immediately and long term. In other words, there exists a direct correlation between a recall of notional units and their hierarchical importance. As would be expected, notions understood by a reader as more important within a text are better remembered than those understood as less important. (Blanton, 1984, p. 37)

Although the article was published,[2] the writing in my estimation fell short. It didn't impress me as the expression of a sophisticated mind. But I doubted I could push myself to a more abstracted level, to write sentences like these:

> Professional self-monitoring, adjudication, or accounting can be directed at a field's problem definition, proposed problem solutions, or methods and criteria for drawing inferences and identifying relevant sources. In the case of Renaissance Historicism, each of these three has been found problematic by one or more critics. Feminist critiques of the field's problem definition, as well as critiques of anecdotes and inferences, all point to the field's lack of

---

[2]I was grateful then, and still am, that the article was published. And I don't intend here to ridicule the article or *ESPJ*'s decision to include it. My point is rather that I realize now that as a writer and person, I am ill suited to certain genres and styles. But I certainly concede the right of discourse communities to set their norms and expectations, while maintaining my right to challenge them.

well-developed traditions or mechanisms for carrying on a sustained, pro-
gressively developing disciplinary conversation for arguing about the field's
focus and methods. The kind of disciplinary self-monitoring and adjudicat-
ing that professional forums allow is usually performed through epistemic
language, but the articles in my sample appear to take differing positions on
the value of epistemic language. (MacDonald, 1994, pp. 120–121)

I am not mocking, really I'm not. For all I know Susan MacDonald wrote
as she did for some of the same reasons I wrote as I did. And I am not saying that everyone must write as I now try to. A greater diversity of accepted
academic styles and genres would be good. A broadening of what's considered good academic writing would be useful. Allowances for essays of
opinion as well as articles of fact would be beneficial.

What I am saying is that I wrote the way I did because I thought that's
what was professionally expected of me (as contrary as that was to my self)
and that was what got published. Writing any other way, my thinking went,
would neither get me published nor allow me to be considered academic,
or at least academic enough (as in *good enough*). True, I could have gone
off to wait tables, but I had thrown my lot into academe, and at a certain
point changing horses mid-race didn't make sense. Because, constricted as
I was, I didn't know what to say to peers, and writing with nothing much to
say is torture (ask our freshman composition students), I put my energies
into writing textbooks, where I felt comfortable speaking to students.

Obviously, I didn't see things then the way I see them now. As I was living my life forward—building a marriage, raising a child, teaching a heavy
load, working for tenure and promotion—I was just doing what I could.
But—to rephrase Kierkegaard—life, while being lived forward, can only
be understood backward. And understanding backward gives the impression it was all simpler and more straightforward than it was.

Understanding my struggle to write for peers, to write for scholarly publication, took another turn in the road when I read Jane Tompkins (1990).
Writing about an academic phenomenon she calls the *performance model*,
Tompkins claims that teachers, including herself, are socialized into performing, to show how much we know, to the detriment of creativity—to students' creativity, as well as our own (p. 654). She further claims that
academics' fear of exposure, of being found out as inadequate in intelligence or knowledge, has no basis except in the performance model itself,
which has created for us a separation between our academic behavior and
our selves, creating basically false selves. The article sent me reeling.

Tompkins' words struck me this way: I was reading something I knew
but hadn't realized I knew. At the same time I recognized that this truth,
like a dirty, little family secret, wasn't supposed to be revealed. I had to remind myself to breathe. Graduate students of mine were reading the same
article, and I didn't know whether to go to class the next day and defend
myself or throw up my hands and admit the jig was up.

What struck me most was that Tompkins dared to risk herself to write so directly, honestly, and openly (even negatively) about herself—her "awkward lunge" in changing her teaching, sitting in "abject terror" as she waited to be interviewed for a Woodrow Wilson Fellowship, feeling "guilty" when her students did the work of a course (and she wasn't performing), teaching a course—while she was trying to change her way of teaching—that turned out to be a "nightmare." I was further shocked that she equated teaching to S-E-X—"something you weren't supposed to talk about or focus on in any way ... but that you were supposed to be able to do properly when the time came" (p. 655). I figured she, unlike Corder, couldn't get away with it.[3]

As it turns out, she didn't. Responding to Tompkins' writing, in particular to her memoir *A Life in School* (later published in 1996), Adam Begley, a book columnist, ripped her up one side and down the other. "What looks to Tompkins like self-expression ... looks to others like self-indulgence" (1994, p. 57). In a tone only to be described as sexist and mocking, Begley persisted in demeaning Tompkins by referring to her physical body. He said that Tompkins was "marching under the banner of the naked *I*." And he pointed out that, during an interview, Tompkins emphasized higher education's failure to put students in touch with their inner selves by "tap[ping] her breastbone" (p. 56). Even Begley's title—calling Tompkins a critic who "exposes herself"— shocked me by its hostility and disrespect.

Before leaving her professorship at Duke University to work at a restaurant—and to write as she felt she must—Tompkins published a scathing essay in which she defended her way of writing and her decision to view academe through a feminist lens. Claiming she had been hiding a part of herself for a long time largely because she knew there was no place for it within the academy, Tompkins asserted:

> What is personal is completely a function of what is perceived as personal. And what is perceived as personal by men ... is different from what is felt to be that way by women. For what we are talking about is not the personal as such, what we are talking about is what is important, answers one's needs, strikes one as immediately *interesting*. (Tompkins, 1991, p. 1089)

On her way out the door, Tompkins claimed that the public–private dichotomy, which she calls a public–private "hierarchy," is a founding condition of female oppression. That the reason she felt embarrassed at her own attempts to speak personally in a professional context was

---

[3]"Getting away with something" implies, to my mind, being met with—at a minimum—a benign response from one's peers and superiors. Above all, it implies an avoidance of public attack. In challenging professional norms that "rule out certain domains of thought" and expression, Ruddick, in a recent (2001) *Chronicle* essay, speaks of the paralyzing power of the "fear of attack" (p. B8), a fear I share.

that she'd been conditioned to feel that way (p. 1080). Her parting shot was "to hell with it."[4]

In part because of the depth of my reaction to both Tompkins' content and style, I began to feel a shift in my own determination to speak. To speak in a way that allowed me to connect my thoughts and experience to words on a page. I began to realize—I'm not sure fully when or why—that I had cut myself off, leaving me with little to say. Some of my realization came about while working with immigrant (U.S.-educated) English as a second language (ESL) students, the 1.5 generation,[5] whose full literacy experience in English lay in trying to write five-paragraph, expository themes in generic school voices on topics they neither knew nor cared about. They too had cut themselves off.

I also realized that both my students and I were operating in a double bind. My students couldn't express themselves through school writing, because at its worst, nobody can. And they were cut off, at school and in English, from the languages and cultures in which they had gained their primary and most valued experiences in the world. And some things don't translate, especially if the writer is less-than-proficient in the school language and the writer's only literacy experience is school writing.

As for myself, I felt, like Tompkins, that the academy is a male-determined place in its norms, forms of expression, and modes of evaluation—a place where I didn't (often still don't) feel nurtured or valued. And from my birth culture—a nonintellectual, sometimes even anti-intellectual, minority culture—I had been socialized to view displays of superior knowledge and engagement in talk over people's heads as negatives, even as cause for social ostracism. No wonder both I and my students, for different reasons, operated behind masks, or at times preferred silence. Or, even when speaking, felt compelled to discuss certain matters "with a caution bordering on ventriloquism," to borrow Lisa Ruddick's phrase (2001, p. B8).

---

[4]Tompkins did not stay gone from academe. She is currently listed on the website of the University of Illinois at Chicago as a member of the graduate faculty in their College of Education. And she was listed as a speaker at the 2001 Modern Language Association Conference. Tompkins' return to academic life does not, however, invalidate my point about the risks she took in countering professional and rhetorical norms. Despite her academic stature, she, in fact, didn't "get away with it": she was publicly "flogged" for the stance she took and dragged into defending herself. It is of no consequence that the one publication I cite—the one in which she was thoroughly excoriated—is not considered a scholarly journal. Begley's attack on Tompkins was indeed public—it appeared in print—and his pointed claim was the outrageousness of some academics and their writing.

[5]The term *1.5 generation* was first used by Rumbaut and Ima (1988) to characterize U.S.-educated learners of ESL whose "traits and experiences ... lie somewhere in between those associated with the first or second generation" of immigrants (cited in Harklau, Losey, & Siegal, 1999, p. vii).

Yet, to return to Tompkins, if a lesson was to be taken from her writing experience, she had not gotten away with it. Like Hester Prynne, she had been publicly branded with a letter. Only in her case, it was *I*. Although I didn't liken myself to Tompkins—I didn't have her high profile or the intensity of her anger—I did consciously set out, in my own tentative way, to narrate myself back together. To take a risk. Look behind the mask. See what was there. And to find a voice in which to speak professionally in order to have something to say.[6]

My first effort resulted in the article "Discourse, Artifacts, and the Ozarks: Understanding Academic Literacy" (Blanton, 1994), which I sent off to the *Journal of Second Language Writing* with considerable trepidation. (By this time, I had been teaching for almost 30 years.) I knew the article had crossed the line into the personal. I had after all brought my grandmother into it, and publicly acknowledged I was from the Ozark Mountains, a fact I hid, by omission, throughout my high school and undergraduate years in Southern California. (To obscure my origins, I had changed dialects.)

I also knew the article had transgressed into a reflective format, where I attempted to instruct through telling my own classroom story—"Here's what happened to me, and here are some of the things I've been thinking about." And I knew the article left me feeling vulnerable—"Here's what I'm wrestling with, although you intelligent readers probably sorted these things out ages ago." Yet I knew the article was honest and open, and it held true to the adage I offer as guidance to my writing students: Write a paper that, if you were your audience, you would like to read.

I steeled myself for the negative reviews I was sure would follow. And they did. One reviewer said the paper:

---

[6]*Voice* interests me greatly, but I see it as a subject I hope to explore elsewhere. Discussing it here would take me too far off track. I do want, though, to acknowledge its complexity and the disagreement in current literature about the validity of voice as a viable concept in writing instruction. Bowden (1999) claims that voice is a particularly Western concept, even an American one, that has persisted beyond its usefulness. Ramanathan and Kaplan (1996) claimed that voice is largely a culturally constrained notion that's inaccessible to students who aren't participants in the culture in which they're asked to write (p. 22; noted in Johns, 1999, p. 159). (An even more current interest in voice is evidenced by the combined issue—Numbers 1–2, Volume 10, February/May 2001—of the *Journal of Second Language Writing* devoted to the subject.) As for me, I agree that certain voices, registers, and dialects may meet the expected norms of some discourse communities more than others. And, yes, novice writers, speakers new to public forums, and writers and speakers aiming at crossing cultures have to work at developing an *ear* for what a new audience expects. But I disagree that voice exists simply as a meta-linguistic notion created to fit an outmoded instructional paradigm. For me, voice has a tangible and palpable reality. Voice (actually a range of ways of voicing myself) must be felt within me; otherwise I have no way of shaping, even generating, something to say, on paper or elsewhere. (And I am not conflating speaking and writing. I am quite aware of the complexities of difference.) In this volume, Dwight Atkinson, Ryuko Kubota, and Paul Matsuda all address voice in one way or another.

seems to lose focus … and … gets lost in divergences. Some of the most salient points come across almost as asides.… The effort goes astray with too
many excursions.… The paper lacks clarity and focus on a single, dominant
thesis.… Overall it comes across as a rather disjointed collection of introspective observations.

Although this reviewer didn't chastise me for nakedly exposing myself,
he or she did deal a stinging blow in saying that I "reveal[ed] naïveté about
the real world role of ESL at the university level."

On reading these comments, I felt rather like the child I'd heard
Courtney Cazden, of the Harvard School of Education, once talk about.
The girl had written about special treats her grandmother had organized
for her, including a birthday party. In response, the girl's teacher said the
piece of writing lacked coherence, made no sense, and was otherwise a
pointless hodgepodge of details. "But, but," the little girl cried, "I just
wanted to show you how wonderful my grandmother is, how much I love
her." Cazden's point was that cultures vary in the discourse structures they
privilege. The child's preferred structure was *episodic*, as opposed to the
hierarchical structure the teacher expected, probably without awareness
of other possibilities, or even of her own expectations.

Two other reviewers, to my great relief, read my submission differently.
One called it "groundbreaking" and speculated it would prove to be a
"much-cited and seminal piece." (I quote here with humility.) The second
recognized a subtlety I had hoped to achieve: "The style reflects the content." This reviewer went on to write that "after years of reading manuscripts, [she] could finally say 'accept' the first time around." So far, so good.
The journal accepted the article. The negative judgments were known only
by the editors, reviewers, and me. Maybe I had gotten away with it.

At the Teachers of English to Speakers of Other Languages (TESOL) Conference in Baltimore (1994), a month or two after the essay was published, I
stepped into an elevator—minutes after arriving in town—with someone I
vaguely knew, a college professor and published author. We exchanged
greetings, and then he offered that he'd read "my home-spun little article in
the *Journal of Second Language Writing*." I said something stupid like
"thank you," as if he had paid me a compliment, and got off the elevator. I
wasn't sure which letter I had just been branded with, but it felt like *F*, for *female*. So, I hadn't gotten away with it, but it didn't matter. Others later said
they liked the article, had learned from it, and thanked me for its clarity.[7]

More to the point: through the writing of the piece, I had taken a stride in
integrating myself, in bringing the personal and professional together. For
the first time, I felt I had reached a point of having something public to say
and a means of saying it that wasn't contrary to who I am as a teacher,
scholar, and human being in the world. That said, I acknowledge that I,
and the little girl in Cazden's story, both have to work at negotiating who

---

[7]I was honored later to have the article anthologized (Zamel & Spack, 1998).

we are with those around us. Everyone does—that's the nature of cultures—but those brought up outside the mainstream have more to negotiate if they aspire to acceptance, even success, out of their home cultures. ("But, but," the little girl might cry, "that's not fair. It shouldn't be ei-ther–or—your way or none.")

For myself, I cannot simply tell stories and then leave possible interpretations and applications up to others, as I was socialized to do.[8] Although it feels as if I don't respect the intelligence of readers to individualize their own connections, I do accept that—if I want academic peers to hear me—I have to offer commentary. I cannot (just) leave my stories free-standing. Because instructing through storytelling is already anomalous in the public arena in which I ply my trade, I cannot—for the sake of communication—reasonably expect to add one anomaly to another.

So, being heard is an issue in how I choose to speak—whether or not my way is acceptable or accepted. But I want to raise the ante: Storytelling—that is, speaking of one's life experiences—is, I think, also an issue of mental and public health. Let me close with a larger concern about the role of personal stories, of being heard as individuals, in our professional lives. John Lahr (1994) said it better than I can:

> What we call "I"—the self that we spend a lifetime making and remaking—is really a story we tell ourselves and that is reflected back to us by the world. When both versions of this narrative are more or less in synch, you have sanity; when they aren't, you have madness. And when, for neurological reasons, the mind can't even assemble the plot of its story, you have the discombobulated world that Oliver Sacks famously describes in his collection of essays *The Man Who Mistook His Wife for a Hat*. "To be ourselves we must *have* ourselves—possess, if need be *re*possess, our life stories.... We must 'recollect' ourselves, recollect the inner drama, the narrative of ourselves. A [person] needs such a narrative, a continuous inner narrative, to maintain [her] identity, [her] self." (p. 104)

In narrating myself, in composing an identity and a writing life, I need to (re)collect my life stories. Culturally, that rings true to me, but—and here is where crossing cultures goes both ways—it may benefit others as well.

---

[8]I better understand the conflict between my own upbringing and others' norms through explanations such as this:

> The extent to which adults verbalize connections across events or between intentions and behaviours varies across cultures and socialisation patterns. However, groups whose societies place high value on formal schooling appear to stress such explanations more than those who have only recently begun to make education in schools widely available and requisite (Scribner & Cole, 1981; cited in Heath, 2000, p. 125).

My birth culture did not value formal schooling, although that is now changing. During my childhood, in fact, I constantly heard *too much booklearnin'* as a reason why someone failed to make sense—or have common sense. And little was worse than an absence of common sense.

Obviously Tompkins thought it must, and Corder wrote as though it did. When we scratch the surface, we may find, as Heath claimed in the opening quote to this essay, that "the narrative form of shaping the self ... appears to be universal." If Heath is right, each of us must take care that in narrating ourselves—both publicly and privately—we don't, somewhere along the way, lose the plot. I say, let the little girl tell her story.

REFERENCES

Begley, A. (1994, March/April). The I's have it: Duke's "moi" critics expose themselves. *Lingua Franca,* 54–59.

Blanton, L. L. (1984). Using a hierarchical model to teach academic reading to advanced ESL students: How to make a long story short. *The ESP Journal, 3,* 37–46.

Blanton, L. L. (1994). Discourse, artifacts, and the Ozarks: Understanding academic literacy. *Journal of Second Language Writing, 3*(1), 1–16.

Bowden, D. (1999). *The mythology of voice.* Westport, CT: Heinemann Boynton/Cook.

Corder, J. W. (1986). Learning the text: Little notes about interpretation, Harold Bloom, the *Topoi,* and the *Oratio. College English, 48*(3), 243–248.

Corder, J. W., & Baumlin, J. S. (1987). Opinion is, of course, bad; research, on the other hand, is quite good: The tyranny (or is it myth?) of methodology. *Journal of Higher Education, 58*(4), 463–469.

Harklau, L., Losey, K. M., & Siegal, M. (Eds.). (1999). *Generation 1.5 meets college composition: Issues in the teaching of writing to U.S.-educated learners of ESL.* Mahwah, NJ: Lawrence Erlbaum Associates.

Heath, S. B. (2000). Seeing our way into learning. *Cambridge Journal of Education, 30*(1), 121–132.

Johns, A. (1999). Opening our doors: Applying socioliterate approaches (SA) to language minority classrooms. In L. Harklau, K. M. Losey, & M. Siegal (Eds.), *Generation 1.5 meets college composition* (pp. 159–171). Mahwah, NJ: Lawrence Erlbaum Associates.

Lahr, J. (1994, June 13). Losing the plot. *The New Yorker,* 103–106.

MacDonald, S. P. (1994). *Professional academic writing in the humanities and social sciences.* Carbondale and Edwardsville, IL: Southern Illinois University Press.

Ramanathan, V., & Kaplan, R. B. (1996). Audience and voice in current L1 composition textbooks: Some implications for L2 writers. *Journal of Second Language Writing, 5*(1), 21–33.

Ruddick, L. (2001, November 23). The near enemy of the humanities is professionalism. *The Chronicle Review* of *The Chronicle of Higher Education,* B7–9.

Rumbaut, R. G., & Ima, K. (1988). *The adaptation of Southeast Asian refugee youth: A comparative study.* (Final report to the Office of Resettlement). San Diego, CA: San Diego State University. (ERIC Document Reproduction Service No. ED 299 372).

Scribner, S., & Cole, M. (1981). *The psychology of literacy.* Cambridge, England: Cambridge University Press.

Tompkins, J. (1990). Pedagogy of the distressed. *College English, 52*(6), 653–660.

Tompkins, J. (1991). Me and my shadow. In R. R. Warhol & D. P. Herndl (Eds.), *Feminisms: An anthology of literary theory and criticism* (pp. 1079–1092). New Brunswick, NJ: Rutgers University Press.

Tompkins, J. (1996). *A life in school: What the teacher learned.* Reading, MA: Addison-Wesley.

Zamel, V., & Spack, R. (Eds.). (1998). *Negotiating academic literacies: Teaching and learning across languages and cultures.* Mahwah, NJ: Lawrence Erlbaum Associates.

12

Writing for Publication/Writing for Public Execution: On the (Personally) Vexing Notion of (Personal) Voice

Dwight Atkinson
Temple University Japan

It is rare in the field of language education to get a chance to deal directly with existential questions. But in order to address the topic I have chosen regarding my own academic literacy practices—whether I "have" a written voice, and if so how to characterize it—the following questions must be engaged: *Who am I? What am I doing? What is going on here?*[1] But let me begin with some background.

In past, mostly theoretical work on the notion of written voice and associated concepts (Atkinson, 1997, 2001; Atkinson & Ramanathan, 1995;

---

[1]The last of these questions—"What is going on here?"—is the classic social science question: What "deep action" is going on beneath the surface of the social practices and scenes?

I will not, in this essay, attempt to define the notion of voice as I use it. Readers are referred to Ramanathan and Atkinson (1999), where voice is discussed and defined at length. It should be mentioned, however, that the notion of voice referenced here accords most closely with "personal voice" or "authentic voice" as used by Peter Elbow and others in composition studies (see Berlin, 1987; Bowden, 1999). For different versions of the voice concept, see Yancey (1994), Bowden (1999), and Belcher and Hirvela (2001); for suggestions that some of these may still implicitly contain the notion of personal voice, see Atkinson (2001).

I would like to thank Andrea Simon-Maeda for helpful comments given on an earlier version of this paper.

Ramanathan & Atkinson, 1999), Vai Ramanathan and I have claimed that it is intimately linked to a particular ideology of the individual: Euro-American *individualism*. This ideology has been characterized by many; for example, Pierre Bourdieu (1984, p. 414) described it as

> the whole range of institutional mechanisms, especially the intellectual and educational ones, which help to encourage the cult and culture of the "person," that set of personal properties, exclusive, unique and original, which includes "personal ideas," "personal style" and, above all, "personal opinion." It could be shown that the opposition between the rare, the distinguished, the chosen, the unique, the exclusive, the different, the irreplaceable, the original, and the common, the vulgar, the banal, the indifferent, the ordinary, the average, the usual, the trivial, with all the associated oppositions between the brilliant and the dull, the fine and the coarse, the refined and the crude, the high (or heightened) and the low is one of the fundamental oppositions … in the language of bourgeois ethics and aesthetics.

Bourdieu located this ideology particularly in the world of education, and it is partly there too that I want to discuss its role. But, as with other dominant social practices, a larger frame or context must first be provided.

Theorists often trace the birth of Euro-American individualism to the aftermath of the European Renaissance, when God had initially been questioned as the source and arbiter of all things. Thus, Michel Foucault understood the making of modern "individuals" as part of the Enlightenment project of rationalizing humankind. Prior to the Enlightenment, humans were seen as deriving their identities primarily from their relation to a "high center" (Anderson, 1983)—God, or his immediate earthly representative, the king. The farther away you were from the king physically or socially (and most were very far away), the more you were part of the undifferentiated mass of subjects. But all subjects came under the king's absolute power, which was exercised mostly through negative means—direct physical imposition and violence. As part of the Enlightenment, however, new economic realities as well as the waning power of kingship itself necessitated a revolution in means of government—by locating and disciplining bodies in physical and symbolic space, human beings began to be "individuated," that is, reconceived and reconfigured, fundamentally, as individual or autonomous subjects, which allowed for their greater control. Thus, hospitals (Foucault, 1975) and prisons (Foucault, 1977a) became places in which patients and inmates were individually treated and rehabilitated, rather than simply excluded from society en masse. More centrally, schools and factories began to be organized around the quantifiable performance of individuals, who underwent a rigorous disciplinary regime:

> The chief function of the [modern] disciplinary power is to "train"… Instead of bending all its subjects into a single uniform mass, it separates, analyses,

differentiates, carries its procedures of decomposition to the point of necessary and sufficient single units. It "trains" the moving, confused, useless mul-
titudes of bodies and forces into a multiplicity of individual elements—small,
separate cells, organic autonomies, genetic identities and continuities,
combinatory segments. Discipline makes individuals; it is the specific tech-
nique of a power that regards individuals both as objects and as instruments
of its exercise. (Foucault, 1977a, p. 170)

Thus, far from being simply a move toward personal freedom and the
inalienable rights of (individual, rational) "man," as innovators of the modern democratic tradition like John Locke would have it, the fostering of an
individualist ethos from the Enlightenment onward was part of a more
general movement to discipline and control him—to colonize progres-
sively larger parts of his life, to subjectify him. Again in the words of
Foucault (1982, p. 212), such disciplinary power "applies itself to immediate everyday life which categorizes the individual, marks him by his own
individuality, attaches him to his own identity, imposes a law of truth on
him which he must recognize and which others have to recognize in him."

Now what does this have to do with writing for publication? Perhaps not
much, at first glance. But the concept of author, according to Foucault (1977b)
and others, is intimately tied up with that of the individualist individual. And
this in fact would seem to bear out historically—the birth of quasilegal systems of textual ownership appears to have been a product of the Enlightenment, though not fully realized until closer to the present day. Certainly, up to
and indeed through much of the Enlightenment, there was easy and promis-
cuous plagiarism and textual appropriation (to use modern, individualist
terms), while it was not uncommon for texts of many varieties to be published anonymously (e.g., Kronick, 1988). In the first modern scientific journal, *The Philosophical Transactions of the Royal Society of London*, for
instance, anonymous articles appeared commonly in the 17th century but
virtually disappeared starting in the 18th (Atkinson, 1999b; Kronick, 1988).

The "author function" (Foucault, 1977b) was thus produced by an indi-
viduating system or network of power relations that positioned the writer
of a particular text (even this latter formulation seems a modern, individualist one, because composition has always been such a *putting together* of
different things, as the word itself tells us) as the sole owner of that text and
the words and ideas contained therein. The author in this way was irre-
versibly tied to her or his "own" words and ideas, for which she or he was
then held responsible (and sometimes as a result also punished).

MY PERSONAL ACCOUNT OF WRITING FOR PUBLICATION: BACKGROUND

All this must still seem far away from the topic of voice, and from what is
supposed to be basically an autobiographical account. Let me therefore

shift gears radically, and discuss in this section and the next my own experience as a writer.

In fact, Foucault's description of the birth of the modern (Euro-American) subject and its history of progressive individuation is light-years away from my own personal experience as a writer. In this "commonsense,"[2] or "naive," view, there is little doubt in my mind that I write first and foremost to know more about myself—to find out what I think on a particular topic—and then secondarily to share this view with others. There is also no question that I *enjoy* writing, both the abstract thinking processes that it requires and enables and the more kinesthetic activity of moving ideas, words, and sentences around, or finding better ideas, words, and sentences, until they are "just right"—a kind of literate puzzle-solving. I am convinced beyond a doubt that if I did not naturally enjoy writing, I would not now be doing it.[3]

If I were to try to reconstruct my personal history—always a dangerous activity[4]—vis-à-vis writing, it would begin with an early infatuation with *reading*, especially adventure fiction. It would then move on to a seemingly natural transition from reader to writer in early adolescence, with absolutely no encouragement at all, as I recall, from educational authorities. As an adolescent I wrote freely, if perhaps irregularly: poetry; short stories; long, highly descriptive letters. These first attempts to write, I am sure, were heavily conditioned by what I was reading—Hemingway strongly influenced a story set on an Indian reservation in Maine, for example, just as Ray Bradbury inspired a poem with a carnivalesque theme. In my senior year of high school I was co-editor of the school literary magazine, not a very popular or desirable position in southern Virginia in the early 1970s. But by then I was getting encouragement from several teachers, and the next year I was off to Kenyon College—a place with something of a literary reputation—thinking I would be an English major, and secretly desiring to be a writer. As much as anything in my first two decades, then, reading and writing—pursued by and large for the joy they provided—dominated my life.

---

[2]"Commonsense" views of reality have been studied by philosophers and social scientists (e.g., Berger & Luckmann, 1966), who generally find that commonsense experience is just as socially constructed as other epistemological vantage points, the main difference being that we experience it as a kind of irreducible, "ground" reality.

[3]In this connection it was striking, in a workshop conducted by Chris Casanave at Temple University Japan in February 2000, that of the 40-plus participants polled by Casanave as to whether they enjoyed writing, only two—of whom I was one—raised their hands.

[4]The sense-making function of narrative autobiography has been extensively investigated in the social sciences and humanities, the core finding being that people "remember" their pasts in terms of their present realities. Therefore, to consider individuals' autobiographical accounts as true in any literal sense would be, to say the least, a gross misunderstanding of how they function in their lives.

As an academic writer-in-training in college, however, I had less success. A perfectionist by upbringing, I gradually developed a writer's block. I vividly remember sitting with yellow legal pad and pen, or sometimes at a friend's typewriter, simply trying to get the first sentence of a paper down and done with. But even that I found an impossible task. When I graduated from college in 1979, I left something like 14 papers unwritten; I was allowed to graduate, I believe, only because I did well in other areas, and because it was the permissive 70s. But it had not been a pleasant experience, and I did not expect to see the inside of a college classroom again.

By the mid-1980s I was back in the college classroom, this time studying Teaching English to Speakers of Other Languages (TESOL) in an effort to upgrade my status as an English as a Second Language (ESL) instructor in Japan. My teachers at Temple University Japan were caring, nurturing, and seemed unconcerned when I was sometimes unable to hand in assignments on time. However, I did do my assignments, which were much more practical (and perhaps for that reason easier, or at least more possible) than those left undone as an undergraduate. When I returned to the United States in 1987 to do a PhD in applied linguistics, I therefore did have an approach to dealing with academic writing assignments, though a labored and uncomfortable one. In fact, the approach still involved yellow legal pads and pens, but in the meantime I had discovered that wonderful invention, white-out: I would write my papers on the yellow pad, carefully whiting-out and revising what seemed like every second or third word or phrase. In my first year of PhD studies, I remember sometimes feeling dizzy from white-out fumes; and my fellow graduate students nicknamed me "Dwight-out" for my exemplary use of the stuff.

In 1988 or thereabouts, my classmate John Hedgcock (also a contributor to this volume) introduced me to word processing and thereby changed my life as a writer. In one stroke (actually, it took time, as I am a slow learner and was strongly addicted to the white-out), I was suddenly able to revise and reorganize effortlessly. It was then I believe that I began to find my comfort zone as a writer and started to enjoy it as a puzzle-solving game.

Let me now step back and comment on what I have written in this section. First, this commonsense view of why I write and how I became a comfortable academic writer clearly leaves out a lot, quite apart from the accuracy of what it does describe. For instance, missing is the fact (not a prominent feature of my subjective experience) that I need(ed) to write to be taken seriously in my academic field, at least beyond the confines of my home institution. Also missing is the fact that the topics I choose hardly appear out of thin air—rather, they have to have some currency in the field. A third point not accounted for in my subjective experience is that the larger part of my professional identity—formed substantially in graduate school, I believe, but by no means unrelated to my eminently middle class, mainstream upbringing (see Heath, 1983, chap. 7, for the place of literacy in such upbringings)—is as a researcher. It can further be noted that my account leaves out the research process completely, suggesting that my writing takes place as an independent activity.

Second, I find it interesting (and possibly troubling) that so much of my account seems to focus on writing-as-inscribing, that is, as a *getting down of words*. In college, this is what my writing block reduced to, subjectively speaking: the virtual impossibility of engaging in the *physical act* of writing. And, as a more mature academic writer, this is the core of the task as I experience it—putting down *words*, juggling them around, finding better (or fewer, or simpler, or more apposite) ones, and then feeling at last that I have things "just right." It is possible, I suppose, that my subjective obsession with words is due to the fact that all the other stuff—the cognitive processes, the subliminal intertextuality, the intense (if sometimes faceless) sociality of writing for an academic audience or community—is not readily available to personal reflection. But perhaps it is also more, as I hypothesize later in the chapter.

Third, it is sobering to note how closely my commonsense description articulates with the expressivist view of writing promoted by Peter Elbow, Ken Macrorie, Donald Murray, and others. In her cross-cultural study of the Peoples' Republic of China and U.S. high school writing teachers judging student essays from both countries, Li (1996, p. 91) captures this view perfectly in describing the evaluative orientation of the latter:

> The primary function of writing for [the U.S. writing teachers] is the exploration and expression of "self." As [one of the teachers] expounded eloquently, "It is very important for writers to deal with life, to reflect, to look into themselves and the meaning of their lives. That's the whole purpose of writing as far as I am concerned."

Although I do not believe I follow this principle literally in writing for publication—in theory at least, I write *about something*, not just, or even primarily, about myself—I feel strongly that the exploration is nearly always an intensely personal one—a personal attempt to know, and thereby to refashion, my/self as a human being by expanding and complicating my horizons.

The realization that my subjective experience accords closely with a view of writing as more-or-less pure self-discovery/individual knowing suggests of course what I believe to be true: This view is as much an ideological product as that of Elbow and his compatriots, and that it is furthermore a product of the *same* basic ideology: individualism. The power of ideology is in fact exactly this—to reframe, or "naturalize," what is actually a "social relationship between men [as a] a [natural] relationship between things" (Marx, 1889/1978, p. 321). I examine my own place in this ideological formation later in this essay.

Finally, I should note that talking this abstractly about one's subjective experience of writing for publication has its obvious limits. Let me therefore turn now to recurring themes and incidents in my life as an academic writer, which may shed light on whether I have a voice.

MY PERSONAL ACCOUNT OF WRITING FOR PUBLICATION: RECURRING THEMES AND INCIDENTS

My past experience with writing for publication suggests that I guard my texts jealously—that I will inevitably come into conflict with any editor who seeks, from my point of view, to substantially change them. But "substantially" here in fact denotes quite a low threshold of sensitivity—at base I believe that almost *any* change to something I have written is in principle a violation of my sovereignty—my rights and responsibilities as a writer. Arguments I have used in the past to justify (to myself, mostly) this possibly radical position are: 1) I tend to work over texts exhaustively, drafting, redrafting, tinkering, and fine-tuning until, as mentioned earlier, I have things "just right." Having done my effortful best, I am unlikely to be happy when someone else takes my essay apart with a red pen in an hour or two; 2) I pride myself on being a "good writer"—someone at least who takes great care and puts great effort into making sure my writing makes sense. I have often thought that I am probably a *better* writer in this regard than most copyeditors and perhaps some journal editors. I do not, therefore, find very valid or fulfilling editorial comments questioning, for example, my use and knowledge of commas, word choice, paragraph structure, or passive voice; 3) I regard many conventional strictures on academic writing as efforts to stifle individual expressiveness and creativity. Although I can accept a general point here—if we were all to do only our own thing in academic writing, the resulting literature would probably not be usable for the purposes we typically use it for—neither do I wish merely to sacrifice my own interests (i.e., my own best efforts to express my current thinking on a particular topic) to this "greater good." To give the idea a Foucauldian twist, it is in each of our interests to resist attempts at subject(ificat)ion and homogenization by dominant discourses, even if the "opportunity space" for doing so may ultimately be small, or even nil (e.g., Foucault, 1988; St. Pierre, 2001); 4) It often strikes me that copy editors are ignorant of the conventions of the specialist fields in which they edit. A significant number of their corrections, therefore, although perhaps right in some abstract, style-guide type of sense, are simply wrong vis-à-vis the conventional practices of particular fields; 5) Many of the manuscripts I read for journal and book editors are not, to my eyes, very well or carefully written. I tend to feel, therefore, that my work should not be classed with them, or subjected to the same kinds of summary treatment.

More concretely, these convictions have brought me into conflict with different editors. To relate only the most extreme instance, a few years ago I received page-proofs back from a well-reputed journal in my field—one that in my experience has a history of being extremely literal in interpreting dictates of formal correctness and style—with perhaps 150 corrections on it. I went through each of these and accepted perhaps a third, and then wrote the editor that I could not accept the rest because they affected my basic arguments, justifying my position in strong terms. A rather sharp phone conversation ensued, and the paper was eventually published with most (but not all) of the original language intact. Although my relations with this editor seemed somewhat strained afterwards, I was happy to see that a paper accepted by the same journal a year or so later was much less heavily edited, although prominently stated in the editor's letter of acceptance was that the journal reserved the right to edit according to style requirements, and that it was up to contributors to abide by this agreement.

One or two observations about this experience, and I will move on: First, it seems fairly clear to me (in keeping with my earlier emphasis on writing-as-inscribing) that the objections I have to editors' comments usually concern the specific language in a piece, rather than its larger ideas. That is, I don't seem to be opposed, in principle, to changing content—at least to the same degree I am to changing form.[5] I'm not sure what to make of this, but one possible explanation is that my papers are usually accepted (when they are) *on condition of* certain changes in content; it is only afterwards that the more detailed editing takes place. When I argue with an editor about wording or punctuation, I may therefore subconsciously be banking on the fact that the paper has already been accepted, and possibly therefore also slotted into plans for a particular issue. At any rate, violations of my voice—if in fact I have such a thing—seem here to revolve around issues of language and form rather than content.

Second, I do not consider myself an argumentative person, generally speaking, though self-concept in such cases is of course highly unreliable. It is therefore curious to me that I take such umbrage at having (from the purely subjective point of view, once again) my language interfered with. The feeling of violation is almost primal, visceral—not unrelated, perhaps, to having had a very strong mother who persistently corrected my "bad English." "My language is mine!" the feeling is: "Correct it at the risk of alienating me or not getting my cooperation." This, to me, is a substantial argument—though possibly based on idiosyncratic experience—for the existence of something like voice.

Let me now describe a second recurrent experience I have had with writing for publication—that signified by the "Writing for Public Execution" part of my title. For reasons I am not very aware of, my academic writing

---

[5]The one real exception I can see to this point is that I tend to strongly resist changing the content of a piece when I feel that an editor or reviewer hasn't read my paper on its own terms—that is, that they would basically have the whole thing reconceptualized to fit their personal preferences and biases. But papers read in this manner rarely get accepted, leaving the issue of how or whether to revise moot.

seems frequently to involve me in controversy. Two conceivable explanations are (a) I tend to take up topics that are magnets for disagreement, and/or (b) I express myself in writing in ways that tend to breed controversy, whether in fact my views are so controversial or not. A third possibility I won't discuss in any detail (but see, e.g., Charney, 1996) is that I am part of a dying paradigm in language education which assumes that received categories like culture or empirical research still have utility in the field, and I am not afraid to say so (see Atkinson, 1999a, 1999c). In this view I represent—rather than an active seeker of controversy—a useful target for supporters of the new (let's call it "critical") paradigm, who are naturally interested in carving out their own territory.

A concrete example is the ongoing conflict I have with Ryuko Kubota (another contributor to this volume) over whether and to what degree we can make generalizations about "Japanese" or any other culture, and whether by so doing we are simply reproducing a racist, colonial discourse of othering (Atkinson, 1999a, 2002; Kubota,1999a,1999b, 2001). Kubota has claimed that some of my own work (particularly Atkinson, 1997; Ramanathan & Atkinson, 1999) participates in such harmful stereotyping, especially when it features concepts like "critical thinking" and "groupism." On my own behalf, I can say I did not consciously seek out controversy; I can also say I believe I have learned something from Kubota and others in the interim, perhaps particularly regarding the potential stereotyping power of cultural description. But this is by no means to admit that I now think the idea, for example, that groupist ideology strongly influences Japanese society is simply a matter of racist, postcolonialist labeling, or that cultural generalization should automatically be banished from language education. Rather, my way of looking at such ideas and generalizations has been complicated—a new layer has been added to my understanding of their possible motivations and uses.

As for my own predilection to attract controversy, my best guess is that it results from a combination of things—perhaps all the points I've mentioned so far: an attraction to topics that are somewhat controversial, for whatever reason; a form of expression in which things tend to be put strongly, and therefore arguably; and, yes, perhaps even the paradigm shift in language education that I briefly speculated on earlier. Of course, any academic writer whose work is not simply ignored probably generates *some* disagreement (e.g., Myers, 1989), so the controversy surrounding my work may not be so different in kind or degree. In other words, as with most everything else I've described so far, the fact that my writing, especially, attracts controversy may be more a matter of subjective experience.

DO I HAVE A WRITTEN VOICE?

This brings me, by a meandering course, to the main topic of this chapter—whether in my writing I have a "voice." But my course, although meandering, has by no means been idiosyncratic—it is the conventional course of the essayist versus the researcher, the humanist over the social scientist—a distinction patent to anyone who reads applied linguistics side by side with work from, for example, composition studies (see also Atkinson & Ramanathan, 1995; Santos, 1992). Although oppositions like humanist versus social scientist are themselves problematic, the differences in preferred genres are neither insubstantial nor insignificant—and this is where I bootstrap my way into talking more directly about "voice."

The historical innovator and popularizer of the essay genre was Michel de Montaigne. According to Paradis (1987), Montaigne was attempting to develop a radical voice of direct, subjective experience—almost a "voice from the soul," a pre-Enlightenment precursor to stream-of-consciousness. The paradox, of course, is that by consciously innovating and popularizing the essay genre, Montaigne also began the institutionalization of a *social category*: a conventional social expression of (what he conceived to be) intensely personal experience, or at base even self. Like other genres, the literate essay certainly has its conventions—personal reflection, ease of style, singularity of expression, leaps of logic, a studied informality, a resistance to set generic forms (Heath, 1987), and so forth—and no single one of these features need be or will be instantiated in any particular essay, yet they nonetheless conventionally mark the genre. This archtypical expression of self in writing therefore participates as much as any other in conventional expectations that are socially constructed, socially regulated, and socially known.[6]

This is not necessarily to say that there is nothing "personal" in written expressions of self such as the essay. It *is* to say, however, that the personal and the social are intimately linked in the production of *self*-expression. More generally, as Mikhail Bakhtin among others has revealed, language in general is so quintessentially socially produced and owned that the notion of personal expression is at least a highly complex and convoluted one, even if Bakhtin himself maintained (at least in some of his work; Atkinson, 2001, note 4) that personal expression was still possible—that language could ultimately be made one's own. I myself am less confident that such is the case—as has often been pointed out elsewhere (e.g., Atkinson,

---

[6]Roland Barthes makes some enlightening comments in discussing the advisability of publishing one's private journals—comments that hold equally, it seems to me, for the essay:

> [The] aims traditionally attributed to the intimate Journal ... are all connected to the advantages and the prestige of "sincerity" (to express yourself, to explain yourself, to judge yourself); but ... sincerity is merely second-degree Image-repertoire.... What a paradox! By choosing the most "direct," the most "spontaneous" forms of writing, I find myself to be the clumsiest of ham actors. (Quoted in Geertz, 1987, pp. 89–90)

2001), our linguistic resources are fundamentally *co-owned*, so that any form of "personal expression" is perforce also a social one, leaving us with, among other things, the severely reduced possibility of expressing a prelinguistic or alinguistic self.

And if we then go one step farther and adopt the postmodernist view that autonomous, originary individuality was an invention of the last three centuries—or even the relatively weaker position that an ideology of individualism has pervaded Europe and North America over approximately the same time period—there is very little left indeed to indicate the probability of unique, highly personal voice. In sum, these are some of the main reasons—laid out cogently in a wide range of writing in recent years (e.g., Bakhtin, 1990; Bellah, Madsen, Sullivan, Swidler, & Tipton, 1985, Berlin, 1987; Bowden, 1999; Foucault, 1972, 1977a, 1977b, among others; Heath, 1991; see also Ramanathan & Atkinson, 1999)—why I have a difficult time allowing for the possibility of personal voice.

Yet there *are* arguments and experiences that *do* suggest a place for personal voice, or at least some variety of "voicist" (Hirvela & Belcher, 2001) theory in understanding how and why we write. First, there are clearly writers who leave a characteristic "footprint" in at least some of their work, the most obvious being literary stylists such as Hemingway and e.e. cummings. Ironically, perhaps the clearest sign of their originality is the fact that they tend to be widely imitated. The term "style" (which has sometimes been contrasted with voice—e.g., Sheppard, quoted in Safire, 1992, p. 14—but is more typically used as its synonym) captures well the seemingly conscious efforts of such authors to set themselves apart; voice skeptics might note the similarities between such writing and attempts to distinguish oneself by dressing outlandishly or adopting highly stylized forms of speech. The skeptic might even wish to categorize such apparently diverse behaviors under the same general socially constructed phenomenon—"distinction"—delineated by Bourdieu (1984), as quoted at the beginning of this chapter.

But literary writers are not the sole purveyors of written voice or style. Academic writers also exist who can doubtless be identified on the basis of their style, at least some of the time. My favorite at the moment is Andy Clark, a so-called neural philosopher who writes on recent research in cognitive science, particularly in the areas of connectionism and the embodied mind (e.g., Clark, 1997). What is distinctive about Clark's style, as far as I can tell, is less purely linguistic than with the great literary stylists: a combination of content (connectionism–the embodied mind), theoretical position (pro-connectionist—though not exclusively so—and pro-embodied mind), a slightly wacky but delightful sense of humor, extreme clarity of exposition, and apparent mastery of his subject. All these add up to what rhetoricians might call a compelling ethos or persona—yet other terms that seem to hover in the air around voice.

A second reason not to summarily dismiss the voice notion, to my mind, is that I think I do have something like a voice as an academic writer. The sense in which I think I do, however, is quite a limited and literal one, having much to do with my obsessive attention to wording and phrasing when I write. That is, I believe I choose words in part based on their sound and rhythm—how they fit together as a kind of sound image—what is to me at least a certain euphony of collocation.[7] Neither my means of or rationale for selecting language on this basis are normally readily available to my consciousness—it's a "feel" sort of experience more than a consciously guided procedure. But I am most consciously aware of it when I read my prose to myself out loud, almost always in order to help me choose one word or phrase over another. I believe I do this less than formerly, which suggests to me that the process may be becoming more automatic as I gain more experience as an academic writer. Once again, however, this is a very limited sense of voice—it does not likely translate into writing that one could read and, with a flash of recognition, announce: "That's Dwight Atkinson." Rather, it is an essentially private experience of something more-or-less related to the expressivist notion of voice.

Third, finally (and perhaps ultimately), the reason why I would not like to dismiss personal voice from the landscape of writing studies is that it seems to accord so well with my subjective, personal experience of writing. Certainly, subjective experience as a legitimate means to knowledge has been severely critiqued in scientific and quasiscientific circles, and its socially constructed and ideological nature has been revealed by philosophers, sociologists, anthropologists, and, most recently, postmodernist theoreticians. It is, nonetheless, from a phenomenological and emic point of view the primary way in which we know of and actively exist in our world and so should not be easily dismissed. My subjective experience overwhelmingly suggests to me that I have or *am at least searching for* a personal, individual self, and that this self is not reducible simply to a social construction, or an intersection point of Foucauldian discourses. Yes, I no doubt derive my basic understanding of myself and my actions from those around me; and, certainly, I live in a highly constructed social world. But the phenomenological experience of being inside my own skin and head and no others, and the sometimes painful realization of being branded with both my own personal history and my own feeble, ongoing efforts to make sense of the world, do not allow me to dismiss the notion that I as an individual-in-process have the possibility of unique, personal expression and knowing. To put it more concretely, if still speculatively, who else could dream the exact dreams I have when sleeping, no matter how commonly patterned human dreams may be? Or, specifically in regard to writ-

---

[7] I owe this idea to my reading of Darsie Bowden's stimulating *Mythology of Voice* (Bowden, 1999), especially pages 88–93.

ing, who else could write precisely the paper that I am now writing/you are now reading, even if the semiotic resources for doing so, as well as much of the knowledge and thought on which it is based, are clearly at least co-owned with my social world? In the end, therefore (no matter how ideologically guided), I would give a certain privilege to the "reality" or at least immediacy of personal experience and seeking—the ego in its ongoing efforts to make sense, as it were—and resist efforts to completely banish the notion of personal voice.

Foucault (1972, p. 17), that explorer of human paradox who both declared the individual dead and deified individual seeking and sense-making, deserves the penultimate word here:

> What, do you imagine that I would take so much trouble and so much pleasure in writing, do you think that I would keep so persistently to my task, if I were not preparing—with a rather shaky hand—a labyrinth into which I can venture, in which I can move my discourse, opening up underground passages, forcing it to go far from itself, finding overhangs that reduce and deform its itinerary, in which I can lose myself and appear at last to eyes that I will never have to meet again.... Do not ask who I am and do not ask me to remain the same: leave it to our bureaucrats and our police to see that our papers are in order. At least spare us their morality when we write.

It may not be in expressing whatever well-developed, static self we already possess, then, that the notion of voice has its true power and utility, *but in seeking for and creating our/selves as we write.*[8]

CODA

No description of writing for publication which ignores the crucial role of editors can be taken seriously, particularly in a book with "behind the scenes" in its title. I would therefore like to conclude by describing my understanding of the editors' roles in the process of writing this paper. This account is meant to provide one further angle on professional writing processes in general, to the extent that the current case is representative; it is also meant to refocus my account on the social side of writing, and to take one final stab at understanding voice and self.

As with all "individual" human products, this paper by no means originated in the head of the author. At the 2000 TESOL convention in Vancouver, British Columbia, Canada, Chris Casanave described to me how I could contribute to a book project that Stephanie Vandrick and she were putting together. Without imposing any strict limits on the content of this

---

[8]Compare Stirner (1844, quoted in Critchley, 2001, p. 28; italics added): "I am *not* nothing in the sense of emptiness, but I *am* the *creative* nothing, the nothing out of which I myself as creator create everything."

piece, Casanave suggested that I might think about how my own writings have involved me in controversy, in regard to assumed-to-be culturally sensitive phenomena such as critical thinking and voice. This idea dovetailed with some of my own reflections on being a professional writer, and I took on the project eagerly; I relished the challenge of writing a different, more personal kind of piece.

Evolving plans for the paper were subsequently written up in an abstract, which was submitted to the editors and responded to by them with comments and suggestions (my memory of the exact process is not good—it may even have involved writing and submitting multiple abstracts at different times, or at least a title and an abstract). The plan for the present paper was therefore hatched in close collaboration with this volume's editors, in a sort of "outside-in" form of cognition (Shore, 1996); that is, its origins were hardly internal and individual, and its development took place substantially in social space.

In the end, however, the content and shape of the paper were left to me to determine. I write "in the end" here, but in fact this process continues even as I write. One of its critical moments was when the editors read and commented on the paper's first draft. Beyond the usual congratulations on writing a stimulating piece, they made five main "comments/suggestions" (the ambiguous speech act status of editors' comments are of course one of their sources of power): (a) Make the beginning more personal—it reads a bit impersonally for a book on individuals' writing experiences; (b) similarly but more generally, cut down on the theoretical nature of the discussion, at the same time adding in more of "me"; (c) cut down on the number of footnotes and references; (d) delete discussion of my adversarial relationship with Ryuko Kubota, and especially an endnote on her use of the term "racism" to describe the belief systems of ESL teachers (see Atkinson, 2002); and (e) adjust my tone in places where I talk about my confidence and possible superiority as a writer.

I find these comments extremely important and revealing as to what might be meant by "self" and "voice" in writing, and so will conclude by briefly discussing them. The first three points relate directly to the overly "academic" approach taken in this paper—the foregrounding of others' views and the building of an argument of sorts based on them—while including less of "me" than is consistent with the tone of the volume. I understand and appreciate this point. On the other hand, my deeply held conviction is that this *is* "me"—an academic obsessed with books and who ultimately finds his bearings in the work of others, particularly these days postmodernist scholars like Foucault and Bourdieu. To present a substantially different version of self would therefore be inauthentic, if ultimately we can talk about authenticity at all regarding anything as fundamentally social as self. Certainly, it would be to present a *different* version of self than the one I have laboriously constructed here, and which is apparently the one I am most comfortable with. I have therefore chosen to retain the basic tone of the essay, while nonetheless of course trying to modify where I feel I can.

Comment 4, on my academic disagreements with Ryuko Kubota, mentioned that the tone of my writing was "soured" by including personal details of a disagreement. Here, very interestingly, I am being asked by the editors to be *less* personal: There clearly seem to be more and less appropriate versions of the self at work in these comments, as would be expected if self in reality is a highly social category, as I have been attempting to argue. In fact, in discussing the details of an academic disagreement I was well-aware that doing so was beyond the bounds of normalcy or polite etiquette in academic writing. Still, this is the experience I had as an academic writer, and one I want to share with my readers.

Comment 5, on my confidence and possible feelings of superiority as a writer, again urged modification of the person or voice expressed in this essay. As with the Kubota example, I had here as well been endeavoring to capture my feelings as an academic writer—and once again as well with the awareness that the resulting portrait might not be a particularly attractive or socially acceptable one. Modesty is a conventional requirement in academic writing and one with a long history behind it; in some of its more "scientific" versions (e.g., Myers, 1989; Atkinson, 1999b, chaps. 4 and 6) the effect may even be self-abnegation. Yet as a middle-aged, middle-class, "Native"-English-speaking Anglo-American man I feel generally empowered and enabled in my academic world, and my (over)confidence as a writer is probably a direct result. To purge my writing of such details would be, again from my personal point of view, to present an inauthentic version of self.

To conclude, I have found the editors' comments, as well as my own considered responses to them, an interesting and important additional opportunity to reflect on what having a "self" or a "voice" in academic writing could mean. That the editors were even interested in impression management at all reveals that voice and self are anything but individual, personal categories—that they are extremely sensitive to audience beliefs and expectations. By the same token, my reactions to their comments once again suggest that my own subjective experience is one of actually *having* an authentic self or voice—that I am not simply the sum of a complex of social forces. These points of view further enrich my understanding of what it is to have a "self" or a "voice," of who I am in the world, and—when we engage in the often straightforward-seeming task of academic writing—of the vast, paradoxical complexity of "what is going on here."

REFERENCES

Anderson, B. (1983). *Imagined communities.* London: Verso.

Atkinson, D. (1997). A critical approach to critical thinking in TESOL. *TESOL Quarterly, 31,* 71–97.

Atkinson, D. (1999a). Response to Ryuko Kubota's "Japanese culture constructed by discourses: Implications for applied linguistics research and English language teaching." *TESOL Quarterly, 33*, 745–749.

Atkinson, D. (1999b). *Scientific discourse in sociohistorical context: The Philosophical Transactions of the Royal Society of London, 1675–1975.* Mahwah, NJ: Lawrence Erlbaum Associates.

Atkinson, D. (1999c). TESOL and culture. *TESOL Quarterly, 33*, 625–654.

Atkinson, D. (2001). Reflections and refractions on the *JSLW* special issue on voice. *Journal of Second Language Writing, 10*, 107–124.

Atkinson, D. (2002). Comments on Ryuko Kubota's "Discursive construction of the images of U.S. classrooms." *TESOL Quarterly, 36*, 79–84.

Atkinson, D., & Ramanathan, V. (1995). Cultures of writing: An ethnographic comparison of L1 and L2 university writing/language programs. *TESOL Quarterly, 29*, 539–568.

Bakhtin, M. (1990). From *Marxism and the philosophy of language.* In P. Bizzell & B. Herzberg (Eds.), *The rhetorical tradition: Readings from classical times to the present* (pp. 928–944). Boston: Bedford Books.

Belcher, D., & Hirvela, A. (Eds.) (2001). Special Issue on Voice. *Journal of Second Language Writing, 10.*

Bellah, R. N., Madsen, R., Sullivan, W. M., Swidler, A., & Tipton, S. M. (1985). *Habits of the heart: Individualism and commitment in American life.* Berkeley, CA: University of California Press.

Berger, P., & Luckmann, T. (1966). *The social construction of reality: A treatise on the sociology of knowledge.* Garden City, NY: Anchor.

Berlin, J. (1987). *Rhetoric and reality: Writing instruction in American colleges, 1900–1985.* Carbondale, IL: Southern Illinois University Press.

Bourdieu, P. (1984). *Distinction: A social critique of the judgement of taste.* Cambridge, MA: Harvard University Press.

Bowden, D. (1999). *The mythology of voice.* Portsmouth, NH: Boynton/Cook.

Charney, D. (1996). Empiricism is not a four-letter word. *College Communication and Composition, 47*, 567–593.

Clark, A. (1997). *Being there: Putting brain, body, and world together again.* Cambridge, MA: MIT Press.

Critchley, S. (2001). *Continental philosophy: A very short introduction.* London: Oxford University Press.

Foucault, M. (1972). *The archeology of knowledge and the discourse on language.* New York: Pantheon Books.

Foucault, M. (1975). *The birth of the clinic: An archeology of medical perception.* New York: Vintage.

Foucault, M. (1977a). *Discipline and punish: The birth of the prison.* New York: Vintage.

Foucault, M. (1977b). What is an author? In *Language, countermemory, practice: Selected essays and interviews by Michel Foucault* (pp. 113–138). Ithaca, NY: Cornell University Press.

Foucault, M. (1982). The subject and power. In H. Dreyfus & P. Rabinow (Eds.), *Michel Foucault: Beyond structuralism and hermeneutics* (2nd ed., pp. 208–226). Chicago: University of Chicago Press.

Foucault, M. (1988). An aesthetics of experience. In *Politics, philosophy, culture* (pp. 47–53). London: Routledge.

Geertz, C. (1987). *Works and lives: The anthropologist as author.* Stanford, CA: Stanford University Press.

Heath, S. B. (1983). *Ways with words: Language, life, and work in communities and classrooms.* Cambridge, England: Cambridge University Press.

Heath, S. B . (1987). The literate essay: Using ethnography to explode myths. In J. A. Langer (Ed.), *Language, literacy and culture* (pp. 89–107). Norwood, NJ: Ablex.

Heath, S. B. (1991). The sense of being literate: Historical and cross-cultural features. In R. Barr, M. L. Kamil, P. B. Mosenthal, & P. D. Pearson (Eds.), *Handbook of reading research,* Vol. 2 (pp. 3–25). New York: Longman.

Hirvela, A., & Belcher, B. (2001). Coming back to voice: The multiple voices and identities of mature multilingual writers. *Journal of Second Language Writing, 10,* 83–106.

Kronick, D. (1988). Anonymity and identity: Editorial policy in the early scientific journal. *Library Quarterly, 58,* 221–237.

Kubota, R. (1999a). Japanese culture constructed by discourses: Implications for applied linguistics research and English language teaching. *TESOL Quarterly, 33,* 9–35.

Kubota, R. (1999b). Response to comments on "Japanese culture constructed by dicourses: Implications for applied linguistic research and English language teaching." *TESOL Quarterly, 33,* 749–758.

Kubota, R. (2001). Discursive construction of the images of U.S. classrooms. *TESOL Quarterly, 35,* 9–38.

Li, X. (1996). *"Good writing" in cross-cultural context.* Albany, NY: SUNY Press.

Marx, K. (1978). Capital, vol. 1. In R. C. Tucker (Ed.), *The Marx–Engels reader* (2nd ed., pp. 294–438). New York: Norton. (Original work published 1889)

Myers, G. (1989). The pragmatics of politeness in scientific articles. *Applied Linguistics, 10,* 1–35.

Paradis, M. (1987). Montaigne, Boyle, and the essay of experience. In G. Levine (Ed.), *One culture: Essays in science and literature* (pp. 51–91). Madison, WI: University of Wisconsin Press.

Ramanathan, V., & Atkinson, D. (1999). Individualism, academic writing, and ESL writers. *Journal of Second Language Writing, 8,* 45–75.

Safire, W. (1992, June 28). The take on voice. *New York Times Magazine,* p. 14.

Santos, T. (1992). Ideology in composition: L1 and ESL. *Journal of Second Language Writing, 1,* 1–15.

Shore, B. (1996). *Culture in mind: Cognition, culture, and the problem of meaning.* Cambridge, MA: Harvard University Press.

St. Pierre, E. A. (2001). Coming to theory: Finding Foucault and Deleuze. In K. Weiler (Ed.), *Feminist engagements: Reading, resisting, and revisioning male theorists in education and cultural studies* (pp. 141–163). New York: Routledge.

Yancey, K. B. (Ed.) (1994). *Voices on voice: Perspectives, definitions, inquiry.* Urbana, IL: National Council of Teachers of English.

CHAPTER
13

The Privilege of Writing
as an Immigrant Woman

Aneta Pavlenko
Temple University

The stories they are waiting for—of a brave but disadvantaged immigrant woman trying to understand an unfamiliar language, missing the customs and the foods of the homeland, overcoming one 'culture shock' after another—have nothing to do with me. I resent being expected to tell such stories because I have none to tell and also because, even when they are the true stories for many first-generation immigrant women, there is something self-congratulatory or condescending in most listeners' attitudes. The stories of immigration are often heard by nonimmigrants in the spirit of 'I am so lucky that I was always an American.' They are the adult, quality-of-life versions of 'those poor starving children in China' for whom we were supposed to eat all the food on our plates. (Mori, 2000, 138–39)

This chapter is supposed to be about academic writing. However, I cannot help but think that who we are is extremely relevant to how we write and what we write about and that every time we write something, we put our own selves on the line. Thus, what follows is my own story, which is not only about how I have written and published a number of chapters and articles, but also about what took place behind the scenes—what led me to academic publishing, what made certain topics more important than others, and what made me react in particular ways to interactions with editors and publishers. It is also a story of ways in which I gained membership in a scholarly community and constructed an authoritative voice, with a trace of an accent (which I prefer to see as bilingualism and double vision). In telling this story, I will try to demonstrate that an "immigrant woman" is not a singular subject position: Whereas for some aspiring scholars it can be a source of disempowerment, for others, myself included, being a refugee, an immigrant, and a female is a privilege and an ultimate source of strength, critical consciousness, and multiple perspectives.

A REFUGEE JOURNEY: LEARNING TO DARE
WITH NOTHING TO LOSE

Two distinguishing features of successful academic writers are, for me, a belief in what you have to say and an ability to start over, time after time, revising and rewriting draft after draft. What helped me most to learn how to do both was the experience of starting my own life over from scratch with nothing but symbolic capital (Bourdieu, 1991) and a deep belief that this time things could be different. This experience also informed my views on gatekeeping, helping me differentiate between actual gatekeeping and critical—but constructive—comments.

My life took a major turn in the summer of 1988 when I unexpectedly got pregnant and made a decision to raise the child as a single mother. At the time, I was between jobs and living in my native city of Kiev, Ukraine, one of the oldest and most beautiful cities in Europe. It was also one of the most anti-semitic ones, offering very few educational and employment options to Jews in general, and even fewer to Jewish women. In 1981, after graduating from high school with what would be considered in the United States a 4.0 grade point average, I had enormous difficulties entering college, in my case Kiev Pedagogical Institute of Foreign Languages. Despite the fact that I got *A*s on all my entrance examinations, was a winner of a regional competition in French language proficiency, and spoke five other languages, my name was not on the list of those admitted. My mother, an alumna of that college, and I stood outside the entrance doors, together with other hopefuls, reading admission lists, straining to find my name. Nope, I was definitely not admitted—but I did see a few names of those who took the tests with me and got *B*s and *C*s (privacy of information did not mean much in the U.S.S.R.). Mom and I hugged each other and cried.

Luckily, my grandmother, who had a number of connections in the Ukrainian Ministry of Education, took a less passive approach, and soon, in a typical Soviet fashion, my name appeared on the "additional list" with all others who had to take a roundabout approach to get into college. Ironically, whereas some have been accepted despite their low grades, I needed connections to be accepted despite my ethnicity. Five years later, in 1986, I graduated summa cum laude and even more in love with languages and linguistics. All I wanted to do was to continue research and go on to graduate school. I had, however, reached a glass ceiling—even the roundabout approach and the Ministry connections did not help this time—the graduate school of my alma mater already had a token Jew and had no interest in or need for another. I encountered a similar attitude when applying for jobs: People who knew me and seemed extremely interested in employing someone with the knowledge of several languages would become disappointed when they opened my passport and discovered that I was listed as Jewish (in all fairness, my being Jewish did not matter to many of them all that much; what mattered was the line in the passport—to have a listed Jew was not good for their personnel records). Thus, prospective employers would immediately remember that the position had already been filled and thank me for my interest, wishing me lots of luck in the future.

Meanwhile, that future behind the Iron Curtain seemed rather hopeless. While the West was becoming increasingly excited about our new leader, the Soviets were rather skeptical about Gorbachev's efforts, and even now many remain convinced that the U.S.S.R. fell apart not because of his attempts to establish a more democratic government but because of his inability to keep the house of cards from tumbling over. The only effort of his that many of us appreciated was the reestablishment of immigration policies of the 1970s that allowed Soviet Jews to leave the country because of religious and ethnic persecution or for reunification with real or fictional relatives in Israel. For me, in 1988, after almost 2 years of unsuccessful attempts to get into graduate school or to find a professional job, to leave the country seemed like the only way out. This desire became even more imperative when I got pregnant—my life might have been over, but I did want my unborn child to have a better future, one that included options and possibilities. On the other hand, both my mother and I were concerned about finding work in the United States, where we hoped to go. Our main field was languages, and the knowledge of English may have been somewhat valuable in Kiev, but in the United States everyone else spoke English, too. Nevertheless we decided to try, and in the Fall of 1988 applied for exit visas. At that time, immigration departments were overwhelmed with applications, and the waiting period took months and months, which gave us time to ponder over our decision while giving private English lessons to other potential refugees.

My son was born in April of 1989; the exit visas were still not there, and our doubts about our future in the West grew. And then the relatively peaceful world of Soviet citizens was shattered by events in Georgia, Armenia, and Azerbaijan, where ethnic hatred finally boiled over and where militia and the military failed to protect ethnic minorities from murder, rape, and other forms of violence, at times conspiring with the persecutors instead. In May of 1989 the ethnic unrest reached Kiev, and rumors of an upcoming pogrom started circulating among the population. We gave no heed to such rumors (What *pogrom*, we do not live in tsarist Russia!) until one fine morning when there was a knock on the door of our apartment. A Russian neighbor we knew only superficially stood there and asked for

permission to come in. When we locked the door behind her, she whis-
pered that she and her husband had heard the rumors and wanted to hide
us in their apartment during the upcoming pogrom (she knew as well as
we did that the government and its militia would not be of much help if the
pogrom were to occur). It was then that the possibility of a pogrom became entrenched in our minds and our decision to leave the country became irreversible (the pogrom ultimately did not occur—but everyone
believes that it could have). I had reconsidered my ambitious dreams and
firmly stated that I was ready to wash dishes for the rest of my life in order
to ensure that my son was safe, sound, and happy. (All this was to change
very soon, as the reader will see—once in the United States, I refused to
wash dishes for a living, and nowadays it is my son who—albeit safe,
sound, and happy—makes dinners and washes dishes while his mom is
working on yet another important academic paper. Thanks, Nik, for being
the best son an academic woman could have!)

Finally, in November of 1989, we received our exit visas. There was one
problem, however: Emigration with refugee status was officially over and
we had a choice of leaving the country almost immediately with no possessions or staying to see whether the new regulations would allow us to
leave. My mother and I looked at each other and decided that we might as
well leave everything behind. And so we did, leaving a fully furnished
apartment to relatives to deal with and embarking on our historic journey
with $300 and three suitcases filled mostly with old family pictures and
cloth diapers. The 2-day trip from Kiev to Vienna with a stopover in Poland
culminated in the Vienna airport where we sat, smelly and tired, in our
heavy Russian coats, surrounded by our earthly possessions, awaiting the
arrival of the representatives of the Hebrew Immigrant Aid Society (HIAS),
who were supposed to meet us and take us to some hotel or other. The
representatives did not show up. Here we were in the West, and the beautiful people were passing us by trying to avoid the pathetic refugee family,
and we had no idea what to do next.

Soon, however, little Nik made his needs known, and I wandered
around in search of a bathroom where I could change his diapers (by
now, we were down to a single cloth diaper). While looking for a bathroom, I noticed another family that seemed equally pathetic and even
more firmly ensconced in the airport, and attempted to talk to them. After
having tried a couple of languages, I eventually succeeded with French
and a smattering of Arabic, finding out that these people were refugees
from a war-torn Lebanon, with no papers, and had spent 2 days in this airport trying unsuccessfully to communicate their ordeal to authorities.
Finally there was something I could do! Even if I couldn't help myself I
could help these people, and so I immediately took charge and acted as a
translator between the family and the customs officers who, in turn,
called the Red Cross representatives. The family was successfully exited

from the airport, and I realized that stripped of all my social identities and material possessions, I still carried around some cultural and linguistic capital that could be put to good use. Hey, if necessary, I could ask the same Red Cross to take care of me and my family. This was, however, unnecessary, as the HIAS representatives finally arrived, and transported us in a little van to a refugee-populated hotel in a working-class area of Vienna. Our new life in the West had officially begun.

Like many other refugees, we stayed in Vienna for a month; then, after we declared our desire to go to the United States rather than Israel, we were transported to Italy to stay in a refugee settlement waiting for some Jewish community in the United States to sponsor us. The arrival in Rome was quite grand—our refugee-filled plane was met by the carabinieri with dogs and machine guns in order to protect us from possible terrorist attacks. This sight filled us with both sadness and gratitude—how ironic that another country cared more about our safety than our former motherland! Soon, the journey that started with apprehension became an adventure. Although we may have been staying in refugee settlements and working at low-paying jobs for extra cash (a friend and I cleaned apartments for a while), we were also enjoying life as never before, entertaining new hopes and possibilities, partying, and exploring Italy. Before long, the Russian Jewish community of Torvaianica where we were staying organized a school for refugee children, and once again I was in the thick of events, teaching English and translating between English, Italian, and Russian during business meetings between the community leaders, local authorities, and HIAS representatives. I was delighted to see that here as well my linguistic capital had some market value.

Our next stop was Reading, Pennsylvania, where the Jewish community offered to sponsor our refugee family of three. I will be forever grateful to the Jewish Federation of Reading for this kind-hearted decision, as our family did not look very promising in terms of self-sufficiency: an elderly mother, a daughter with no profession but knowledge of English, and a baby. In May of 1990 we arrived in New York City and then flew to Reading where we were met by the members of the Jewish Federation and driven to our own apartment, all furnished with donations from members of the local Jewish community; they even included a playpen for my son with books and toys. Dinner was already on the table, and so were Friday night candles; we were finally home. And so my mom and I looked at each other—and yeah, there we went crying again.

Unfortunately, the relationship between us and the Jewish Federation soon turned sour. I was offered what seemed like a dream job back in Kiev—washing dishes and cooking kosher food in the Jewish wing of the local hospital (simultaneously, I was sent on a couple of blind dates). The problem was that by that time, having realized the value of my education, I no longer wanted to wash dishes, nor was I interested in dating. And so I refused, pointing out that my cooking abilities would only further damage the hospital patients (and the marital prospects). I asked for a 3-month extension during which I could look for a job on my own. Our sponsors kindly agreed, and so I went to the local library where I copied down addresses of all colleges in Pennsylvania that offered Russian, or for that matter French or Spanish, and started applying for jobs, regardless of how far away the colleges were and regardless of whether they were actually looking for anyone (job ads were at that point an unfamiliar concept). Even though I had no firm understanding of how higher education in America worked, I knew that I had nothing to lose by trying (the kitchen job was still waiting) and everything to gain.

As a result of my letter-writing campaign, I got seven job interviews and four offers to take part-time adjunct positions in various languages. This outcome firmly reinforced my belief that now I could do whatever I put my mind to. In contrast, our sponsors were in despair trying to point out that I would be unable to support myself and my family on an adjunct salary with no benefits (yet another unfamiliar concept). I, on the other hand, was elated to be considered acceptable for a job in my field and was already thinking about the next step—becoming a full-time academic (with benefits, whatever those might be). In shock, our poor sponsors tried to counteract and set up a meeting for me with a local college professor who told me his own story of 7 miserable years in graduate school. Luckily, what was considered poverty from a middle-class American perspective was a very acceptable standard of living for a newly arrived refugee. In my mind I also figured that if it took the professor 7 years to finish his dissertation, I could probably do it in 5. And so, 4 months after my arrival in the United States, I was working two part-time jobs, teaching Spanish in one college and Russian in another, and getting ready to take my Test of English as a Foreign Language (TOEFL) and Graduate Record Examinations (GREs). Three months into the fall semester I took the tests, got my scores back, and started applying to graduate schools—to become an American academic. So what if some schools do not accept me, maybe others will—what have I got to lose?

BECOMING AN AMERICAN ACADEMIC: THE JOYS OF DOUBLE VISION

Yet another advantage of my refugee background is the inside perspective on the immigrant experience, second language (L2) socialization, and bilingualism that allows me to walk back and forth across the divide that in the field of Second Language Acquisition (SLA) often separates "us" (academics) from "them" (L2 learners and users). Perhaps, if I were to remain a foreign language user, I would not be so tempted to rebel against each and every tenet of the field and to search for alternative approaches that reflect ways in which our languages are so tightly—and at times painfully—interlocked with our multiple identities and desires.

This rebellion was about to take place at Cornell, the school where in the Fall of 1992, 2 years after my arrival in the United States, I started yet another new life, that of a graduate student. I had selected Cornell as one of the few schools to which I applied on the basis of a description in yet another catalog in the local library in Reading, Pennsylvania. The notion of "Ivy League education" and various stratifications in American higher education did not mean anything to me at that time, and so my search was guided by the focus of the particular programs. Ever since my undergraduate years in Kiev, I had been interested in the study of SLA and in psycholinguistics, and so I selected programs that specialized in either one or both. A particularly appealing one was offered by the University of Delaware, where the professors seemed to be interested in Soviet psycholinguistics. My essay described my own background and familiarity with the work of Leontiev and Vygotsky, and soon I got a phone call from one of the faculty members at Delaware, Professor James Lantolf, telling me that I was accepted into the program. He also told me at that point that he was leaving Delaware for Cornell. Because Cornell was on my initial list anyway and I did want to work with James Lantolf, whose articles really impressed me, I forwarded an application there and was accepted as well—even though I had to wait another year to get a teaching assistantship before going to Ithaca.

And there I was in the picturesque city of Ithaca—29 years old and finally fulfilling my own dreams of being in graduate school (long gone my desire to sacrifice myself to my son's better future). My first course, in L2 reading, required a final paper that would be 'publishable'—whatever that meant. The concept was somewhat mysterious, and our professors did not disclose how one might go about creating something publishable. I was determined to succeed, however, and so, once again, the library seemed like the place to find an answer. During that first semester, I examined what journals existed in SLA and what type of work they published. Since I also needed to learn to write scholarly work in English, I studied closely how other people constructed sentences and which pronouns, qualifiers or verbs they chose. By the end of that first semester I had conducted my first case study of reading development of a learner of Arabic and wrote a paper that closely imitated the published work I had seen. I tried to impose a similar structure (introduction, literature review, methodology, results, discussion, conclusions), appeal to a similar "objective" manner of presentation (lots of passive constructions), and use similar methods of data collection and analysis. I must have been successful from the point of view of my instructors as I got an *A*. The paper itself, however, left me cold—it wasn't something I was particularly proud of or would ever be interested in publishing. Instead, I had started searching for alternative topics and ways of writing that would take me beyond imitation and repetition and outside the boundaries of the well-known and familiar.

From then on, I spent the happiest years of my life in Olin library: in my carrel, in the stacks, and in the computer and copy rooms. I was greedily absorbing knowledge, trying to learn all I could about various databases and bibliographies, reading and compiling information on various areas in- and outside of SLA and poring over the debates in the field. My desire to be systematic led me to explore the areas one after the other, familiarizing myself with every possible aspect of SLA, from individual differences in L2 learning, to language-learning strategies, to neurolinguistics of the bilingual brain. All my extra earnings from tutoring and translation were spent on books and on xeroxing what I thought were the key papers in various areas, which I then put into binders by topic. My desire to be comprehensive also led me to write some of the longest papers my professors had ever been subjected to. Ultimately these explorations taught me a lot about what's hot and what's not in the field, pointing to some areas that had been underresearched and underexplored. They also allowed me to internalize the basics of expository writing.

Unfortunately, my reading also led me to conclude that I deeply disliked both mainstream linguistics and SLA. The scholarship simply did not reflect me nor anyone I knew, living, breathing individuals, at the nexus of multiple power relations that often determined what—and how much of it—gets or does not get acquired. Nor did it recognize the fact that more than half of the world population was multilingual which made monolingualism and monolingual-like competence an exception rather than the rule. The departmental emphasis on mainstream generative linguistics seemed absurd and meaningless to my novice eye, and while my classmates were diligently solving syntax problems, I struggled to understand what the point of the problems was. Similarly, my SLA readings seemed to suggest that most SLA studies focused on questions that to me were incredibly minute and trivial and avoided the "real" issues of power, access, and identity. And so I slowly started asking questions and voicing opinions in my graduate classes. Oftentimes my questions and statements were ignored, and I was beginning to wonder about their validity. Then I enrolled in a graduate seminar where the process of my "devoicing" took a particularly humorous form. I consistently made points that would be brushed off by my professors. Then, a few turns later, my male classmate would make the same point—worded differently—and would be rewarded with "Yes, Rich, that's absolutely right—this is an excellent point." (To Rich's credit, I must say that he always tried to interject that Aneta had just made the same point.) I was upset, frustrated, and grateful for the lesson—I had learned that my points were valid indeed but that I didn't have the necessary linguistic capital to make them heard. Thus, I set out to develop ways in which I could make my points and be heard. And because in academia being published is often paramount to being heard, I focused on strategies that would make my arguments legitimate in writing.

To begin with, I enrolled in a course in the writing program with an unforgettable Barbara Legendre, who continued to meet with me one-on-one for 2 years, long after the course ended and up until the point of my defense (I am forever indebted to her for this generosity.) Reading through my dissertation chapters with Barbara taught me how to look at texts from a reader's perspective and forced me to think about cohesiveness, coherence, and reader-friendliness in ways I never did before. Another helpful experience was coediting *Cornell Working Papers in Linguistics*, with a classmate, Rafael Salaberry, in 1996. The process, from a call for papers, to review, to acceptance of revised papers, was an extremely informative one. Of particular importance for me was learning how to write reviews of others' work, starting with what kinds of things one might comment on and ending with how one might word the comments in supportive and constructive ways. It was also revealing and uplifting to see that native speakers of English were not necessarily better writers than nonnative speakers: Some also had problems imposing logical structure on the text and maintaining coherence and cohesiveness. From then on, I have always divided the writers into experts and novices, rather than native and nonnative speakers, and my later editing experiences only reinforced this perspective. Yet another helpful experience was reviewing conference proposals for the American Association for Applied Linguistics (AAAL) and the Second Language Research Forum (SLRF) and manuscripts for *Applied Linguistics*. This experience made me think about multiple ways in which people position their scholarship within the field and link it to the work of others.

Simultaneously, I started looking for a theoretical framework that would accommodate my multiple questions and for an academic community that would legitimize them. There, being a former Soviet citizen was tremendously helpful once again. Unlike many of my classmates, I was completely at ease rejecting dominant mainstream theories as ideologically oppressive discourses. Nevertheless, the critical route I chose was not an easy one, and I would probably have dropped out of graduate school were it not for my wonderful mentor, Jim Lantolf. A maverick and a critic of mainstream SLA practices himself, Jim never imposed on us his own chosen theoretical framework, sociocultural theory, and encouraged all our attempts at critical thinking and reading outside of the "accepted body of literature," introducing his students to critical theory and poststructuralism. And so I read on, embracing first social constructionism and then feminist poststructuralism and looking for an academic home where the questions I was interested in could be raised. Eventually, I found such a home in the interdisciplinary field of bilingualism, where poststructuralist approaches seemed as welcome as functionalism or Universal Grammar, where conferences entailed friendly and collegial exchanges, and where many scholars were openly concerned with issues of language, power, identity, and social justice. My immigrant past once again served me well—I was not afraid of changing tracks or fields, even midway through the graduate program. Once again, I proceeded to read work and conduct empirical studies in diverse areas of bilingualism, creating more binders, acquiring more books, and formulating questions I would eventually want to ask in my dissertation.

My five years of graduate school were filled with exciting reading and multiple learning experiences, yet they were far from idyllic. The professor from Reading was right in warning me that one cannot survive on a teaching assistantship and moreover support a family. And so I once again ventured into the world and landed a part-time job in a local Refugee Assistance Program, working as a job developer and translator with Russian, Ukrainian, and Bosnian refugees. In addition, I subbed as an ESL instructor, worked as a court and medical interpreter, and taught Russian for the local adult education program, while my mother helped me out babysitting my son. And even though wearing so many hats was time-consuming and frustrating, and being a good student and a good mother seemed like options that canceled themselves out, I continued feeling grateful for the privilege of being a student in an institution that accepted me on my own merits, rather than because of—or despite—my ethnicity. What may have seemed like misery and drudgery to the Reading professor, seemed like a luxury to me—and I reveled in it. I was finally doing graduate work, while my teaching assistantship and my other part-time jobs kept me firmly grounded in the reality of learning and using additional languages.

Eventually these multiple experiences allowed me to identify several lacunae in the scholarly literature and I attempted to address one of them in my dissertation, which examined the implications of the theory of linguistic relativity, or the Sapir-Whorf hypothesis, for bilingualism (Pavlenko, 1997). This dissertation also gave birth to my first published articles—and my first rejections. In what follows, I will discuss my first attempts to write for publication and to develop an academic voice that would reconcile authority (i.e., the right to impose reception, in Bourdieu's terms) with authenticity (i.e., the right to retain my own accented feminine voice and my multiple perspectives, those of a researcher and an L2 user, a Russian refugee and an American scholar, an academic and a feminist).

WRITING ABOUT BILINGUAL WRITERS: LEARNING TO VENTRILOQUATE

The first strategy I developed in trying to become an academic writer was to make my points through ventriloquism. In untangling the complexities of multiple academic debates, I learned about existing camps and found ways of positioning myself, trying to state my views not in my own words but in those of others (e.g., "as X (1986) convincingly demonstrates"; on learning academic ventriloquism, see also Chris Casanave's chapter in this volume). This strategy worked to an extent as long as other people were addressing the same issues I was interested in. But as time went by, I accumulated a number of important concerns that did not seem to have been raised in the literature or at least not in the way I saw fit. One such issue was the nature of success in second language learning. Although there was a whole body of scholarly literature addressing "the good language learner," this literature—similar to the rest of mainstream SLA scholarship—seemed extremely limited in its focus on the language classroom and exceedingly patronizing in its division into "us" (researchers, teachers, academics) and "them" (language learners, refugees, immigrants). The whole focus of the field of SLA seemed to be on the mythic "language learner" who somehow never became a "language user" or, even less likely, a "bilingual." And although the field of bilingualism encompassed SLA research with ease (see, e.g., Appel & Muysken, 1987; Baker, 2001; Hamers & Blanc, 1989), the field of SLA resolutely ignored research on bilingualism as completely irrelevant to its own endeavors.

It dawned on me that I was on a mission—to bring the two together (filling out a number of gaps in the process). Ideally, I would have liked to use my own experiences in doing so, but that somehow seemed "unscholarly," "biased" and "subjective" (the terms I later learned to revere). And so I looked for others who may have had similar experiences—learning to be adults in their second language—and who had also talked about them, creating a particular brand of narrative truth I could juxtapose to the scientific truth of SLA research. To my relief, I found a whole treasure trove of language-learning memoirs written by bilingual writers and scholars whose experiences, in my opinion, were directly relevant to the field of SLA, but whose voices, up until then, had not been heard. And so I set out to write a dissertation chapter and then a paper where I used these personal narratives to argue that there were numerous successful L2 users out there in the real world and that their language learning was intrinsically linked to their identities. I derived great pleasure from manipulating these voices, from arranging them in the order I felt was appropriate and from thinking that now I would be completely hidden behind this choir, conducting it from the shadows.

Once I showed my explorations of bilingual writers' work to my professors, they seemed excited about this new direction. Encouraged, I immediately submitted my paper to the student-run *Issues in Applied Linguistics*. I also sent it to some of the bilingual writers whose narratives I appropriated, to make sure I had not misstated their points or erroneously depicted their experiences. I got very positive feedback from those I could reach (in particular Anna Wierzbicka, with whom I have remained in touch ever since). I was particularly elated when one day I saw a package in my mailbox addressed to me by my idol, a Romanian-American writer and radio personality, Andrei Codrescu. In that package was Andrei's latest book with an autograph and a letter stating that I had not misstated his points. What shocked me was the last sentence of his letter: "You are, of course, writing your own autobiography in this essay, a bit like a hand surgeon operating on a hand." So, Andrei did see through me after all, and my attempt to whisper my points "objectively," while hiding behind other people's life stories, had failed. It was a lesson I never forgot—one that forced me to acknowledge my own subjectivity as an interested and invested scholar rather than a hidden puppet-master, and one that several years later gave an impetus to this chapter. And although nowadays I still work with language-learning autobiographies, I no longer use them to tell my own story; rather I try to examine the multiple stories they reveal and hide, including the ones that may be quite distinct from my own experiences.

COLLABORATING WITH EDITORS: LEARNING TO REVISE

Soon the article on bilingual writers was accepted for publication with minor revisions. As it was about to come out in the summer of 1998 (Pavlenko, 1998), I was moving to a new phase in my life—my first tenure-track position, as an Assistant Professor of Teaching English to Speakers of Other Languages (TESOL) at Temple University in Philadelphia. There, I had to face academic publishing on my own, as it no longer seemed appropriate to run for help to Barbara and Jim. And in doing so, I had learned critical lessons on how to create new networks of support and on how to view editors and reviewers as gate-openers rather than gate-keepers—lessons that made me into the writer I am today.

   The story of my first major publication started when I was still in graduate school and tried to describe the results of my dissertational research in a paper on linguistic relativity and second language learning. Surely, this work, which was extremely positively received at a number of international conferences, would be of interest to journals in the field? I spent a whole summer working on multiple drafts of the paper and then sent the final draft to a major SLA journal. The reviews came back after 6 months, stating that although the article was indeed interesting and refreshing, it would need to be revised and resubmitted, in particular because my arguments lacked statistical support. Undaunted, rather than revise I resent the article to another major journal hoping that perhaps another set of reviewers would understand that my arguments dealt with complex qualitative issues and did not need to be supported by statistics. The next set of reviews was even more damaging—the journal rejected the article straight out, pointing out that I confused language and culture (an argument that sounded too familiar from my graduate school days among generative linguists) and that to support my points I would need to appeal to statistical inferencing.

Although I had an option of revising and resubmitting the paper inserting statistics, I refused to compromise on arguments that were close to my heart and instead decided to address a different audience, that in the field of bilingualism. At that point, Judy Kroll, one of world's leading experts on psycholinguistics of bilingual memory and a coeditor of a new journal, *Bilingualism: Language and Cognition*, suggested that I write a new article spelling out the implications of my research for the field of bilingual memory and submit it to the journal for peer review. The paper was to be submitted for a category of keynote articles, which meant that on acceptance the editors would elicit comments on the paper from well-known scholars and publish them together with the author's rejoinder. This seemed like an appealing prospect, and so I started to work on the new paper, putting away the earlier article in the hope that one day I would find a home for it that would accept arguments not grounded in statistics. The work took me 3 months, and fairly pleased with the end result, in September of 1998, I sent the paper—my first tenure-track submission!—to François Grosjean, the editor in charge of submissions. The four reviews arrived in record time, and in November I heard back from François, who told me that despite the fact that my paper was interesting, relevant, and multidisciplinary, it could not be published in its present format and would have to be revised and resubmitted. The concerns were pretty major: "a certain lack of focus and integration, the absence of challenging ideas, a line of argument that is vague and unconvincing, the presentation of ideas that are not exemplified, a rather weak major line of argumentation, an overall structure that remains unclear, etc." To a novice professor this seemed like a death sentence, and I thanked Grosjean for the reviews deciding to abandon the intricacies of bilingual memory as well and to focus on yet another area of research, that of SLA and gender.

However, while I was trying to do just that—and to negotiate the complexities of my first year in a tenure-track position—François did not give up on me and kept bombarding me with weekly messages asking whether I had started (continued, accomplished) the revisions required. I ignored his messages for several months but eventually realized that to stop the persistent barrage, I should just revise and resubmit the paper. I had finally looked closely at the four sets of comments and was amazed to see how constructive and extensive the comments actually were, all ranging between three and four single-spaced pages. I realized that the purpose of the comments was not to destroy my fragile beginner's ego but to actually engage me in a scholarly conversation and provide me with some guidance (see also McKay's chapter in this volume on the relationship between constructive reviews and successful publications). This guidance included advice on how I could better define my concepts and strengthen

and exemplify my arguments, and suggestions for minor stylistic improve-
ments and additional literature I might want to consider. And so, with the
help of the four reviews, I created a new version of the paper and sent it to
François. In August of 1999, the new reviews arrived: Although all reviewers agreed that the new version was much better and more coherent and
challenging, the paper still needed more revisions to be accepted. Once
again, extensive suggestions were included. By this time, revising had become enjoyable because I could see that, like a sculptor, I was chipping
away at marble only to uncover a statue within. I was delighted to know
that others could envision the sculpture as well and took their time to help
me deal with the marble. And so yet again I revised, e-mailing changes and
more changes to François, to finally have the paper accepted for publication in September of 1999. Even when the paper was deemed ready for
publication the process wasn't over—now it had to be sent out for comments to which I, in turn, had a chance to respond (Pavlenko, 2000). When
the comments arrived I was once again astounded by the highly professional tone and the generosity of my new academic community: Even
people who could have perceived my paper as a critical commentary on
their own research chose to see its arguments as building on and expanding their own and responded in a kind and generous manner. In responding, I got a chance to take part in yet another round of scholarly conversations on my favorite topic.

In the Fall of 1999, during my second tenure-track year, my keynote article was published (Pavlenko, 1999), and soon I started receiving congratu-
latory comments, invitations to submit book chapters, and later on
requests to review articles that built on my theoretical proposals. My rite of
passage was complete—I now knew that "revise and resubmit" means
just that: Revise and resubmit unless you disagree with the direction the
revisions should take (see also Sasaki's discussion of the same issue). I
would never have learned this lesson without the gentle prodding from a
wonderful editor, François Grosjean, and a great team of professionals
working with him in *Bilingualism: Language and Cognition*. Although later
on I would have similarly positive experiences with a number of other journals, and in particular with another highly demanding and equally excellent editor, Claire Kramsch, I credit a lot of my own professional growth
and understanding of professional ethics to the editors of *Bilingualism*
with whom I first interacted as an author and later on as a manuscript reviewer. Looking at the long, detailed, and extremely prompt responses of
the reviewers chosen by François and Judy, I had understood that the goal
of a review is to be constructive rather than judgmental and that one
should not say anything anonymously that one wouldn't say in a signed review. In fact, a number of the *Bilingualism* reviewers, including Judy Kroll,
do sign their reviews, and so from a double-blind process the review becomes a dialogue built on mutual understanding and trust. Another ex-

tremely positive aspect of the *Bilingualism* review (which, according to Judy, is typical for the field of psychology) is the fact that all reviewers at the end get to see all of the reviews (which they can use in case they are reviewing the revised manuscript for the second time). To see what other people had to say about the same paper helped me enormously in finding out whether I was on target in my comments, realizing what I might have missed, and adjusting my tone of voice.

Over the years of being an author and a reviewer for multiple journals, I have learned that revisions are the first chapter in an academic conversation, that not all revisions have to be incorporated and accepted, that many colleagues sacrifice their professional and personal time to socialize novice academics into the profession, and that I can learn a lot from my colleagues' advice (even though at times I may choose not to accept their comments). It pains me to see that this role of editors and reviewers as socializers and gate-openers is sometimes forgotten in our daily grind, and I am happy to say to my editors and to my anonymous reviewers—I enjoyed talking to you!

CONCLUSIONS

So where are we now? In 1998 I had started a tenure-track position with one publication. Four years later I have published—or have forthcoming—17 peer-reviewed articles and 17 book chapters. I have also co-edited an edited volume (Pavlenko, Blackledge, Piller, & Teutsch-Dwyer, 2001) and three special issues of journals in bilingualism. As I am writing this chapter, I am working on two books and on two more coedited volumes. I would never have been able to be so productive if not for multiple individuals—my editors, publishers, reviewers, and my multiple colleagues and friends—who were always there for me with their help, support, and advice. I definitely did not engage in this activity with a tenure review in mind. Akin to Paul Matsuda's (this volume) need to do something *to* and *in* the profession, I was bursting—and still am—with points to be made, new intersections between various areas of research to be created, and new studies to undertake, all of which would reflect second language learning in context, happening to real people. I feel more at peace now knowing that some of my points have been made, heard, and responded to, and that through panels and colloquia, special issues and edited volumes, I have managed to engage in a number of conversations on issues of importance in the fields of bilingualism and SLA. In all of these years, the issue of my nonnative speakerness never surfaced in any but the most trivial manner (typically, in corrections of those pesky articles and tenses). Consequently, I find that calling myself a "non-native" or "peripheral" writer does not reflect the reality of my own academic existence. I feel pretty involved in some of the key conversations in my two fields and am also very aware that my own multilingualism positions me at a very privileged angle.

And so, undaunted, I continue writing and submitting my scholarship for publication. Well, what's the worst that could happen? That an original version of a paper will be deemed unacceptable? As long as I am able to get constructive feedback, revisions do not seem to be much of a sacrifice. Never again will I be told that as a Jew I don't belong in the academy (even though I am very aware that this battle was also fought by Jews in the United States, most notably by Lionel Trilling). Never again will I be sitting homeless in the Vienna airport terrified to face the mythical West. Nor will the thought police appear on my doorstep with a chilly: "Oh, are you the one who criticized Chomsky and Pinker? Please gather your belongings and come with us. Your relatives should send you some warm clothing, it is pretty cold where we are taking you." I am pretty comfortable with the fact that there will always be those who disagree with me, just as there are those who think along similar lines. Some battles will be won and some will be lost. Some arguments will be heard and some ignored. Some articles will appear untouched and some will be significantly revised. I continue to be my own harshest critic, creating multiple versions of each argument, multiple drafts of each paper, and feeling disappointed when outsiders' reviews of my work are not as critical as my own (have they read the manuscript?!). And I still do my best work in revisions and reanalysis (sometimes to the deep exasperation of my coauthors and coeditors). What I have learned as a newcomer to academic writing can be summarized in a few sentences:

- In order to visit the other side of the fence, try to engage in the editing of, and writing for, the student Working Papers in your institution; later on try to edit a special issue of a journal or an edited volume; this will give you invaluable insights into the editing process.
- Try to solicit feedback on your research by presenting at conferences.
- Collaborate with peers who can complement your strengths.
- Find colleagues who could peer-review your work before the actual submission (assuming that you would do the same for them).
- Make sure you are addressing the right academic community (i.e., see which papers the journal has tended to publish in the past few years).
- Do not be afraid to contradict accepted authorities; just make sure you know the research in the field and have a compelling argument.
- Most importantly, do not hesitate to work with highly demanding editors and reviewers; the process of revision could be an extremely enjoyable one—it is a start of a long academic conversation about your work.
- And please, do contribute to the field by reviewing others' papers.

REFERENCES

Appel, R., & Muysken, P. (1987). *Language contact and bilingualism.* London: Edward Arnold.

Baker, C. (2001). *Foundations of bilingual education and bilingualism.* Clevedon, UK: Multilingual Matters.

Bourdieu, P. (1991). *Language and symbolic power.* Cambridge, MA: Harvard University Press.

Hamers, J., & Blanc, M. (1989). *Bilinguality and bilingualism.* Cambridge, MA: Cambridge University Press.

Mori, K. (2000). Becoming Midwestern. In M. N. Danquah (Ed.), *Becoming American: Personal essays by first generation immigrant women* (pp. 138–145). New York: Hyperion.

Pavlenko, A. (1997). *Bilingualism and cognition.* Unpublished doctoral dissertation, Cornell University, Ithaca, NY.

Pavlenko, A. (1998). Second language learning by adults: Testimonies of bilingual writers. *Issues in Applied Linguistics, 9*(1), 3–19.

Pavlenko, A. (1999). New approaches to concepts in bilingual memory. Keynote article. *Bilingualism: Language and Cognition, 2*(3), 209–230.

Pavlenko, A. (2000). What's in a concept? *Bilingualism: Language and Cognition, 3*(1), 31–36.

Pavlenko, A., Blackledge, A., Piller, I., & Teutsch-Dwyer, M. (Eds.). (2001). *Multilingualism, second language learning, and gender.* Berlin: Mouton de Gruyter.

IV

FROM THE PERIPHERY

A Somewhat Legitimate
and Very Peripheral Participation

A. Suresh Canagarajah
Baruch College, City University of New York

> Denying access and limiting the centripetal movement of newcomers and other practitioners changes the learning curriculum. This raises questions—in specific settings, we hope—about what opportunities exist for knowing in practice: about the process of transparency for newcomers. These questions remain distinct from either official or idealized versions of what is meant to be learned or should be learnable.
>
> —Lave and Wenger, 1991, p. 123

When we consider that there is a lot of variability in acceptable discourses in the research articles even within a single discipline and that many of the conventions of publishing are not clearly defined, we begin to realize that the notion of legitimate peripheral participation explains well how we become insiders in our disciplinary communities of practice. According to this notion, developed by Jean Lave and Etienne Wenger (1991), it is not formal study of rules but actually practicing the relevant discourse of the community one wishes to join that leads to one's insider professional status. Think about it—we can't get an authoritative manual where we can read about the "correct" ways to compose a cover letter accompanying the paper, interpret the editor's decision letter and the reviewers' commentary that follow the refereeing process, or write the "follow-up" cover letter after revising and proofreading the original manuscript. Whereas I call them paratextual conventions (Canagarajah, 2002), as they are treated as marginal to the more central construction of research articles, Swales (1996) was more suggestive in calling them "occluded genres." Then consider questions relating to the research article (RA) as a genre: Is the disciplinary discourse of teachers of English to speakers of other languages (TESOL) closer to that of the social sciences, humanities, or the "hard" sciences? Is there a preferred style for our RAs (i.e., do we really adopt the Introduction–Methodology–Results–Discussion structure of the empirical sciences? How far do we diverge from it?). It is true then that it is by engaging in writing with our disciplinary communities that we learn these unwritten rules of publishing and the contingent nature of discourses. This is how we learn, for example, the inner secrets of how one should write for which journal. All that Lave and Wenger (1991) require for one to become an insider in the disciplinary community is to be a potential legitimate member of the community; enjoy the possibility of finding the practices and products of the community transparent; have a certain amount of peripherality which gives sufficient detachment and necessary freedom to approximate the established practices of the insiders; and, above all, keep practicing the discourses of the community in engagement with others.

But the problem for me—when I tried to publish from Sri Lanka—was that I was so off-networked from scholars in the center that my peripherality was far too excessive; the publishing practices of the insiders in the West being insufficiently transparent, the legitimacy of the practices I was adopting was questionable; surrounded by local academics who did not see the value of publishing and were distanced from scholars who were actively publishing, my ability to practice was severely curtailed. How did I still manage to become an insider in the discipline (if I am allowed the privilege of claiming that status)? I must clarify first of all that the disciplinary community—like other communities of practice envisioned by Lave and Wenger—is an invisible community, decentered and translocal, and theoretically anyone can participate in its activities. There is nothing to prevent me from mailing a paper half way across the globe to a respected journal—and also having the possibility of getting it reviewed and receiving feedback. This means, I do have a certain amount of legitimacy, a peripherality like all others, and an ability to participate in publishing, however tenuously. The problem is that certain degrees of legitimacy, peripherality, and participation are constructive, and certain others are not. Lave and Wenger do not fully appreciate the fact that constructs such as "peripherality" and "participation" are not absolute. They are relative and relational. To what degree should one enjoy peripherality in a community in order to be effectively inducted into its practices and become a legitimate participating member? What amount of participation qualifies as acceptance of one as a legitimate member of that community? These are questions not explored fully in the legitimate peripheral participation model.

More importantly, one needs certain resources to participate in one's disciplinary community effectively (see Canagarajah, 2002). If one doesn't have access to a modest number of recent journals, have a decent computer or typewriter to compose on, or enjoy relative freedom from teaching and other institutional commitments to engage in the protracted process of composing and revising the paper, then one cannot indulge in publishing and knowledge production. But Lave and Wenger start from a neutral playing field, where the differing access to resources doesn't seem to matter. Whether their quartermasters have the resources to obtain the alidade that's crucial for their work, or the Yucatec midwives have a means of transportation to reach the pregnant mothers, are not questions they are concerned with. Attempting to participate in one's community of practice from such contexts of limitation brings up many "unofficial" or "unintended practices" (Lave and Wenger, 1991, p.107) of the marginalized that remain unacknowledged and often surreptitious.

CRACKS IN THE ACADEMIC COMMUNITY

It is well known now that however controlled and elitist a community is, there are always cracks that can be exploited by the marginalized to open up the community for critique and change. The crack in the academic community is of the following nature: Cheryl Geisler (1994) observes that there is a disjuncture in the literacy practices of academics. They want other academics to orientate to their writing as a product, but they read the writing of others from a process perspective. Therefore, they erase all traces of the process from their own articles (i.e., the research process that led to their findings; the rhetorical process that led to the final product; and other personal and contingent matters that shaped their research), although it is precisely such information that they use to critique the papers written by others. This practice is also motivated by their intention to create a dependent lay audience that has sufficient knowledge to appreciate their writings but lacks the process information to critique their work or create new knowledge of its own making. As a consequence of all this, the products of academic literacy are freely available, but the processes that led to their construction are known only to the insiders. What this means is that we scholars in the periphery have access (although belatedly) to the journals, books, and other texts that are important in our field, but we are left to guess the research and writing process from faint hints in the products. This situation develops in us a cynical attitude toward academic conventions. We tell ourselves: "I have a story that needs to be shared with the others in my field, but without following the conventions and discourses that are currently in fashion, I can't begin to tell my story. Academic publishing is all about proper packaging. So, by whatever means possible, let me decorate my story appropriately." Of course, the story and conventions cannot be separated this neatly. But this is what we say to empower ourselves to write and to attain publication. More importantly, this attitude encourages us to approximate the conventions and discourses (found in the articles and books we read) in ways that are convenient to us.

In the rest of this chapter, I narrate the strategies that we on the periphery have adopted to find a space for our local knowledge in mainstream journals. The discussion is mainly informed by my academic experience in the University of Jaffna, Sri Lanka. While I taught there from 1984 to 1994, I personally experienced the difficulties that scholars in the third world face in attempting to get their knowledge into print. My observation of the strategies my colleagues at University of Jaffna adopted to get their few articles published, supported by informal interviews and conversations with them, helped me adopt similar strategies in my writing. At other times, the discovery of their strategies helped me acknowledge the practices I was myself using unconsciously to surmount similar problems. In narrating our collective experience in publishing from the periphery, I want to suggest that there appears to be a "publishing culture" constituting such "unintended practices" that is shared by many periphery scholars. Though my own academic status has changed somewhat since I began teaching in New York, I still continue the conversation with Sri Lankan scholars on their problems and prospects in academic publishing.

UNOFFICIAL ROUTES TO INSIDER STATUS

I'll walk through the different sections of the research article to discuss the ways in which my Sri Lankan colleagues and I accomplished the accepted conventions of mainstream publishing.

The literature review is one of the hardest sections to write. After all, it's not any review that passes muster. We have to show an awareness of the most recent studies so that we can create a niche for our own work. But this is difficult to accomplish from a region where only a few journals in a field are available. Even these arrive as much as a year or two late. Similar difficulties obtain for scholarly books. Like most of my colleagues, I was left to guess the state of the art through the incomplete glimpses I got through the available literature. In many cases, I had a general sense of what was going on in the field, although I hadn't read some of the important publications that initiated the movement. On the topic of codeswitching, for example, I found that scholars were gradually moving from a Labovian correlational analysis to a more ideologically sensitive and interpretive orientation. But I hadn't read Heller (1988) or Myers-Scotton (1992), whose book length works were getting cited in the field at this time. What I resorted to doing was to cite these books anyway—withholding the information that I had merely seen them cited in other papers, or that I had found out their content through a brief book review or publication announcement in a journal (see, e.g., Canagarajah, 1995b). (What impression would the referees get if all that I had was "quoted in" and "cited in" for the references in the opening of my article?) This strategy enabled me to project an image of someone familiar with the field and widely read on current developments. I justified this strategy by saying that in an age of intertextuality—when we are comfortable with the notion that texts merge into other texts without distinct traces of the "original" context—where or how I had received these ideas didn't matter.

A related RA convention is the adoption of the appropriate opening moves—that is, showing the centrality of one's subject, creating a niche for the research, and announcing the objectives and plan of the paper (see Swales, 1990). Here again, one needs a clear understanding of the state of the art to accomplish these moves. Though I knew some ways in which I could make a case for my studies, I faced the disadvantage that I couldn't discuss extensively the books and papers I had only heard about through secondary sources. I learned a strategy from an older colleague of mine that I called "the less said the better." This colleague, who got published in respectable journals like *Anthropological Linguistics*, usually had a brief opening paragraph for his introduction. Basically he announced the objective of the paper before he plunged into his data and interpretation. The following is one example:

> The purpose of this paper is to correlate caste and language in the Jaffna Hindu Tamil society. This study is mainly based on data collected from a few sample villages in the Jaffna peninsula where the political and economic ascendancy of the VeLLaaLas (landlords) was very dominant in the recent past. (Suseendirarajah, 1978, p. 312)

The secret was that if one attempted to talk too extensively about the developments in the field, one would invite questions for clarification and explanation from the referees. We knew that we would find it difficult to answer further questions that involved showing more knowledge about publications one hadn't directly read, hence the safe approach of not engaging in complicated discussions of disciplinary discourse. Simply announcing one's research and spelling out the findings was considered adequate. I took this one step further in some cases and alluded to disciplinary developments by using a knowing philosophical–technical language and citations. Thankfully, RAs have limited space for extensive theoretical discussions. Journals are cutting down on the size of the issues and also the length of manuscripts. What is required is to deftly deploy the terms and names that matter in the field. In cases where the reviewers were convinced of my insider status, I managed to get my papers published. But there was one memorable case where a reviewer said "Don't refer to publications and terms you don't discuss extensively" and rejected the paper.

My "less said the better" strategy was also helped by some other current preferences in the RA genre. Increasingly, journals advise contributors to adopt parenthetical documentation rather than footnotes and endnotes. This convention is quite amenable to name-dropping. Showing your awareness of publications becomes sufficient as you don't have to expand any point or conduct tangential discussions about those publications in the notes. Needless to say, if there was an option for parenthetical documentation or notes in a journal, I always opted for the former. The increasing brevity of the RA texts is also of help in this regard. This gives me the excuse that I cannot expand on my references, the studies of other researchers, or the details of new books. With a cursory mention to display familiarity, or a few suggestive citations, I am able to move on to present my own research.

Writing the methodology section in the RA is also uncomfortable for many of us in periphery communities. We don't have the means to use sophisticated hi-tech instruments or conduct extensive controlled experiments to generate our data. There is very little funding available for obtaining new equipment; the available technology is "primitive;" even those available cannot be used because of the intermittent power cuts in the region. To complicate matters further, many of us in Sri Lanka deplored the "tech fetish" in Western journals. We had had the experience of having our papers rejected because they were based on low-tech methods or outdated instruments. In one of the very first papers I submitted from Sri Lanka (after completing my doctoral research in the United States), I reported a study on codeswitching from data I had manually written down in my notebook from observations in local market places. (A related problem was that even the pocket tape recorder I had with me could not be used in the busy marketplace to capture high-quality data.) A reviewer who rejected the paper said:

> The main problem I have at this point is with the methodology. I can't believe that people would address an issue like code-switching in the 1990s without recording actual speech.... Ideally the author should go back and find a way to record some interactions.

It should be mentioned that this paper was written just 2 years after I had conducted a sophisticated sociolinguistic study for my doctorate in the United States, where I audiotaped interviews, recorded in-group conversational interactions, obtained data from online discussions, and collected multiple drafts of writing from my participants. The problem for me was not ignorance about conventions of research processes and reporting, but simply the lack of resources and the conditions of work in Sri Lanka. Fortunately for me, this was also the time that there was developing a resistance against quantitative methods and interest in qualitative studies. Specifically, ethnography was coming into fashion. I decided therefore to make a change in my preferred modes of research to such low-tech low-capital methodologies. Once I latched on to this "art of deep hanging out" (as ethnography was cynically called in my graduate school days) publishing became smoother sailing for me.

I had to make other adjustments in my research orientation as I attempted to represent local knowledge in mainstream journals. This was also the time theory was coming into fashion. I found that there were certain advantages in engaging in theoretical discourse compared with empirical studies. In the latter, you never know whether someone out there in the West (with their greater access to publishing networks) has already done the type of studies you are conducting in your setting and made the argument you are making in relation to your context. You have to be familiar with other empirical studies that have come up in your field in a timely fashion. All this is in addition to the difficulties in obtaining funds and resources for lengthy controlled experiments or observations. In the case of theoretical articles, you simply have to deal with the dominant assumptions and general drift in the ongoing scholarly conversation with the help of a few representative publications. Also, you can engage in theoretical critique against a few seminal books rather than having to obtain empirical studies from all the minor journals your library doesn't subscribe to. Therefore some of us in the periphery started spending more time writing theoretically driven papers. In these papers we could use informal observations and casual conversations as evidence, as they didn't go through the same type of scrutiny as empirical studies.

In a related move, we also discovered the advantages in writing books compared with publishing journal articles. The differences in the discourse of academic books and journal articles are easy to guess. The RA is more focused in scope, reporting specific research projects, assuming careful scrutiny of evidence and methodology from the referees. The book is more holistic, adopting a greater thematic coherence in presentation and integrating a range of previous studies. As early as the heyday of the Royal Society of London, Newton discovered the advantages of writing monographs compared with articles. Wanting to steer clear of unceremonious challenges from the Schoolmen and unproductive arguments with them, he turned to writing monographs rather than articles (see Bazerman, 1988). What we in the periphery found was that in a book you can get away with making powerful claims and adopting radical intellectual moves without being held accountable for exhaustively citing rigorous forms of empirical data. (In fact, the person who let me into this secret was a well-published and respected British scholar!) Despite this realization, in my first book with Oxford University Press (see Canagarajah, 1999), the reviewers criticized me for being far too data-driven. They wanted me to get to my points faster and adopt a more "essayistic" and discussion-oriented style (at least, as I understood them). On the basis of market considerations, they were also concerned that too much data would lengthen the book and unreasonably raise the price of the publication. The tendency to prefer more "essayistic" approaches with less data is of advantage to us in the periphery because we have some powerful insights into social and pedagogical matters but do not always have the technological gadgets to capture or store the data for reproduction. Also, we give a lot of value to findings generated from informal observation, casual interviews, and sheer experience. Such "research methods" don't find acceptance in Western academic circles. But in writing scholarly books, we have the advantage of making our arguments and representing local knowledge with personal, informal evidence.

Exploiting the moment in the academic conversation, we also found that the interest in local knowledge, multiculturalism, and subject position provided us a vantage point for critiquing dominant disciplinary discourses. Working in a periphery context, all that we had to do to make ourselves heard in the scholarly conversation was to consider how the theories and pedagogical constructs exported from the West related to our local classrooms and communities. This approach proved a winning strategy for finding our writings in print. This was not simply a selfish strategy to get published. This opened up possibilities for our local experiences to be represented and to somewhat democratize knowledge production. The multiculturalist discourse in the academic culture could also be exploited to construct a voice suitable to our interests and local discourses. Though I started my publishing career by trying hard to accommodate the dominant ethos of the RA genre, I quickly found that the openness to critiquing the academic discourse, representing one's subjectivity in research, and resisting the mechanical empirical prose of RA could be exploited to indulge in a more narrative, relaxed, involved prose that I was more comfortable with. After a few signals in the opening of the paper, where I invoked values of pluralism and multiculturalism in academic discourse, I found that reviewers were better prepared to tolerate the discourses that they would have otherwise ruled out as nonacademic or simply flimsy.

But I still had to infuse my voice within the RA with some tact. I initially identified sections in the RA that would tolerate a different discourse more easily. In the local academic discourse in Sri Lanka, one has to make a case for one's paper by adopting what I have called a "civic ethos." The scholar has to show that the paper has relevance to the interests of the community and that it addresses pressing social concerns (see Canagarajah, 2002). Therefore in a paper I wrote for *Language in Society*, I showed both relevance to the scholarly conversation and relevance to community concerns in my introduction. This was easy to perform in a paper on the linguistic conflict in Sri Lanka, where the topic lent itself to civic-mindedness (see Canagarajah, 1995a). Some of my colleagues found that the conclusion is another place where you could introduce another obligatory feature in the local academic discourse—moralisms (see

Canagarajah, 2002). So after a very restrained, thoroughly data-driven paper on the connection between caste and language in our local speech community (the opening of which was quoted earlier), Suseendirarajah (1978, p. 319) concluded by moralizing that caste differences should not be maintained and that these linguistic correlates of caste are gradually dying with the infusion of liberal ideologies in local societies:

> In concluding, it may be said that man has awakened. He has a sense of human equality and humanity. He is for better change. Sooner or later we may miss most if not all of the sociolinguistic correlates recorded herein. They are on the verge of dying out.

He guessed, perhaps rightly, that such unconventional moves may be excused in inconspicuous places like the conclusion, after an objective discourse had been adopted in the more important sections of Methodology and Results (to adopt Swales' structure of the RA). This strategy worked: The paper appeared in *Anthropological Linguistics*.

Throughout the paper, as in the case of Western scholars (see Myers, 1990), we too suppress uncomfortable information and highlight information that is advantageous. This is of greater value to us in the periphery because our research processes are more influenced by diverse contingencies. My efforts to conduct a year-long ethnographic study on the attitudes of my ESL students confronted many problems: Classes were interrupted for long durations because of the fighting between the Tamil militants and Sinhala state; the power outages and nonavailability of batteries prevented me from audiotaping the interviews as I had planned; sudden closures of the campus for security reasons forced me to abandon many interviews I had planned with my students; xeroxing facilities were not available, and so I couldn't save a copy of students' work as I had planned. In fact, after a somewhat uneventful course, it was much after the end of the academic year that I discovered the hidden forms of resistance that became the focus of my paper. But someone who reads my report in *TESOL Quarterly* (see Canagarajah, 1993b) won't be able to guess any of this in this seamlessly constructed paper that takes an arrow-straight course of development. After outlining my reservations against scholars who theorize clear-cut cases of student resistance or accommodation, I marshal my data to conduct a nuanced theorization of hidden forms of student opposition. Now, of course, there is increasing openness to acknowledging that all research is shaped by "mangled practice" (see Pickering, 1995; Prior, 1998) and even understanding how these contingencies directly shape the research. My recent book *A Geopolitics of Academic Writing* accommodates the peculiarities of my research context in an unabashed way. But when I first started publishing, these were types of disclosure that were simply not made.

Of course, we in Sri Lanka also indulged in the other well-known practice of shaping the paper for the specific journal. In the now-familiar studies in our field, Myers (1985) and Gilbert and Mulkay (1984) exposed the changes center-based scholars make in their manuscripts (under both direct and passive pressure) to shape their claims and discourse to suit the expectations of the journal. Similarly, in my case, the study described earlier gets reported differently in the *TESOL Quarterly* and *Language, Culture and Curriculum* (a Multilingual Matters publication from Britain). My article in the former is a fairly straightforward research report, with great care given to making balanced and restrained interpretive claims from the data (see Canagarajah, 1993b). I limit myself to "lower level" claims (see Swales, 1990, p.117) and adopt a heavily qualified syntax and tentative tone. I cite "objective" data—constituting interview statements, field notes, and survey statistics. In the latter journal (Canagarajah, 1993a), these forms of data are pushed to the background as I focus on a semiotic study of the graffiti students had written on their textbooks (which is mentioned only briefly in the *TESOL Quarterly* article). There are sweeping interpretive moves, ideological reflections, and explicit politicization of the pedagogical context as I make a dizzying set of "higher level" claims. A paper on the semiotic interpretation of students' graffiti in textbooks is unconventional in both subject matter and methodology for most mainstream journals that are empirically driven. Only a publisher sensitive to ideological issues (such as Multilingual Matters) would tolerate such studies. There shouldn't be any implication that the former type of journals are superior to those like *Language, Culture and Curriculum*. It is fortunate that we have the latter type of journals in our field, as it would have been terribly disappointing for me not to have had an opportunity to convey the larger ideological claims that were crying out to be heard from the students' graffiti.

Such variability in the publishing field we used to our advantage in the refereeing process too. Basically, we played one reviewer off against the other when there were conflicting evaluations. In one case, I found that while two referees had reservations about my submission, they did so for different reasons. In fact, what was objectionable to one was commendable for the other. The referees came from different ideological and methodological camps. The more pedagogically focused referee found my political claims objectionable. The other lauded my ideological grounding but found my pedagogical choices controversial. Though I made some changes in resubmission, I made a successful case to the editor that on alternate matters at least one of the critics was on my side. The paper did get published on the second submission. Experiences such as this have confirmed to us that the refereeing process is highly subjective. We have learned not to feel put down by any rejection letter. More cynically, such experience has created the attitude in us that publishing is all about finding the suitable niche for one's study—the journal, referees, and editor who approximate one's academic interests and ideological values.

In many of these cases it is clear that my colleagues and I found ways of coping with our disadvantages and obstacles and even using them as an advantage for our publishing career. Let me conclude this section with a few other minor ways in which other limitations in the publishing process were turned into a blessing. Note that we in the periphery don't have good peer reviewers to read our manuscripts. Our local colleagues are equally out of date on the published research, distanced from the evolving disciplinary conversation, and alienated from the preferred modes of Western academic discourse. So I had to resort to submitting my papers without peer reviewing. It was the commentary of the referees of the journal that I used as my feedback for revision. Of course, I read and reread their comments to understand the many unstated assumptions and preferences and even tried to infer larger matters like the changes in the disciplinary conversation or nuances in discourse from their abbreviated comments. Though this process reduced the amount of feedback available for use in revision, this made me focus on the criticism that really mattered for getting that paper published in that journal. This situation also increased the speed with which I could submit papers as I wasn't distracted by too much conflicting feedback. Similarly, the limited number of journals we received in Sri Lanka worked to our advantage. We had enough resources to subscribe to only a handful of leading journals in our field. Though this limited the range of journals we could consider for publishing, we were indirectly compelled to aim for the best. In a sense, without getting our resources spread thin and our focus dissipated, we developed a specialized orientation to the discourse and practices of a few chosen journals. This helped us write our papers with a clear sense of where we wanted to submit them for publication.

DECENTERING THE COMMUNITY OF PRACTICE

Although this is a very personal account of how my colleagues and I coped with the publishing conventions from an off-networked and underprivileged location, we find some interesting ways of expanding the useful insights of the legitimate peripheral participation model to explain the ways in which scholars become insiders in their academic communities through publishing. Although too much peripherality and unsustained participation in the activities of the community reduces the transparency of its products and knowledge making practices, even the furthest reaches of peripherality may not lead to total exclusion from the community. Lave and Wenger (1991) use their constructs (such as peripherality, legitimacy, and participation) in somewhat absolute terms and theorized the clear-cut cases of inclusion and exclusion. In the example of apprentice meat cutters who are deliberately denied access to some of the important practices of the profession by the expert butchers, Lave and Wenger consider this as leading to dysfunctional and exclusionary consequences. What my example shows is that the novices may develop many coping strategies to gain useful insights and engage in the workings of the profession. They may adopt unorthodox practices and shortcuts to display proficiency in the discourses of the profession and become participating members. In other cases, they may develop a cynical attitude, demystifying the conventions of the profession and adopting them with a critical awareness. In all these cases, learning is taking place more intensely—and is certainly not reduced (as Lave and Wenger assume in the meat cutter example). Similarly, my colleagues and I in Jaffna latch on to the slightest clues from the published product or editorial correspondence to make inferences about the writing practices or refereeing process that we are alienated from. The rhetorical tactics we adopt to meet the requirements of literature review with inadequate resources (through secondary sources and cursory references) exemplify some of our unorthodox strategies. Suppressing information related to our research process, adopting more convenient research methodologies, or turning to theoretical articles and monographs are other coping strategies we develop to seek legitimacy for our local knowledge in the professional circles.

We don't consider these "illegitimate" methods unethical, though, because we adopt the pragmatic view that we have to negotiate with the dominant conventions and discourses on our terms in order to appropriately package our product and sell it in the intellectual marketplace. To use a different metaphor, we also adopt the playful attitude that academic discourses are "language games" and that the ever-changing discourses don't have to be held on to in religious terms as if they had any foundational status. We may pick and choose, adopt them piecemeal according to our convenience, as long as they enable us to represent our local knowledge and interests. We can't help but play these games and bargain in these markets in order to draw the attention of the sometimes uncaring academic community to serious social and educational concerns affecting remote marginalized communities like mine.

It is not hard to understand how such practices can lead to oppositional knowledge in the scholarly circles. The simple fact that we are not completely inducted into the professional community generates some interesting divergences from the legitimized discourses. In this manner, we can understand how resistance may find a place in the legitimate peripheral participation model. Although Lave and Wenger consider slight variations in the discourses of the newcomers and oldtimers in the community—which leads to change—these changes are largely under control in a cohesive community. The community is still centered (despite the decentering behind the divergent locations of practice of its members). Legitimate peripheral participation functions largely in accommodationist terms. But the atypical modes of peripherality and participation that I have narrated show how even more radical discourses may find a place in the community, leading to the fissures and tensions that generate newer interest groups and discourses. The disciplinary community thus becomes truly decentered, with members in different locations contributing to knowledge in divergent ways, appropriating the dominant discourses and conventions for their own purposes in quite unorthodox forms.

REFERENCES

Bazerman, C. (1988). *Shaping written knowledge: The genre and activity of the experimental article in science.* Madison, WI: University of Wisconsin Press.

Canagarajah, A. S. (1993a). American textbooks and Tamil students: A clash of discourses in the ESL classroom. *Language, Culture and Curriculum, 6*(2), 143–156.

Canagarajah, A. S. (1993b). Critical ethnography of a Sri Lankan classroom: Ambiguities in opposition to reproduction through ESOL. *TESOL Quarterly, 27*(4), 601–626.

Canagarajah, A. S. (1995a). The political-economy of code choice in a revolutionary society: Tamil/English bilingualism in Jaffna. *Language in Society, 24*(2), 187–212.

Canagarajah, A. S. (1995b). Use of English borrowings by Tamil fish vendors: Manipulating the context. *Multilingua, 14*(1), 5–24.

Canagarajah, A. S. (1999). *Resisting linguistic imperialism in English teaching.* Oxford, England: Oxford University Press.

Canagarajah, A. S. (2002). *A geopolitics of academic writing.* Pittsburgh, PA: University of Pittsburgh Press.

Geisler, C. (1994). *Academic literacy and the nature of expertise: Reading, writing, and knowing in academic philosophy.* Hillsdale, NJ: Lawrence Erlbaum Associates.

Gilbert, G. N., & Mulkay, M. (1984). *Opening Pandora's box: A sociological analysis of scientific discourse.* Cambridge, England: Cambridge University Press.

Heller, M. (1988). *Codeswitching.* Berlin: Mouton de Gruyter.

Lave, J., & Wenger, E. (1991). *Situated learning: Legitimate peripheral participation.* Cambridge, England: Cambridge University Press.

Myers, G. (1985). Texts as knowledge claims: The social construction of two biology articles. *Social Studies of Science, 15,* 583–630.

Myers, G. (1990). *Writing biology: Texts in the social construction of scientific knowledge.* Madison, WI: University of Wisconsin Press.

Myers-Scotton, C. (1992). *Social motivations for codeswitching: Evidence from Africa.* Oxford, England: Oxford University Press.

Pickering, A. (1995). *The mangle of practice: Time, agency, and science.* Chicago: University of Chicago Press.

Prior, P. (1998). *Writing/disciplinarity: A sociohistoric account of literate activity in the academy.* Mahwah, NJ: Lawrence Erlbaum Associates.

Suseendirarajah, S. (1978). Caste and language in Jaffna society. *Anthropological Linguistics, 20,* 312–319.

Swales, J. (1990). *Genre analysis: English in academic and research settings.* Cambridge, England: Cambridge University Press.

Swales, J. (1996). Occluded genres in the academy: The case of the submission letter. In E. Ventola, & A. Mauranen (Eds.), *Academic writing: Intercultural and textual issues* (pp. 45–58). Amsterdam/Philadelphia: John Benjamins.

15

A Scholar on the Periphery: Standing Firm, Walking Slowly

Miyuki Sasaki
Nagoya Gakuin University

At 5:30 a.m. on February 11th, 1998, our 3-year-old daughter, Tomo, lost consciousness, and was taken to the hospital by an ambulance that my husband had called. She had been sick for 2 days before that, and her temperature had gone up to 40 degrees centigrade during the previous night. I had taken her to a doctor the day before and had given her the medicine the doctor had prescribed, but it did not improve her condition. Until that day, nobody around her, including the doctor, had known that Tomo had a bad case of influenza. I remained at home with our 2-month-old son, Shou, when Tomo was taken to the hospital. Shou was also showing several bad symptoms, indicating that he might have the same illness as his sister, but at least he was still conscious. Even though I was coming down with the same illness myself, with a high fever and a throbbing headache, I still had to take care of him. It was the longest day of my life. Tomo did not regain consciousness for half a day. The doctor later explained that it was possible that the influenza virus had spread to her brain, perhaps having caused her unusually long loss of consciousness. Lying on a *futon* at home, suffering from the continuous throbbing of a severe headache, in my feverish thoughts I was thinking that Tomo was the last thing I wanted to lose in my life. Later on that day, Tomo regained consciousness, but she was still in critical condition. To make matters worse, Shou became so sick the next day that he had to go to the same hospital. Both of our children were in the hospital for 3 weeks.

On that day, it seemed like I was suddenly forced to pay all the debts I had accumulated during my life. Earlier in the previous year, I had been

211

asked to give a plenary talk at the third Pacific Second Language Research Forum (PacSLRF) in March. It was the first time I had ever been asked to give a plenary talk at an international conference. Because I had just given birth to our son 2 months earlier, I had not been able to prepare for the talk as much as I had wanted. I was hoping to do most of the preparation during the following month. Then, that day, February 11th, came. With a 2 month old and a 3 year old in the hospital, and in light of my own very weakened condition, I wondered if I should cancel my talk. After long consideration, however, I decided that it was too close to the conference and too irresponsible for me to cancel the talk at that point. My name was printed on the PacSLRF flyers that had been distributed 8 months earlier. But after I made that decision, I had to think about how I could manage to prepare my "debut" plenary talk well enough. Now that I think about it, I cannot really recall how I did it. I don't think I was able to prepare to the extent I had hoped, but a month later I did go to Tokyo and I did give the talk. I am thankful for my husband's help, which allowed me to take time to prepare for the talk, but still I remember clearly how trying it was for me to get over my own illness while taking turns with my husband and the babysitters to take care of our children 24 hours a day (which included sleeping on the floor beside their beds) at the hospital for the 3 out of the 4 weeks before the conference.

That experience became a turning point in my life as a researcher. After that, I decided to avoid every possible situation where my life as a mother (and often as a wife) would conflict with my life as a researcher. I learned that being torn between my family and my work is the last thing I want to do. Even before that experience, I was not a very active researcher. I liked what I was doing as a researcher, but I also liked to enjoy my life as a teacher, a wife, and a mother. Especially after our first child Tomo was born in 1994, it had become difficult to be very ambitious as a researcher, whether I wanted to be or not. Because it was (and still is) very rare for a full-time professor to also be a mother at our university (I was actually the first and second person to take maternity leave among the 108 faculty members in the 35-year history of our school), I tried very hard not to make my being a mother an excuse for being unable to function as a full-time teacher. I made every effort not to cancel my classes and to attend all faculty and committee meetings. I tried to make myself available to my students whenever possible. But still, it was impossible for me to put in as much time as I did before our daughter was born. She was sick almost every other day until she was 2 years old. She often didn't want to go to the daycare center and wanted to stay with her mother. I myself wanted to enjoy the precious short period of my daughter's infancy. And my life became even busier after her brother was born in 1997. I wanted more time for everything: raising the children, teaching, doing administrative work, and writing papers.

Canagarajah (1996) reported that researchers in developing countries live in the "periphery" (p. 442) world where "difficulties in getting publications from the outside world, coupled with the unusual delays in receiving mail, greatly reduce access to recently published scholarship" (p. 448), which makes it very difficult for those researchers to publish in mainstream international academic journals. Compared with those in such environments, as a researcher I have lived under much better circumstances that have provided easier access to current publications from the outside world, an efficient mailing system, sufficient "telecommunication facilities and funds to travel" (Canagarajah, 1996, p. 448). And yet I have often felt that I have suffered from difficulties similar to those of the "periphery scholars" (p. 450) because I was unable to use the facilities available since becoming a mother. In this sense, I may have been living on the periphery of the research world after our children were born. Until the day Tomo lost consciousness, however, I had tried hard to work as normally as possible in spite of such unfavorable circumstances. I didn't want other people to think that I had become an incompetent researcher after becoming a mother.

On February 11th, 1998, however, my value system changed. I realized more clearly than before that I could not be happy if my interests as a researcher conflicted with those as a mother and a wife. Trying to do the best possible research while keeping up with the most recent research trends is a good thing to do *only if* it does not get in the way of my life as a family member. And so I decided to slow down the pace of my research even more, but this time I didn't feel frustrated. I knew that this was a decision I made myself and that I could not be happy living my life any other way. Although I admire some of my friends who regularly get their papers published in prestigious journals, organize discussion sessions at conferences, and are involved in research projects with distinguished scholars, I don't have to be like them. For now, I would like to do what is most satisfying in my life, that is, being a good member of my family and writing a good research paper once every year or two (in this sense, I am thankful for the fact that, as is typical at Japanese universities, the university I work for does not have a strong "publish or perish" policy). If I became more ambitious, I would inevitably risk putting myself in a situation like the one I found myself in on that fateful February day, a situation that I hope to avoid for the rest of my life.

Residing in the "periphery" is not such a bad thing, however, and I often wonder why people want to be in the "center" all the time. Being in the center must have its own sources of frustration and disadvantages, too. If I were given enough time to do whatever research I liked with ample (and technically highly advanced) resources to search for the most current related literature, I might be too overwhelmed by the pressure to produce the best kind of research in such an ideal situation. Being invited to work with internationally well-known scholars is exciting, but I might be pressured and frustrated by the fact that I could not work as efficiently as the other members of the team (this has happened to me before). Furthermore, living in a geographically "peripheral" world has provided me with several opportunities (discussed later) to notice things that might not be noticed in the "center," that is, "North American and Western European locations" (Canagarajah, 1996, p. 436). Thus, I enjoy living on the periphery now. I don't know what other people might think about my way of living, but at least to me it is comfortable and worthwhile. In this sense, I am a believer of two teachings of Laotsu: "Those who stand on tiptoe cannot stand long, those who walk with long strides cannot walk far," and "Nothing including what people call goodness and beauty is certain, and it is wrong to be tied to one value system (Kanaya, 1997, p. 81 and p. 18, respectively; the interpretations of the original Chinese sayings were in Japanese and were translated into English by Miyuki Sasaki).

For the past several years, then, I have done my research at my own pace (I never work after 6 p.m. on weekdays and Saturdays, and I never work on Sundays) and have submitted papers for publication as frequently as is comfortable for me. I would now like to write about one of those experiences because the process of doing research and submitting a paper to a journal has been an essential part of what has made my life as a "periphery scholar" happy and worthwhile. The process is long (especially because I work slowly and because I mainly work in English, my second language) and sometimes discouraging (especially when I get rejection notices from journal editors), but I have learned so much in the process, and in the end it is always rewarding in some way, even when the paper is not accepted by the journal in which I originally hoped to be published. I hope that my story will encourage other researchers like me who are forced to live on the periphery of the academic world.

I would like to write about what happened regarding my plenary talk for the third PacSLRF (which I had to prepare during that very tense time after my daughter lost consciousness), because it represents the most recent and typical process of my research work. On March 28th, 1998, I presented a paper titled "Toward an Empirical Model of the L2 Writing Process" (Sasaki, 1998). As I wrote in Sasaki (2001), I had been interested in second language (L2) writing for quite a while by then (partly because I had to struggle so much to be able to write in English myself). I first investigated what factors influenced the quality of Japanese students' expository writing in English in Sasaki and Hirose (1996). I wanted to know "what makes a good L2 writer." Having realized that there was no analytic scale to measure Japanese as a first language (L1) compositions available for that study, my coauthor and I also developed such a scale ourselves through multiple stages of validation (Sasaki & Hirose, 1999).

I then became interested in the *process* by which the quality of such compositions—that is, the writing *product*—is achieved. I searched through previous studies that examined writing process in the fields of both L1 and L2 and realized that many of the studies used what is called a "think-aloud" method to collect the concurrent writing process data. Although it is true that it is practically the only way to investigate what a writer is thinking about while writing, I, as an L2 writer myself, wondered whether a method that forces writers to talk aloud about what they are thinking might not excessively disturb their writing processes. I tried the method on myself and could not complete the task. I asked some of my undergraduate students to do the same. None of them completed the writing task in a satisfactory manner. I realized that the think-aloud method could not always be applied effectively with all types of participants and that it may not be the best method for collecting data from Japanese participants who, so it is said, live in a society where silence is valued (Ishii, Okabe, Kume, & Hirai, 1990). Thinking back on this now, I arrived at this insight because I teach English in a foreign language situation (i.e., where it is not used outside the classroom as a means of communication). As I mentioned earlier, being on the periphery can work as an advantage sometimes!

In search of an alternative way of examining an L2 writer's thinking process, my former coauthor, Keiko Hirose, introduced me to a very promising method that had been developed by Anzai and Uchida (1981) for Japanese L1 writers. Having realized that it was difficult to collect concurrent think-aloud data from Japanese child participants (again, this problem may be culturally rooted), Anzai and Uchida conducted a careful and well-designed empirical study and developed a method for collecting retrospective protocol data that can provide detailed information about what a participant is thinking about while writing. Because the participants were asked to talk just after they had written the first word of the compositions and just after they finished writing, while looking at the composition they had just written, their writing process was not greatly disturbed. They were asked to explain what they had been thinking about at each pause longer than 2 seconds, which had been hand-recorded by a research assistant sitting beside the participants while they were writing. Because a writing process is a continuous and diffusive act, I thought that asking the participants what they had been thinking about every time they stopped writing was a good way of probing their thinking process.

Having been impressed by the high-quality research conducted by Anzai and Uchida (1981), I started to look at other studies published in the *Japanese Journal of Educational Psychology*, where Anzai and Uchida had contributed their study. This process opened a new world to me. I was amazed by the richness of the accumulated knowledge based on the long history of scientific research in the field of Japanese educational psychology. As in the papers written by the "periphery scholars" discussed by Canagarajah (1996), the results of these studies were reported in the local language, Japanese, and thus were difficult for scholars in the "center" to get access to. I regretted that I had mainly looked at studies written in English when I had conducted background literature reviews for the previous papers I had written. Just as Canagarajah lamented the limited distribution of papers contributed to the local journals in Sri Lanka, it would be a pity if researchers outside Japan could not enjoy this treasure trove of knowledge accumulated through Japanese researchers' hard work. But I also felt that this isolation could be an advantage for a researcher like me who could read both English and Japanese: I could learn and cite from literature written in both English and Japanese.

Using the method developed by Anzai and Uchida (1981) for Japanese children was a big success. All of the participants in my pilot study, including a few very shy students, contributed ample data for analyzing their writing process in detail. On the basis of the pilot study results, I also revised Anzai and Uchida's method to better fit my own L2 participants. I used a video camera to record the participants' writing behaviors, including their hand movements, instead of just recording their writing behaviors while sitting beside them. Watching the videotapes of themselves writing and looking at their compositions helped the participants remember what they were thinking about at each pause better than if they just looked at the compositions they had just written.

Having gained confidence in the effectiveness of the main method I would use, I proceeded to conduct the main study in 1996. I investigated the writing processes of four Japanese EFL (English as a foreign language) writing experts (defined as those whose "professional work included regularly writing English research papers while their life was anchored in Japan" [Sasaki, 2000, p. 265]) and eight Japanese EFL writing novices cross-sectionally and longitudinally (before and after 6 months of process-writing instruction). Partly using the coding scheme developed by Anzai and Uchida (1981), I looked at the participants' writing fluency, the quality and complexity of their written texts, their pausing behaviors while writing, and their strategy use. While I was doing a background literature review for this study, I had noticed that there were very few studies that investigated EFL writing experts. Because, by definition, the experts did not live in the center of the academic world, where English is used as a major means of communication, it might have been difficult for the center-based researchers to get access to them. Here again, periphery researchers like me may possibly have an advantage over center-based researchers.

It took me the whole year of 1996 to collect the data from the eight novice writers, and Keiko Hirose provided me with the data from the four experts. Then, in 1997, I started to analyze the data. In the beginning of that year I agreed to give the plenary talk at the third PacSLRF in March 1998. I decided to talk about this analysis of Japanese EFL learners' writing process. Because it was the first plenary talk I had ever been asked to give, I had to gather all my courage just to agree to the invitation to give the talk. I wanted to give a good talk based on good analyses. However, the year of 1997 turned out to be much longer and harder for me than I could have imagined because I gave birth to our second child at the end of that year. Throughout my pregnancy, I was sick. I had to analyze the huge piles of transcribed data in a very weak condition while taking care of our then 2-year-old daughter.

It was just 2 months after I gave birth to our son that the terrible day in February came. I tried my best to prepare for the talk, and at the last minute I jumped on the train for Tokyo (I was in such a hurry that I even forgot the memo that had the name of the hotel where I would be staying that night. I had to call home to find out what it was.) The talk went reasonably well, I thought. On the stage, wearing a pink suit and smiling bravely during my talk, I felt strange that nobody but Setsuko Miyamoto, a friend of mine who came with me from Nagoya because she was worried about my health, knew of my long and hard struggle to get there. To the participants, I was just one speaker who could be easily replaced by somebody else. To them, it was just a 45-minute talk, but to me it was a 2-year-long struggle to stand on that stage.

Just after the conference was over, the new school year started at our university, and I did not have time to write a paper from the speech draft until the summer vacation started that year. To me, writing a presentation draft and writing a paper are two different things. My presentation drafts are usually much shorter and simpler than my written papers. For the former, I only highlighted several points that I thought would be appealing to the audience. When I rewrote the presentation draft for the plenary talk, I had to look at all the data again and add many more details. I also added some additional results from analyses I didn't present in the talk. Because I had by then decided to take my time when working on my research, I worked slowly. During that time, I also had to take care of my baby son and 3-year-old daughter and my husband's sick parents, who had come in the summer of that year from their hometown to stay at a hospital in Nagoya.

The paper, somehow, was completed at the end of December 1998. It took me about 10 months to complete it. I then sent it to Carol Rinnert, an applied linguist whose work I respect very much. She often reads my papers and gives me insightful comments while correcting grammatical errors. After having studied English for almost 30 years, I still make numerous grammatical errors in English, even after I rewrite the draft many times; I need my grammar checked every time I write in English. But Carol does much more than that. As an excellent applied linguist herself, she checks the overall organization and coherence as well as the validity of the content. I am lucky to have several friends like Carol who read my papers both as native speakers of English and as researchers. This time, too, Carol gave me many helpful comments on my paper, and I revised it addressing them and sent it to the *Journal of Second Language Writing* (*JSLW*) on January 23rd, 1999.

Then, at the end of July 1999, I received a letter from the *JSLW* editors. I always feel very tense when I open a letter from the editor of the journal to which I have submitted my paper. I have to take a deep breath before I open it. I opened the envelope and skimmed the cover letter. The sentence "one reader calls for acceptance with revisions; the other, rejection" jumped out from the page. The letter further said

> Because we feel that a well revised version of this paper could make a contribution to the research in second language writing, we would like to offer you the opportunity to revise and resubmit your manuscript for further consideration, with the understanding that this offer implies no obligation on our part to publish a revised version of this paper.

I wonder what other people would do after reading such a response. I must admit I am a coward in this respect. I could not read the reviewers' comments (especially because I was afraid of those from the reviewer who had rejected my paper) for a while, remembering how hurt I have felt after reading such rejection letters in the past. Ever since I sent my first paper to a refereed journal in 1989, I have received comments from many reviewers who rejected my papers. I have learned by now that many of those comments contain constructive and helpful suggestions, but I still tend to be devastated by sentences such as "the study lacks conceptual clarity and a solid basis for formulating specific recommendations regarding ..." or "there are major problems with the theoretical framework, the basic assumptions, and the overly broad research questions."

For this particular letter from the editors of the *JSLW,* I could not make myself read the reviewers' comments until 2 weeks later, and I could not reread them for the purpose of revising my paper until 2 months later. The content of the rejecting review was so shocking to me that I needed some time to gather enough courage to look at it again. The review simply said "I recommend that Manuscript #330 be rejected for the following reasons," and then presented six detailed reasons why my paper was not worth publishing. The comments made the situation look so hopeless to me at first glance that I wondered if it would be worth even revising the paper at all. This must have preoccupied my mind so much at that time that I mentioned it in my e-mail letters to some of my friends. They all encouraged me to revise the paper. I downloaded and posted their messages in front of my computer. My favorite, which I still treasure, came from Kozue Uzawa, who wrote:

> Yes, I can understand that it is very discouraging to read some reviewers' harsh criticisms. However, I usually appreciate them, thinking they are trying to improve my paper. For my paper, which appeared in the *JSLW* in 1996, I revised it, revised it, and revised it so many times before it was finally accepted. And fortunately, it received the *JSLW*'s best article of the year award. So, re-

vising is part of writing, I think. Don't be discouraged, and I am looking forward to reading your article very soon.

I have noticed that many people give up revising and resubmitting their papers when they are rejected for the first time. I would have too if I had not known that many researchers actually begin writing good papers from that point. I have learned this through many friends like Kozue and other people around me. When I was a graduate student at the University of California, Los Angeles, I saw many students, and even professors, having their papers rejected by refereed journals for publication, but they did not seem to be very discouraged. They told me that it is common to have papers rejected or to be told to revise and resubmit them. They even said, "reviewers are not perfect. They can be wrong sometimes. If you cannot accept the reviewers' comments, you can send your criticisms of the reviews to the editors, or send your paper to other journals, too." The other advice I received was "If you decide to resubmit your paper, try to address the given comments as well as possible. You don't have to make your paper perfect. Just follow the reviewers' advice first." Knowing these things, combined with the encouragement of my friends, helped me return to the reviewers' comments once again. As Kozue Uzawa said, reviewers' comments are like bitter medicine I have to swallow if I want to improve the quality of my paper.

So I gathered all my courage together and started to read the reviewers' comments once again in August 1999. After having read the two reviewers' comments several times, I determined that I could probably address both of the reviewers' comments if I spent enough time on them. I decided to resubmit the paper to the *JSLW*. Following the reviewers' advice, I added to the literature review, clarified words, added more explanation, reanalyzed the data, and removed unnecessary parts from the text. Meanwhile, I had to take care of my family, teach classes, and do administrative duties as a faculty member at my university. Looking back now, however, I am surprised how much I learned through that revising experience. Just as with the revising process for the other papers I had eventually gotten published in the past, I discovered several new perspectives from which to look at my data during this time. I also read some related papers in other fields, whose existence I would not have been aware of if the reviewers had not suggested that I refer to them. In the end, the reviews were really good "medicine" for me. This would have been true even if the paper had not finally been accepted. As I had often felt before, I started to feel that this medicine had worked wonders on me, making my researcher's "spirit" healthier and stronger, regardless of whether my paper would finally be accepted. Publication of the paper was just one end product of this long journey.

The revised version was completed at the end of December 1999. Because I wanted to hear comments from experts other than the reviewers, I asked Carol Rinnert and Alister Cumming to read the revised draft. After I revised the paper again on the basis of their comments, I resubmitted it in March 2000. Then on June 28, 2000, I received an e-mail letter from an editor of the *JSLW* again with comments, as well as two additional reviewers' comments. This time both reviewers accepted the paper with revisions. Many of these revisions were minor, but some required me to conduct additional statistical procedures on the data. Because the editor set a deadline of July 7 for my revisions, in the 10 days allowed I tried to concentrate on this work as much as I could. I was happy when I could finally resubmit the final version of the paper on the very day of the deadline.

Up to that point, it had taken me 4 full years to complete the research and write up the results. But it was finally finished. I know that I did not set any record for shortest time for completing a paper in my field, but this way, my way, is the only way that I can be happy and satisfied as a whole person. Furthermore, even at that point, I fully realized that both the research I conducted for the paper and the paper I wrote based on it were far from perfect (I actually did a follow-up confirmatory study later to improve the validity and generalizability of the research; see Sasaki, 2002), but I was happy that I was given an opportunity to make some of the results of my work public. The *JSLW* paper was published at the end of 2000 (Sasaki, 2000). I have received many e-mail comments on the paper since then. Those e-mail messages are the voices I could not have heard if I had not had my paper published in an international journal. I would be content if I could hear those voices every fourth year or so, when a paper is completed. As Laotsu recommends, I would like to stand firmly on own my feet, and walk slowly, but I hope to travel a long way, believing that the world I live in has its own value.

I do not mean to suggest that my story recounts the best way to live as a researcher, but if some readers are wondering how they can live as "periphery scholars," this might be one possibility. You as a researcher might be forced to live in a kind of peripheral world some day, when, for example, you have a family, you fall ill, or you become very busy with something else. I hope that my story will help others to realize that living on the periphery does not have to be a cause of despair, but can in fact be a source of hope.

REFERENCES

Anzai, Y., & Uchida, N. (1981). Kodomo wa Ikani Sakubun o Kakuka [How children produce writing]. *Japanese Journal of Educational Psychology, 29,* 323–332.

Canagarajah, A. S. (1996). "Nondiscursive" requirements in academic publishing, material resources of periphery scholars, and the politics of knowledge production. *Written Communication, 13,* 435–472.

Ishii, S., Okabe, R., Kume, T., & Hirai, K. (1990). *Ibunka Komunikeishon Kii Waad* [Key words for cross-cultural communicaiton research]. Tokyo: Yuuhikaku.

Kanaya, O. (1997). *Loushi* [Laotsu]. Tokyo: Koudansha.

Sasaki, M. (1998). *Toward an empirical model of L2 writing process.* Paper presented at the third Pacific Second Language Research Forum, Tokyo, Japan.

Sasaki, M. (2000). Toward an empirical model of EFL writing processes: An exploratory study. *Journal of Second Language Writing, 9,* 259–291.

Sasaki, M. (2001). An introspective account of L2 writing acquisition. In D. Belcher, & U. Connor (Eds.), *Reflections on multiliterate lives* (pp. 110–120). Clevedon, England: Multilingual Matters.

Sasaki, M. (2002). Building an empirically-based model of EFL learners' writing processes. In S. Randsdell & M-L Barbier (Eds.), *New directions for research in L2 writing* (pp. 49–80). Amsterdam: Kluwer Academic.

Sasaki, M., & Hirose, K. (1996). Explanatory variables for EFL students' expository writing. *Language Learning, 46,* 137–174.

Sasaki, M., & Hirose, K. (1999). Development of an analytic rating scale for Japanese L1 writing. *Language Testing, 16,* 457–478.

16

Writing Across the Theory–Practice Divide: A Longitudinal Confession

Brian Morgan
York University

When I first began teaching in community-based English as a second language (ESL) programs about 13 years ago, my reactions to professional writing in the form of journal articles and academic books were mixed. Sometimes, academic articles inspired me, especially ideas that challenged me to teach in ways that might contribute to social justice. Other times, however, I found myself questioning not only a writer's ideas but also his or her intentions for writing in the first place. Right from the opening paragraphs, I would look for weak links in the chain of reasoning and imagine possible counterarguments I might have to make.

I like to think that my negative reception was more than just a "fear of theory" (Simon, 1992), a reluctance to engage with conceptual fields not directly related to the narrow management of classrooms. Rather, I look back on my early skepticism as a reflection, in part, of personal encounters with the printed word, ones in which the circulation of academic articles had real effects on decision-making in my place of work. That is, in the hands of a particular supervisor or administrator, the "latest research" or "state-of-the-art" teaching method always had the potential of being a weapon of sorts, used to justify a whole range of decisions in our ESL program: the purchase of texts, allocation of classroom space, design of new curricula, and the evaluation of student and teacher performance.

Writing, in this respect, is always more than a set of propositions committed to print. Writing has the power to make ideas seem natural and inevitable, which in turn provides an urgency to modify existing programs and procedures in light of what is being proposed. For practitioners, most of whom are unversed in the textual conventions of academic life, the effect can be a feeling of resignation or powerlessness in the decision-making processes that affect their professional lives. This chapter explores how such feelings are produced both directly and indirectly through writing. To this end, I shall weave together four short personal accounts that trace the history of my developing awareness of the power of writing as it relates to the marginalization of teachers' experiences and ways of knowing.

WRITING–PRODUCING HIERARCHY: A VIEW FROM THE BOTTOM

The first and earliest story took place in a downtown Toronto community center where I taught adult ESL soon after my return from teaching in Chongqing, Peoples' Republic of China, in 1988. Along with a whole range of settlement services for immigrants and refugees, the center had a thriving ESL program for adult students from a variety of ethnolinguistic backgrounds, but predominantly Chinese and Portuguese. Given the high number of Chinese and Portuguese speakers, the center also offered bilingual ESL classes, which were particularly popular with the older students.

Space was always a scarce and highly coveted item at the center, and the classroom needs of the ESL program were often a source of contention amongst coordinators of non-ESL programs. One day, a worrying rumor spread through the ESL staff room. Evan (a pseudonym), the new youth programs coordinator, was inviting a famous applied linguistics professor from the Ontario Institute for Studies in Education (OISE) to attend a meeting at the center and advise us on how to "improve" our bilingual programs. Evan's real agenda, we surmised, was to draw on the expertise and prestige of the invited professor as a means of shutting down or limiting the bilingual classes, thus freeing up more space for other programs. As I was just beginning a master's program at OISE at this time, my panicked colleagues urged me to find out as much as possible about the politics and theoretical orientation of our visitor and potential executioner.

The meeting date was on everyone's mind. Some of the bilingual teachers started talking openly of alternative employment plans. In the meantime, I had spoken to one of my new professors and was relieved to find out that our future visitor was in fact a huge supporter and expert in the areas of French immersion and bilingual education. I passed along this latter bit of information, which relieved some of the anxiety many were feeling prior to the meeting. In the end, the actual meeting turned out to be a painless event for the ESL program. Evan made a bit of a fool of himself, and our academic guest quickly picked up on the somewhat naked power play her reputation was being used to advance. As it turned out, we got some useful advice from our visitor and temporary brakes put on Evan's rampant ambitions.

For me, the whole event was a real eye-opener on the authority that academic theorists have over practitioners. Warranted or not, our nervousness over the future of the program was palpable. As ESL teachers, we truly believed or assumed that the opinion of a professor, whose position and esteem had been certified through academic research and publishing, would have more weight than those of us who actually taught in the classrooms that the academics were theorizing about in their research. On the basis of their command of a particular mode or genre of writing, they had the power to define our work for us.

MOVING UP A FEW RUNGS ON THE LADDER

The second incident took place several years after the first and signals a kind of turning point in my professional life. Although I was still teaching in the same community center, I had now nearly finished a Master's degree and had taken a few tentative steps in the direction of publishing my work. About this time, I began to focus on finding pedagogical applications for the critical theories on language, power, and identity that inspired me in my OISE classes. Texts in the areas of poststructuralism, cultural studies, feminist and critical pedagogy offered a dimension of social possibility that seemed to resonate with my experiences at the community center. Encouraged by my professors and several colleagues, I decided to revise and submit for publication a course paper I wrote on teaching the Gulf War in an ESL classroom (see Morgan, 1998).

The process of submission, editing, and revision was an extremely difficult one (see Morgan, 1997). I originally sent my manuscript to the flagship theoretical journal of a major, international English language teaching organization. The editor of the journal promptly returned it, advising me to resubmit the manuscript to the organization's new teaching journal because my submission was primarily focused on practice. This required substantial reduction of a 25-page paper into a much smaller work conforming to the criteria of the practitioners' journal at this time ("between 1,000 and 3,000 words in length" with a focus on "teaching and classroom research"). In this shorter format, I decided to remove a theoretical overview of poststructural notions of discourse and subjectivity as well as a short historical discussion of conventional theory formation in applied linguistics and its limitations for community-based, critical ESL pedagogies.

Without adequate theoretical support in my article, I believe, points of contention between the editors and me were inevitable. In several areas of the manuscript, what I assumed were relevant practices on the basis of my readings in critical pedagogy and poststructuralism, the editorial team saw as jargon or activities unrelated to my ESL responsibilities. Most importantly, as I had learned in the staff meeting described earlier, what was at stake in this debate was more than the final version of a single submission. Writing could have effects that went beyond the immediate reader-ship of a journal. It could reinforce the status quo in a profession, or it could initiate alternatives to the dominant notions of what a teacher should see, say, and do, and how he or she might respond to the exchange of mean-ings that interconnect classrooms, communities, and societies.

EDITING DEBATES

Because the major points I want to make revolve around editing issues, it is worthwhile revisiting a couple of specific examples along with the social context from which the manuscript emerged. My adult ESL class at this time actually took place in a spare classroom at a local public primary school in which several of my students' children studied. As the Gulf War escalated, many of my students expressed their concern regarding the various posters depicting bombs and planes dotting the hallways. These depictions, several students complained, treated the war "like a game," and as survivors of revolution and civil war, they were troubled to see this in a Canadian school.

In response, one day, I arranged a meeting between my class and the sev-enth-grade students next door. Their teacher and I thought it might be useful to have the younger students hear personal accounts of what it is like to live through war. When I approached my students with the plan, however, sev-eral stated that their English limitations prohibited them from participating. I was surprised given that the students were quite advanced, but realized after some discussion that my class was the only place in which some students used English. In my manuscript, I speculated on the underlying causes of this situation in the concluding remarks of the introductory section.

> One of the main reasons is a cultural sense of identity where the structural form of public speech, if incorrect, devalues both the content of the utter-ance and the dignity of the speaker. How my students presented themselves in public was important to them and, in some ways, inseparable from what they intended to communicate. My students' concerns also made me realize how I have developed a way of filtering the spoken word, where judgment of content is rarely subordinated to the precision of form.

Immediately after this piece of text, I summarized the introduction with the following two sentences: "These were the emerging concerns that helped create the pedagogical strategy for my first lesson on the Gulf War. Each subsequent lesson was contingent on the strengths and weaknesses of its predecessor." The referents I assumed for "emerging concerns" were several interconnected issues in the Introduction: (a) the organiza-tion of support (e.g., posters) for the war at the primary school; (b) notions of social identity, dignity, and public language requirements that inhibited the participation of several students; (c) my own assumptions regarding both of these issues and how they might influence my role as a teacher. Most importantly, in my mind, language learning was organized in support of social needs and outcomes, not the reverse. And in this respect, I tried to develop a set of lessons that increased students' awareness of how their new L2 might be used to "manufacture consent," in Noam Chomsky's memorable phrase, for public policies that favor dominant interests.

The editorial revisions that concluded my introduction stated: "My students' concerns helped me structure strategy for our lessons on the Gulf War. I built lessons on sticky language forms into three speaking, reading, and writing classes that focused on the students' experiences of war." This subtle shift in priorities, from discursive notions of identity (cf. Norton, 2000; Toohey, 2000) and the achievement of social outcomes through pedagogy, toward affective barriers and skills-based instruction, of itself, was not substantial. But throughout the manuscript, deletions were subsequently made because certain ideas became "peripheral" or "new" to the priorities that the editorial team had attributed to me in the introduction.

An important example of editorial deletions and shifted priorities involved my portrayal of the meeting with the seventh graders, which turned out to be a difficult session. Whenever my students personalized their experiences of war or mentioned the terrible conditions that the children of Iraq might encounter, the seventh-grade teacher interrupted them and tried to redirect attention toward geopolitical concerns specific to the Gulf War. In the summation of this lesson, I wrote in the manuscript:

> Initially I found this to be a very depressing and wasteful experience. But after a while I realized that many positive things occurred. For the grade sevens, it was probably their only opportunity to hear different perspectives, however harassed, about the nature of warfare. For these children, the existence and recognition of dissenting opinions is an essential prerequisite for developing new social possibilities if they so chose.

In the editorial revisions that I received from the journal's staff editors, the entire last sentence was deleted and the following sentence inserted in its place: "At the same time, my students saw that they were able to express themselves—when they weren't being interrupted." As an explanation for the change, the annotated comments stated: "Segue would link this section to the initial goals you set forth in the introduction to this article, that is, meeting your students' need to communicate without embarrassment."

During a phone conversation with the staff editors, I said I was opposed to the revised concluding sentence because my focus for this lesson had been primarily social rather than affective or linguistic, narrowly defined. In response, one of the editors stated that it would be inappropriate for me to talk about children in Grade 7 "developing new social possibilities." Eventually we agreed to keep both sentences, the editors' and mine, with mine at the end. However, in the fax I received the next day my concluding sentence had undergone an unexpected adjustment: "(Reflecting on dissenting opinions is a prerequisite for developing a sense of social responsibility and the possibility of social change.)" I immediately faxed back and argued that the parenthetical placement of this statement made it seem incidental or like an afterthought rather than an intended social outcome produced by a pedagogical strategy of bringing together my students and the seventh graders. Eventually, we settled on wording that we could all live with.

Another significant deletion, from my perspective, was made in the article's conclusions. The following paragraph was a particular point of contention:

> Regardless of one's opinion on the Gulf War, it has set into motion many new realities that are frightening for the future. For the young, war has become indistinguishable from a football game, cartoon show, or video arcade. Contrary to New World Order rhetoric, the ignorance of war's reality is a disturbing legacy for the future, in which a public desire to resolve dispute through aggression becomes, once again, the norm rather than the exception. Considering the proliferation of ever more efficient means of technological destruction, our legacy to future generations would seem to border on the apocalyptic.

I would never presume that this paragraph could not be improved by editing. However, the key point is that the entire paragraph was edited out because of content. The reason stated: "Conclusion is weakened by introducing these new themes peripheral to the lessons. Delete." In a subsequent telephone conversation, I had to justify the inclusion of the above paragraph by referring back to questions my students had developed for their meeting with the seventh graders. Examples such as, "Do you think this will provide a good future for the next generation?" and "Why not buy oil from Iraq instead of Kuwait?" challenged the assertion that I was introducing new themes to the paper.

Elsewhere (see Morgan, 1997), I have provided a more thorough account of the give-and-take that shaped this latter paragraph and several other areas of the manuscript. The process was difficult and time consuming. It seemed that we would never resolve our differences, and we openly discussed the withdrawal of the article from the journal on several occasions. The editors, I am certain, felt that they were dealing with an inexperienced and overly sensitive author unwilling to cooperate with normal editing procedures. I am sure, as well, that the editorial team felt that as a practitioner I was venturing into conceptual areas in which I was not qualified to participate. On more than one occasion, I was told, "That's not done in ESL; it's conjecture—not academic." From my perspective, I felt that ideas that were foundational to my way of teaching were either being removed or trivialized in the editing process.

To repeat, I think that the editorial disagreements that occurred were advanced by the spatial restrictions and focus of the journal at that time (1993). Without theoretical foregrounding and explication, a primary emphasis on language and power, or critical literacy skills that examine government, would appear incompatible within the general scope of most ESL teaching journals. Subsequently, it would not be unreasonable for the editors in this context to put forward the changes they wanted to make. I would not presume that it was ever the conscious intention of anyone to manipulate or distort my work. But I do believe that given the self-image of neutrality and pragmatism that predominated then and still continues in much of the ESL field (see Benesch, 1993, 2001; Pennycook, 2001), it was the desire of the editors to disengage language from politics and ideology as the pedagogical priority of my article; or in other words, to help "make [my] ideas clearer" for the journal's readers.

THE SUPPORT OF A CRITICAL COMMUNITY

The fact that this debate took place at all is why I characterize this experience as a turning point in my relationship to writing. At an earlier stage in my professional career, I doubt that I would have been so unaccommodating and persistent in challenging the changes being offered. I would likely have been too thrilled by an offer of publication to challenge the parameters assigned to me as a practitioner. What sustained me, in fact, was the support of a strong critical community at OISE. During this time, a small group of graduate students, at various stages including Tara Goldstein, Helen Harper, Ryuko Kubota, Angel Lin, Bonny Norton, Alastair Pennycook, Alice Pitt, Arleen Schenke, and professors such as Jim Cummins and Roger Simon, met on a regular basis to share our ideas, inspirational texts, and our own work as we tentatively explored what it might mean to do critical ESL pedagogies.

I still think of this study group as providing one of most vibrant and formative learning experiences I had at OISE, and it was this critical community that helped give me the confidence to question the authority by which my practice was being named in the journal. On a more personal level, many in this group had read my manuscript and were equally shocked by the changes being proposed. A few said I should pull the article immediately, submit it elsewhere, and/or write about my concerns. The advice with which I felt most comfortable was that I should decide which aspects of the article were essential for me and which were not; then I should be prepared to negotiate and provide careful, reasoned arguments to support my positions.

To this end, my participation in this critical community also provided me with the means—a language of critique—by which a more persuasive, academically sound argument might be formulated. In our many discussions at OISE or over a beer at our favorite local pub, we talked about the history of our profession, its ideological, (neo)colonial and corporatist dimensions (see Canagarajah, 1999; Corson, 1997; Pennycook, 1994; Phillipson, 1992). We used new terms or attached new meanings to old ones: discourse, deconstruction, subjectivity, difference, textuality, to name a few. We also imagined new principles and focal points for ESL: the situatedness of knowledge, the decentered subject, the multivocality of texts, as examples. Realizing the partiality of my profession was fortifying in a sense. Common ways of doing things were not the only ways available, and the key question I could pose was not what is or what is not ESL, but rather, "How did it get to be that way, and why should it remain so?" Such questions helped me argue for the importance of practitioners' experiences and forms of knowledge in ESL theory-formation.

Still, it was probably Foucault's (1982, 1997) work and especially his conceptualization of power/knowledge that was the most influential at this time of critical curiosity. In this configuration, power is not simply a formalized set of laws, institutions or coercive practices that can be periodically shut out of the classroom. Power is always present and produced through the workings of knowledge—in the creation and division of disciplinary fields, systems of measure and evaluation, hierarchies, and continua that define progress and failure, and the spatial arrangements, gestures, and forms of interaction that define our classrooms.

Foucault made me feel that power was not just everywhere, but also somewhere, immediate, and subject to my own small moments of agency. Writing could be both an act of conformity and an act of resistance. The wording and framing of an article did matter, maybe not so much in terms of unveiling new "truths" about language but rather in the sense of limiting the influence of older ones on the critical imagination of practitioners. In my mind, I anticipated other staff meetings in other community centers where a teacher might respond to a supervisor's critique by saying "I tried out this approach after reading an article by Morgan in [a known ELT journal]." Such thoughts made the challenging process of revising my article seem worthwhile.

BRIDGING THE THEORY/PRACTICE DIVIDE

To reiterate, the article on the Gulf War reflected a major shift in my attitude toward academic publishing. Whereas in my earlier encounters, I was sensitized to particular effects of writing—a potential arbiter selectively used by administrators in community programs—the Gulf War publication gave me new insights into the types of rhetorical moves that give writing its authority within a university culture and, subsequently, the criteria by which its effects might be potentially mediated or resisted. As I published more and became more immersed in academic life, I became more responsive to the benefits of writing and the positive changes in habits of thought that can result from the circulation of academic articles. Especially for community ESL practitioners, many of whom work in isolation and have little opportunity for professional development, writing has the potential of introducing exciting and challenging ideas into settings that have become overly familiar.

Nearer the completion of my doctoral studies, I came to look on writing as having dual purposes for my teaching colleagues in community ESL programs. I was too immersed in theories of postmodernism to believe that the ultimate truth or final answer to the "mysteries" of language would ever be discovered, yet I saw writing as a means of provoking new understandings that had important transformative possibilities. At the same time, I continued to recognize the low status of practitioners in the profession and that those who had access to the most current theories and descriptors had authority over those who didn't. In short, my new operating assumption was that writing could always be potentially "dangerous" but also potentially emancipatory, either in terms of what people thought, or in terms of helping them strategically convert those thoughts into action. Accordingly, depending on what was happening at the community center, or what types of issues were being raised in the staff room, I increasingly started bringing articles into work, casually leaving them around the staff table, and commenting on them when someone asked me about their contents.

Two important incidents come to mind. The first involved the issue of homosexuality. The backdrop was Gay Pride week in Toronto, 1998, which every year attracts hundreds of thousands of visitors to the city and heightens awareness of social differences and the need for understanding and tolerance. For most of the students at the center, the week comes as a shock to common-sense values, especially as they witness the semi-official endorsement of the week's events by government—the mayor often leads the parade—and read positive coverage of the same in the mass media. Invariably, students ask teachers questions. My response has always been to emphasize that being gay is more than sex, or love, or what you do in your bedroom, and that it is a "culture" in the same way we view all cultures: a different way of being, responding, and creating. "That's why we need a whole week to celebrate," I tell my students. Some accept this, and others don't.

One of my teaching colleagues was demonstrably unaccepting, and this became an issue in the staff room as she spoke openly of her refusal to do anything but condemn gay lifestyles in front of her students. One day, I decided to bring in a couple of copies of Vandrick's (1997) article, "The Role of Hidden Identities in the Postsecondary ESL Classroom." One of the key recommendations in the article is that instructors take an active role in "demystifying" hidden identities and "attempt to create classrooms where people feel safe and feel they can be open about various aspects of their lives and identities, even if they do not choose to do so" (p. 157). A couple of teachers read the article, and we talked about it informally in the staff room before class and at lunch. In many ways, the article enabled the conversation to occur. It provided focal points and issues to talk about. Most importantly, our colleague realized that many of her peers did not support her prejudices and that expressing them in front of her students, some of whom might be gay, was not a responsible way to perform her duties.

The second incident involved a disagreement between Cindy (a pseudonym), a teacher in a bilingual basic ESL class (Cantonese), and a program supervisor who observed her class for 15 minutes one day and subsequently criticized her for using too much L1 in her instructions. Cindy (personal communication) objected to this criticism on a number of grounds on the basis of her longtime experience at the Chinese community center. First, almost all of the students in her class were seniors, most of whom had had limited formal education in their L1. Cindy told me that as much as she tried to introduce alternative learning strategies into her classroom, her students preferred oral drilling, copying from the blackboard, and the translation and memorization of key vocabulary. In fact, most of her class viewed L1 translation, compilation, and memorization of vocabulary lists as synonymous with learning a second language.

Second, Cindy pointed out that all of her students either live in Chinatown or with their children. From health needs, shopping, or banking to entertainment, information-gathering, or socializing, every aspect of their lives is experienced and communicated through Chinese. Thus the notion that they are motivated to acquire a generic set of tasks, functions, or competencies in their L2 bears no reality to their lives. Yet, they come to class every day. In Cindy's words (personal communication), "They have little expectation of themselves in studying English. To them studying English means going to English class on time and without absence. They want to be certain of everything and do not like to take any risk." Obliging this need for certainty, given the setting and students involved, involves using a comparatively large amount of L1 in the classroom. Not to do so would risk driving students from the program and the closing of the class because of reduced numbers.

After Cindy told me about her supervisor's criticism, we talked about different strategies that she might use to get her students to try using English in class. Later, I gave her a copy of Auerbach's (1993) "Reexamining English Only in the ESL Classroom," and lent her my copy of Cummins' (1996) *Negotiating Identities: Education for Empowerment in a Diverse Society*. I talked about how these two publications in particular had helped me to rethink the place of Chinese in my lessons at the community center. I talked about specific lessons in which I allowed my class—the advanced class at the center(!)—to use a lot of Chinese if they needed because the issues were serious for them and required clarification in L1 first. These kinds of activities made me realize, as Cummins' (1996) text passionately details, that an L1 is not just a set of structures and vocabulary, but is an integral part of one's social identity and dignity.

I cannot say whether my colleague confronted her supervisor with any new insights she garnered from these texts and our discussions. I see the supervisor's error as symptomatic of a foundational problem too common in our profession, and one to which this chapter is addressed: the presumption that personalized and context-adaptive knowledge of a particular setting (i.e., teachers' knowledge) is somehow less rigorous or reliable than the objectifying, rule-generating knowledge that characterizes most academic work (see, e.g., Crookes, 1998; Johnson & Goettsch, 2000; Lynch, 1996; Murphy & Byrd, 2001). At the least, in this incident, I hope that our discussions and the texts gave my colleague more confidence in her own judgment and a willingness to theorize about her experiences and draw on this knowledge when discriminating between competing forms of advice at the community center.

CONCLUSION

From my current vantage point, a completed doctorate behind me, and a new faculty appointment ahead, I appreciate the degree to which a public voice gained through writing has increased my confidence and status in my field. However, in my role as an academic researcher and writer, I still feel a bit of the frustration that I first felt at the start of my teaching career. I resent the fact that practitioners' knowledge and experiences remain undervalued in our profession. I get frustrated when I see TESL organizations promote academic standards in teacher certification but slide around the comparable issue of standard codes of conduct for employers of ESL teachers.

I'm too much of a Foucauldian at heart to think that as a critical applied linguist or a critical ESL pedagogue—a moniker I've never warmed up to—my research and writing will overcome what Mark Clarke (1994) once aptly characterized as a dysfunctional relationship between theorists and practitioners in ESL. As I become immersed in the demands of my new position, I recognize how all-encompassing an academic life can be. Whether or not one is a poststructuralist or a psycholinguist, the danger of becoming self-absorbed in one's own conceptual world is a professional liability to watch out for, especially when working with language practitioners. Similarly, I am also unsure as to whether present or future critical discourses (e.g., postcolonial, cultural, and feminist studies) can ever resolve the issue of "authentic" representation of other voices left by the wayside in academic publishing. Gaining approval from one's critical peers can itself be a form of gatekeeping, where those outside the perimeter come to know themselves—especially what defines them as critical, moral, or ethical—within the terms of inclusion dictated by group membership.

Of course, something gets left behind when we craft for ourselves a critical and ethical identity or voice through writing, and perhaps reflection on this displacement or dispossession can be one of the most insightful aspects of the writing process. In reflecting on the incidents I've described and recognizing the professional transitions in my career, I hope always to retain a small amount of wariness or caution similar to the skepticism with which I first viewed the written word at the community center. On the one hand, this might keep me humble in terms of the emancipatory claims I make for my work. On the other, it may also remind me that whereas current theories limit authorial control in meaning production, it is still my responsibility to take care in the construction of my texts and reflect on their circulation and potential (mis)application in sites of practice.

REFERENCES

Auerbach, E. R. (1993). Reexamining English only in the ESL classroom. *TESOL Quarterly 27*, 9–30.

Benesch, S. (1993). ESL, ideology, and the politics of pragmatism. *TESOL Quarterly, 27*, 705–717.

Benesch, S. (2001) *Critical English for academic purposes.* Mahwah, NJ: Lawrence Erlbaum Associates.

Canagarajah, A. S. (1999). *Resisting English imperialism in English language teaching.* Oxford, England: Oxford University Press.

Clarke, M. (1994). The dysfunctions of the theory/practice discourse. *TESOL Quarterly, 28*, 9–26.

Corson, D. (1997). Critical realism: An emancipatory philosophy for applied linguistics? *Applied Linguistics, 18,* 166–188.

Crookes, G. (1998). On the relationship between second and foreign language teachers and research. *TESOL Journal, 7*(3), 6–11.

Cummins, J. (1996). *Negotiating identities: Education for empowerment in a diverse society.* Ontario, CA: California Association for Bilingual Education.

Foucault, M. (1982). The subject and power. In H. Dreyfus & P. Rabinow (Eds.), *Beyond structuralism* (pp. 208–226). Chicago: University of Chicago Press.

Foucault, M. (1997). Various works. In P. Rabinow (Ed.), *Michel Foucault: Ethics, subjectivity and truth.* New York: The New Press.

Johnston, B., & Goettsch, K. (2000). In search of the knowledge base of language teaching: Explanations by experienced teachers. *Canadian Modern Language Review, 56,* 437–468.

Lynch, B. K. (1996). *Language program evaluation: Theory and practice.* Cambridge, England: Cambridge University Press.

Morgan, B. (1997). The politics of publishing: Positioning critical voices in an ELT Journal. *College ESL, 7*(1), 14–31.

Morgan, B. (1998). *The ESL classroom: Teaching, critical practice, and community development.* Toronto, Ontario, Canada: University of Toronto Press.

Murphy, J., & Byrd, P. (Eds.). (2001). *Understanding the courses we teach: Local perspectives on English language teaching.* Ann Arbor, MI: University of Michigan Press.

Norton, B. (2000). *Identity and language learning: Gender, ethnicity and educational change.* White Plains, NY: Longman/Pearson Education.

Pennycook, A. (1994). *The cultural politics of English as an international language.* London: Longman.

Pennycook, A. (2001). *Critical applied linguistics: A critical introduction.* Mahwah, NJ: Lawrence Erlbaum Associates.

Phillipson, R. (1992). *Linguistic imperialism.* Oxford, England: Oxford University Press.

Simon, R. (1992). *Teaching against the grain.* Toronto, Ontario, Canada: OISE Press.

Toohey, K. (2000). *Learning English at school: Identity, social relations and classroom practice.* Clevedon, England: Multilingual Matters.

Vandrick, S. (1997). The role of hidden identities in the postsecondary ESL classroom. *TESOL Quarterly, 31,* 153–157.

17

Crossing Over: Writing a Life in Two Genres

Martha Clark Cummings
The University of Aizu

Here is my life: I am sitting at the plenary session of an international publisher's conference in a Middle Eastern country where I have been sent by a U.S. government agency. I am listening intently and taking notes as the Director of the Ministry of Education gives a speech on the importance of joy and autonomy in learning. He is my kind of speaker, and I am thoroughly engrossed in his admonishments to teachers to have clear and transparent aims, to set time limits, to make tasks interdependent. But I know myself well enough to take notes on only the right side of my notebook, leaving the left side for the images, colors, sounds that will inevitably come to my attention when my intellect is engaged.

The other list begins:

"If you wear a skirt in this country, it looks like your options are skin-tight boots the color of mustard or black boots with six-inch stiletto heels."

"A number of the women in the audience have hair the color of a ripe plum."

The list continues, including expressions involving clothing that the presenter, not a native speaker of English, uses to make his point:

"We must pull up our socks and roll up our sleeves."

"We were caught with our pants down."

There is a story here. Something about the loneliness of the "specialist" on assignment, the isolation of the "expert" in a foreign country. I continue making notes, all the while listening carefully enough to the presentation, so that afterward, when he asks me how I liked it, I can tell him exactly which parts made the most sense to me.

I am delighted to have come this far. I am a respected professional in two very different worlds, and I wouldn't have it any other way.

I went to Teachers College in 1982 to get an MA in teaching English to speakers of other languages (TESOL) because I wanted to find a way to support myself while I pursued my career as a fiction writer. I was not a scholar. I knew that from the start. But I had been teaching ESL to Swiss Bankers and diplomats from the Iraqi mission to the United Nations for $6.00 an hour when one of my fellow teachers told me that I could earn $30.00 an hour (an enormous sum at the time) if I got an MA. So I went. But all along I felt I was pretending. I wasn't really an academic, not the kind who would go on to publish scholarly articles about theories.

As Joan Didion (1976) put it in her essay, "Why I Write," when she described her own forays into academia, "My attention veered inexorably back to the specific, to the tangible, to what was generally considered, by everyone I knew then and for that matter have known since, the peripheral" (p.18).

I sat in my English Grammar class, thoroughly intrigued by the mysteries of count and noncount nouns, but equally interested in the peculiarly uneven knot in my professor's tie, the spectacularly rumpled look of his eyebrows, the exact angle at which his glasses sat on the bridge of his nose.

I loved graduate school. I loved thinking and reading and spending hours in the library. It was the most fun I'd had in years. And I was good at it. My professors, although bemused as they were with my obsession with inconsequential details, told me I would be doing a disservice to the field if I didn't go on to get a doctorate and then apply for a full-time, tenure-track position in TESOL. I had never been happier, so I stayed. While listening with one ear, I began writing short stories in class. I discovered that all I needed was to be obliged to stay in one place for an hour and a half, with a pen in my hand and a piece of paper in front of me, and a professor lecturing on a topic I was deeply interested in—words—and images would appear in my mind that I had to write down.

Didion (1976) suggests that these images may be what distinguish fiction writers from other writers. We are obsessed with images that hover in our peripheral vision and instead of pushing them away and getting back to the business of thinking about ideas or just plain living our lives, we write them down. At first, most of these images were tied to my childhood. One of the earliest ones went like this:

> The first horse I ever rode was named Velvet. Velvet was an enormous, silky-smooth roan mare, sway-backed and lop-eared and the most beautiful thing I had ever seen in my life. Velvet had a long skinny neck and a scraggly mane but when I looked into her large brown eyes, I knew this animal would change my life forever. I stood on the mounting block, that day after my sixth

birthday, breathing in the rich smell of hay and manure, and watched Shirley, the riding instructor, lead Velvet out of the dark stable. The metal shoes on Velvet's hoofs made sparks fly from the cement floor. She came out into the sunlight, the dust thick in her coat, her soft black nose rising slightly as she ambled over to where I was standing, waiting to be hoisted onto her back. I remember the creak of the leather as I settled into the saddle, the thick, sticky reins that Shirley placed between my fingers, the way she angled my feet to get them into the stirrups, adjusted as short as they would go. Then Shirley swung onto her own horse and took hold of Velvet's bridle to get her started. We were moving! A slow walk felt like a miracle!

I published my first short story the year I graduated with my EdD and got my first tenure-track position at a community college teaching ESL. My dissertation, called "What We Talk About When We Talk About Writing," the title inspired by Raymond Carver's (1980) short story, "What We Talk About When We Talk About Love," was a study of an excellent writing teacher and four of her students talking together in one-to-one writing conferences. It was a combination of ethnography and conversation analysis and informal narrative that was compelling if not traditional and allowed me to take the next step in my academic career.

I had always loved teaching. Although a full-time, tenure-track position was not at all what I had in mind at the outset, the "process" approach to the teaching of writing was in its heyday, and it did and still does make a great deal of sense to me. I wrote with my students. The leading experts in the field—Lucy Calkins, Donald Graves, Donald M. Murray, Ann Raimes, Vivian Zamel—suggested that this was appropriate behavior. I spent the next 4 years writing with my immigrant and refugee students, developing our voices, expressing our feelings, experiencing the creative surge that comes with large doses of encouragement and support. What I wrote in class with my ESL students I eventually worked into both fiction and nonfiction pieces of writing. I will always be grateful to them for helping me become a better writer.

It didn't really matter to my colleagues at the community college whether I wrote and published academic work. What mattered very much to me, of course, was that I continued to be a writer. When I define myself as a writer, I am saying that the act of writing is my access into my own mind and heart. Writing helps me know what I think and feel; it helps me distinguish the significant from the trivial. The only times in my life that I have felt deep despair were times when I was not writing.

When I began winning literary prizes, my colleagues grew suspicious. How was I finding time to write stories good enough to win a grant from the New York Foundation for the Arts? What about my teaching? What about my committee work? And where was that one major contribution I was supposed to make that would change the college forever? When would I find the time to do that?

The answer was that I didn't. I moved to California to teach graduate school instead and was lucky enough to find an institution that did not have rigorous requirements about large numbers of scholarly publications in small numbers of years, an institution that valued teaching. In addition, I was lucky enough to find colleagues and editors, such as Kathi Bailey and David Nunan, who saw the value of the subjective view of life in the classroom. I felt I had been given a second chance.

I left the community college not because I didn't like the job or because I was working toward academic advancement. I still miss my pre-academic ESL students and wish somehow I could have brought them with me. I left the community college because of the stifling busy-work—the endless committee meetings, curricular revisions, written reports on projects that would make no difference. It was, as Donald M. Murray and others have said, "like being bitten to death by ducks." And it seemed to me that teaching graduate school might be very much like eternally attending it, and that both sides of my mind could function well there.

As a person in academia who has the "backstage" life of a fiction writer, I have something to offer students that some other academics perhaps do not: I can partake in their utter bewilderment at the world of abstractions. When I teach second language acquisition, I candidly look up from an article we're discussing, from a section that reads (with apologies to the author),

> Some linguistic knowledge, such as several rules for English articles, and subtle aspects of the use of the T/V distinction to mark power and solidarity in Romance and other languages, is too abstract, complex, or semantically opaque to be understood by linguistically naive learners. Some, such as gender-marking in French and English dative alternation involve too many irregularities and fuzzy categories, and some, such as subject–auxiliary inversion after preposed negative adverbials and uses of whom, are too rare or perceptually nonsalient. (Long, 1996, pp. 426–427)

I ask, sincerely, "Can anyone tell us what this means?" Some students, one or two, react with annoyance. Why am I teaching the course if I don't understand the articles either? Most of them, though, are tremendously relieved. Academia is not an elite society of which they will never become members. Academia is a puzzle, a problem that has a solution. As with my ESL students, my students and I are on a joint venture, trying to understand a way of thinking and expressing ideas that we have not quite found access to yet. But we apply ourselves, each of us wanting to be the one who can solve the mystery for the rest of the class. In my graduate classes, students are likely to jump out of their seats and go to the white board to draw a diagram. "Is this it?" they ask. Others will get up to draw another circle, another arrow. Soon we are feeling both confident that we do in fact understand and tremendously proud of ourselves.

I hold my divided life together by being as true to both sides of myself as I can. Over the years, I have developed a number of habits that allow me to do this. I keep my journal with me at all times. Whether what I write is ultimately published as fiction or nonfiction is not the issue. Maintaining a habit of mindfulness is. And when I see something I can use, something incidental, peripheral, seemingly insignificant, I am ready.

For example, in a story I've been working on lately, a group of people in a cabin on a lake in Maine end a birthday party with a game of "Blow the Feather." The players sit on the floor and stretch a sheet tight between them, holding it up to their chins. It's a little like they're all in a big round bed together. Then one player drops a feather into the middle of the sheet and the other players blow as hard as they can until the feather goes over another player's shoulder. The person whose shoulder the feather goes over must remove an article of clothing. The winner is the person who is wearing something, anything at all—one sock, for instance—at the end of the game.

Observing my colleagues with this particular scene in mind makes faculty meetings infinitely more entertaining, as well as getting the job done of populating the story with realistic characters. Eventually, I come up with a scene like this:

> The feather danced. It was a large fat feather Phoebe had yanked from one of the pillows on the bed upstairs. We puffed out our cheeks and blew, hard, until it sailed, like a drunken moth, over Walter's shoulder. Walter blushed, the red blotches starting on his chest and swiftly traveling up his neck, his cheeks, to the roots of his hair. His wire-rimmed glasses glinted so that we couldn't see the expression in his eyes. He smiled awkwardly and hesitated. Walter was from Germany and spoke more languages than everyone else in the room put together, but for the moment he was speechless. Then he surprised us all by unbuttoning his tan cardigan sweater and shrugging it off his shoulders, slowly, like a stripper.

I look for opportunities to hone my writing skills. I am always happy to do observations of my colleagues, and they are no longer surprised to find segments like this in the drafts of my observation reports:

> Estelle lumbers in, 6 minutes late, her heavy self swathed in a sweat suit. She sits at the end of the conference table, as far as she can get from Irene, the teacher, and looks at her, intently, unsmiling. She leans so far back in her chair it seems it might tip over backwards. And she answers every one of Irene's questions, whether called on or not, sometimes in a voice loud enough to be heard, sometimes sotto voce.

> She stares, unblinking, unsmiling, as if she wants to pin Irene to the wall like a specimen. Actually she makes me think of a sex criminal in a mystery starring Helen Mirren. I would be nervous if I were Irene.

Estelle sighs audibly, squirms in her chair, rocks back and forth. Her eyes are still; the rest of her can't stop moving. It seems to me she wants to be the teacher's pet and the rebel at the same time. She wants to misbehave and still be loved. She wants to get all the answers right and still be able to reach under the table for her bag, over and over again, fumbling through it for a pen, then a drink, then a piece of gum. She wants to flip through the pages of her notebook loudly, interrupt Irene in the middle of an explanation to ask a question, whisper to the student next to her as soon as Irene turns away to write on the board, and still be the favored student.

I steal, and encourage my students to do likewise. I learned about using other writers' work as models from Raymond Carver, who stole from Chekhov. I realized this when I read Carver's story, "What We Talk About When We Talk About Love," and then read Chekhov's story, "Concerning Love," and saw how very similar they were. This discovery was a great relief to me, taking away the pressure of trying to be original. I decided to try my hand at this kind of modeling. Carver's story starts like this:

My friend Mel McGinnis was talking. Mel McGinnis is a cardiologist, and sometimes that gives him the right.

The four of us were sitting around his kitchen table drinking gin. Sunlight filled the kitchen from the big window behind the sink. There were Mel and me and his second wife, Theresa—Terri, we called her—and my wife, Laura. We lived in Albuquerque then. But we were all from somewhere else. (Carver, 1980, p. 137)

The beginning of my story, "Love Stories," starts like this:

Kevin lingers in the doorway, his red bathing suit still damp, his eyes blood-shot, as if unable to decide if he wants to come in or not. Then he has decided and the screen door slaps shut behind him. Outside, the scrub pines hunch on the edge of the lawn and the sun shines golden as it nears the horizon. Bobby and I are sitting in the small room off the kitchen that should be a sun porch but isn't. We are visiting our friend, Ann, on Martha's Vineyard. Ann gave up a tenure-track position at the same university we all teach for to work as the cook at a health food store here. We can't decide if she's lost her mind or if she's the only one of us with any sense. She puts her glass of Scotch down so hard that some of it flies out of the glass and spills onto the table, seeping into the old wood. But she's always been a heavy drinker.

I share these secrets with my students. I remind them again and again that they don't have to be original, that there are models everywhere, just waiting to help them get started, whatever kind of writing they want to do.

I keep writing by searching out other writers who want to give and receive feedback, finding audiences and allies. At home I have my partner, Lisa Vice, a first-rate novelist and short-story writer, who believes in me and my work totally and is willing to support and nurture me every step of the way. She can tell me in very specific and concrete ways what she loves about my writing, and I find I cannot do without her immediate and articulate feedback.

When I was away from home, teaching at the Monterey Institute of International Studies in California, and my colleague, Renee Jourdenais, expressed an interest in getting some writing done, I pounced. Renee is a scholar and her writing is academic, but she was willing to work with me because I promised her serious feedback. As an audience for a scholarly writer, I am as demanding a reader as can be. I need every concept defined and exemplified. I need the prose to be crystal clear. I refuse to deal with jargon. I want my worldview to be altered. Renee and I set up a schedule, gave each other deadlines, read each other's drafts, and kept writing.

In this matter of writing for publication, audience is crucial: a personal and supportive audience to begin with, followed by a larger and largely anonymous audience, where our voices can be heard. And there is room in academia for more voices than are being heard now. We are not all going to publish articles in *TESOL Quarterly* or *Language Learning*, nor are we all going to publish short stories in *The New Yorker* or *The Atlantic*, but there is a vast world between those extremes, waiting to hear from us. There is also a world between the extremes of David Lodge's hilariously funny novels describing academia, such as *Changing Places* (1975), and *Small World* (1984), and David Mendelson's (1999) tremendously moving "Untunneling Our Vision: Lessons From a Great Educator." There is room in the world of academia for all kinds of writers.

We must find our own voices and make sure they are heard. Somewhere between the folly of pretending that scholarly writing doesn't matter and the rigidity of insisting it matters more than anything, we must find our answer, searching always for the clearest path to our own intellectual and creative powers.

I can't say that I understand why I must live this divided life, with only "a foot in the world of ideas" as David Nunan put it (1999), but I have come to accept myself without doubt, blame, criticism, or resistance. If I must be a fiction writer working as an academic, so be it. I have tried to give up one for the other and have been unable to. I will live the rest of my life divided. And I will keep writing.

REFERENCES

Carver, R. (1981). What we talk about when we talk about love. In *What we talk about when we talk about love* (pp. 137–154). New York: Knopf.

Didion, J. (1976, December 5). Why I write. *The New York Times Book Review,* pp. 2, 98–99.

Lodge, D. (1975). *Changing places.* New York: Viking Penguin.

Lodge, D. (1984). *Small world.* New York: Macmillan.

Long, M. (1996). The role of the linguistic environment in second language acquisition. In W. Ritchie, & T. Bhatia (Eds.), *Handbook of second language acquisition* (pp. 413–468). San Diego, CA: Academic Press.

Mendelsohn, D. (1999). Janusz Korczak. Untunneling our vision: Lessons from a great educator. In D. J. Mendelsohn (Ed.), *Expanding our vision: Insights for language teachers* (pp. 174–186).Toronto, Ontario, Canada: Ontario University Press.

Nunan, D. (1999). A foot in the world of ideas: Graduate study through the Internet. *Language Learning & Technology, 3,* 52–74. Retrieved January, 2000 from: http://llt.msu.edu/vol3num1/nunan/

AUTHOR BIOSTATEMENTS

DWIGHT ATKINSON

I am a middle-aged, middle-class, white, male American academic, with all the constraints and advantages that this social position provides. My experiences as an academic writer are no doubt very much influenced by this positionality. At the same time I hope and believe that my views on writing do not reduce merely to my placement in various social categories. I hope that something in my experience as a writer is generalizable and can be shared with others. Or else what is the point of writing?

I am presently employed as a visiting professor at Temple University in Tokyo and Osaka, Japan. I work largely with doctoral students in Second Language Education, and a substantial part of what I do, from my perspective, is teach writing. That is, my students learn the ropes of academic writing by investing themselves seriously in developing their identities as academic researchers. This is, I believe, how most if not all serious learning takes place, in writing as in all other areas—by trying to "be somebody," by trying to "join a club."

Books that have inspired me as a writer:

Heath, S. B. (1983). *Ways with words: Language, life, and work in communities and classrooms.* Cambridge, England: Cambridge University Press.
Clark, A. (1997). *Being there: Putting brain, body, and world together again.* Cambridge, MA: MIT Press.
Foucault, M. (1977). *The archeology of knowledge.* New York: Pantheon.
Geertz, C. (1973). *Interpretation of cultures.* New York: Basic Books.

LINDA LONON BLANTON

Writing suits me. I say that because it lets me be public, but not too public. On paper, I can be bold. I can be funny. I can speak. Then I can retire. But standing in front of an audience, my knees shake. I get butterflies. I cannot think on my feet.

Yet in terms of participation and identity, my difference between writing and speaking publicly was not always evident to me. It had no way to form, to be. Although I recognized my shaky public speaking voice, my public writing struck me as having no voice at all. In it, I could not discern myself. So, for much of my now-long professional life, I was not sure that public writing suited me at all. It fit me like someone else's suit ... a generic, gray one, or actually more like armor.

Then I came across the writings of other academics that challenged views and voiced opinions I had not been bold enough to challenge or voice. Academic writers like Susan Miller, who argued that compositionists foster their own cultural marginalization by assuming their assigned self-sacrificial identity. Writers like Andrea Fishman, whose qualitative research on literacy helped me understand how individualized—how nongeneric and thoughtful—both research and writing for publication can be. Writers like Jane Tompkins, who approached—head on—issues of gender, academic writing, and individualized voice. And like Shirley Brice Heath, who showed me that academic research and writing, in addition to voicing its author, can give voice to those who don't or can't speak for themselves. Encouraged, I began to work at actualizing a writing place, an identity, for my self. Now I can say that—to a greater degree—writing suits me. Even public writing.

Books and chapters that have inspired me:

Fishman, A. (1988). *Amish literacy: What and how it means.* Portsmouth, NH: Heinemann.
Heath, S. B. (1983). *Ways with words: Language, life, and work in communities and classrooms.* Cambridge, England: Cambridge University Press.
Miller, S. (1991). *Textual carnivals: The politics of composition.* Carbondale and Edwardsville, IL: Southern Illinois University Press.
Tompkins, J. (1991). Me and my shadow. In R.R. Warhol & D.P. Herndl (Eds.), *Feminisms: An anthology of literary theory and criticism* (pp. 1079–1092). New Brunswick, NJ: Rutgers University Press.

GEORGE BRAINE

Growing up in Sri Lanka as a bilingual, I read voraciously in both English and Sinhala. I have no doubt that the love of reading and the need to tell my own stories motivated me to write. As far as academic–scholarly writing is concerned, I had no instruction in terms of writing courses, not even in graduate school in the States. I learned to write by teaching freshmen composition (a step ahead of my hapless students) and by modeling my articles on the ones I liked in scholarly journals.

Now in Hong Kong, I teach a graduate course in second language writing, which provides the incentive for me to keep up with the scholarship in the field. I still read, but almost entirely in English. In the pressure cooker that is Hong Kong, I retain my sanity with the help of *The New Yorker*, with its long-winded and meandering articles.

Over the years, I have lost the ability to write at length in Sinhala. I continue to read Sinhala newspapers and magazines, though I doubt if they influence my writing in any way.

A. SURESH CANAGARAJAH

My educational and professional lives have involved constant shuttling between communities in the East and West, which has generated some unresolved conflicts for my writing practice. I had my secondary and tertiary education in Sri Lanka in the vernacular (with English as an additional subject). There was little meta-talk about processes of writing there. The implicit standards were expressive. When I moved to the United States for my graduate studies in 1985, I was surprised to discover that there were rules for academic writing and that readers here had a keen sensitivity to the finished product. Though I greeted the punitive editing of my essays by my instructors with disbelief and amusement, I was attracted by the research attention given to writing here.

Conducting a study of the literate practices of African-American students for my doctorate and presenting my findings in a rigorously constructed dissertation, I thought I had mastered the conventions of academic writing. When I returned to teach in my hometown at the University of Jaffna in 1990, I was surprised to find that my thoughtful thesis statements and topic sentences created an image of someone self-centered and overconfident. The preferred opening moves there emphasized humility and respect for the reader in a largely end-weighted structure of development. Rediscovering the laudable values behind my vernacular discourse, I strove to use a discourse that accommodated my vernacular background. Perhaps the early 90s were too early for rhetorical experimentation in papers I published in journals like *TESOL Quarterly* and *Language in Society*. Being a newcomer to the academic publishing scene didn't help either. It would take articles in *ELT Journal* and *Written Communication* in the late 90s for me to do anything mildly experimental in my research writing. My forthcoming *A Geopolitics of Academic Writing* (University of Pittsburgh Press) is the most daring in my rhetorical creativity. Still, each piece of writing presents challenges of its own, and I haven't resolved all the conflicts I face between the vernacular and English, the Sri Lankan and Anglo-American, in me.

The publications that have proved useful for my understanding of writing are not those dealing with writing per se, but those indirectly dealing with the place of writing in other fields of study:

Foucault, M. (1972). The discourse on language. In *The archeology of knowledge* (pp. 215–237). New York: Pantheon.

Geisler, C. (1994). *Academic literacy and the nature of expertise: Reading, writing, and knowing in academic philosophy.* Hillsdale, NJ: Lawrence Erlbaum Associates.

Marcus, G., & Fischer, M .M. J. (1986). *Anthropology as cultural critique: An experimental moment in the human sciences.* Chicago: University of Chicago Press.

Myers, G. (1990). *Writing biology: Texts in the social construction of scientific knowledge.* Madison, WI: University of Wisconsin Press.

CHRISTINE PEARSON CASANAVE

While finishing up doctoral work at Stanford as an "older" student, I spent a year teaching in the TESOL program at the Monterey Institute of International Studies, where I had also gotten my MA. It was then that I realized that I was a language teacher educator at heart. I then headed off for what I guess turned out to be my main career as an English language and applied linguistics professor at a Japanese university and as a part-time instructor in the MATESOL program at the Tokyo campus of Teachers College Columbia University. True, I needed a job and the one at Keio University came along at the right time, but as a language teacher I also wanted to experience what it was like to be a zero-level totally illiterate learner living in a foreign country. Describing this masochistic experience would require a book in itself. However, I did not immerse myself in Japanese language and culture the way a Krashen fan would. My work with students and colleagues was nearly all in English, and never knowing for sure when I would be returning to the States, I was determined to keep up my researching and writing for publication as a way to keep myself involved with the field. For over a decade, then, I was both a language learner (self-study) and a "student" of second language education, studying, reading, and writing in order to stay connected with issues and people in research and scholarship, particularly in the area of second language writing. I also think that something has always attracted me about immersing myself in books and articles and ideas and then trying to squeeze out lines of words in print, as agonizing as this process often is for me. I think the most interesting part of my more recent professional life has been learning how the book and article publishing process works, the social and political parts of it in particular.

Some of my favorite books and articles about writing and research:

Brodkey, L. (1996). Writing on the bias. In L. Brodkey, *Writing permitted in designated areas only* (pp. 30–51). Minneapolis, MN: University of Minnesota Press.
Dillard, A. (1989). *The writing life.* New York: HarperCollins Publishers.
Heilbrun, C. (1988). *Writing a woman's life.* New York: Ballantine Books.
Rosaldo, R. (1987). Where objectivity lies: The rhetoric of anthropology. In J. Nelson, A. Megill, & D. McCloskey (Eds.), *The rhetoric of the human sciences* (pp. 87–110). Madison, WI: University of Wisconsin Press.
Rosaldo, R. (1989, 1993). *Culture and truth: The remaking of social analysis.* Boston: Beacon Press.
Van Maanen, J. (1988). *Tales of the field: On writing ethnography.* Chicago: University of Chicago Press.
Woolf, V. (1929). *A room of one's own.* New York: Harcourt, Brace, Jovanovich.

MARTHA CLARK CUMMINGS

What can I tell you about myself that I haven't already said in my chapter? As I write this, I am between jobs, sitting in my log cabin in Thermopolis, Wyoming, getting ready to pack everything I own, rent the house and move to Aizu-Wakamatsu, Japan, where I will again take up an academic position, and again hope that it will inspire me as a fiction writer. My partner, Lisa Vice, the greatest writer I know, will be there with me.

Sources that have inspired me as a writer, writing teacher, and teacher educator (a few others appear in Appendix E: Selected Resources on Writing and Publishing):

Berthoff, A. (1984). *Reclaiming the imagination: Philosophical perspectives for writers and teachers of writing.* Upper Montclair, NJ: Boynton/Cook Publishers.
Murray, D. (1989). *Expecting the unexpected :Teaching myself—and others—to read and write.* Portsmouth, NH: Boynton/Cook.
Ray, R. (1994). *The weekend novelist.* New York: Dell Publishing.
Rose, M. (1989). *Lives on the boundary.* New York: Viking Penguin.
Solotaroff, T. (1987). *A few good voices in my head.* New York: Harper & Row.
Stafford, W. (1987). *You must revise your life.* Ann Arbor, MI: The University of Michigan Press.
Vice, L. (1995). *Reckless driver.* New York: Dutton.
Vice, L. (1998). *Preacher's lake.* New York: Dutton.

JOHN HEDGCOCK

In my early days as a graduate student, I viewed writing as a means to an end: I wrote papers because they were assigned, and I knew they were assigned in order to evaluate my skills and knowledge. It did not occur to me that to become a competent academic, I would eventually have to carve a niche as an author. I began my graduate studies in Romance Languages and Literatures, composing the majority of my writing assignments (including an MA thesis) in a foreign language. From the outset, writing for me was complex and intense because the process was tied not only to my emergent role as a reader and thinker, but also to my identity as a language learner.

After enrolling in an applied linguistics doctoral program, I had a frightening epiphany: My professional life would henceforth involve a lot of writing. At the time, I was teaching undergraduate and graduate courses on English for Academic Purposes. How could I teach academic writing when I wasn't even an accomplished academic writer of English myself? After all, I had received no explicit writing instruction (in any language). Not unlike many in the TESOL profession, I learned by doing, discovering along the way that I loved teaching writing and that I also loved the challenge of working through problems in my own academic prose. In reflecting honestly on the factors that have most tangibly shaped my identity as a writer, I realize that I came into the practice of writing through a back door. I owe most of what I know about writing to the experience of teaching it. I still wonder about that paradox: It seems to me that a teacher, especially a teacher of a skill as complex and important as writing, ought to undergo formal training and then practice that discipline before accepting the privilege of teaching it. That's not what happened to me, yet I now realize the significance of what I have learned from my student writers over the years. I suspect that I have perhaps learned much more from them than they may have learned from me.

Sources that have inspired me as a writer, writing teacher, and teacher educator:

American Psychological Association. (2001). *Publication manual of the American Psychological Association* (5th ed.). Washington, DC: American Psychological Association.

Elbow, P. (1981). *Writing with power: Techniques for mastering the writing process.* New York: Oxford University Press.

Smith, F. (1988). *Joining the literacy club: Further essays into education.* Portsmouth, NH: Heinemann.

Smith, F. (1994). *Writing and the writer* (2nd ed.). Hillsdale, NJ: Lawrence Erlbaum Associates.

RYUKO KUBOTA

As a native of Japan, I received my education there, from elementary school through undergraduate. I began writing actively for publication in my late 30s with the motivation to keep my university teaching position in the United States. As writing became my daily habit, I came to enjoy its challenge. I am currently an associate professor at the University of North Carolina at Chapel

Hill. As one of only a few Asian professors, I face some unique challenges. People around me often comment how "tiny" I am. They perhaps see me as a small, quiet Asian lady, rather than an intellectually capable researcher. A student teacher I supervise introduces me to his high school class, "This Dr. Kubota. A very smart lady." It must be hard for some to believe by looking at me that I am a scholar and a teacher educator. In my daily life, I work against such stereotypes. Writing, however, frees me up from this obstacle. Because my appearance is invisible to the readers, I am judged on the basis of what I write and how I write it, rather than how I look.

I have been inspired by many authors with their brilliant, innovative, and provocative ideas as well as their magical techniques to make abstract ideas accessible. These authors include Harumi Befu, Jim Cummins, Rosina Lippi-Green, Sonia Nieto, Yoshio Sugimoto, and Guadalupe Valdés.

ENA LEE

I'm currently pursuing a PhD degree in the Department of Language and Literacy Education at the University of British Columbia and am indebted to my supervisor, Bonny Norton, for inviting me to contribute to the writing of this chapter. This is my first publication, and I'm excited and relieved that it was written in collaboration with her, as she was able to "show me the ropes" from its initial conceptualization to its fruition here. I'm sure very few are able to start off their academic writing careers in such comfort!

In terms of my writing, I'm inspired when I'm able to see and hear writers in their work; bell hooks is one such author. The passion in her words and ideas seems to emanate from the page. Also, in readings I've done thus far as a graduate student, I've also come to really appreciate writing that is both thought-provoking and insightful but at the same time clear and concise. Here, Alastair Pennycook and Elsa Auerbach come to mind.

Regarding the technical side of my writing, I've been at a loss to find a book that has really assisted me with my academic writing aspirations, but this is where I hope this very collection can fill this void. I expect this book will be the "bread and butter" that I and other graduate students like me can finally refer to and count on throughout our academic studies. Publishing world, here I come!

The books that have inspired me:

Auerbach, E. R. (1995). The politics of the ESL classroom: Issues of power in pedagogical choices. In J. W. Tollefson (Ed.), *Power and inequality in language education* (pp. 9–33). New York: Cambridge University Press.

hooks, b. (1994). *Teaching to transgress: Education as the practice of freedom*. New York: Routledge.

Pennycook, A. (2001). *Critical applied linguistics: A critical introduction*. Mahwah, NJ: Lawrence Erlbaum Associates.

ILONA LEKI

My very first teaching job was in France teaching English without any real training in how to do that. Then, after teaching French for several years (something I did know how to do), I started teaching L2 writing, again, like most others at the time, before I really knew much about that either. Despite my ignorance, I wanted to help my L2 students write more easily and successfully, and frankly I also wanted to spare myself the excruciating boredom of reading the sad, stilted papers about nothing that were coming out of my writing classes. I was lucky enough to tune in to the professional conversation just at the time that people like McCrorie and Elbow were suggesting ways to rid L1 writing classes of those same sad, stilted papers about nothing. My own academic writing textbook grew out of that constellation of encounters and eventually so did my desire to participate in that professional conversation. The next step for me came as I realized how little my junior colleagues and my colleagues teaching L1 writing understood what it was like to try to create academic texts in L2. Thinking that I now did know something about this issue myself, I worked towards publishing what I knew. Realizing then that in fact I hardly knew anything about the real academic writing tasks facing my students outside my L2 writing classes, I have most recently turned toward trying to understand better what challenges they face and how they are able to meet them as they move through the university curriculum. I have come to recognize that although final answers to questions about human language learning and behavior won't be forthcoming in my lifetime, we have, nevertheless, come a long way thanks to the efforts of those who have been willing to share their insights by engaging in the (often laborious, sometimes painful) job of scholarly research and publication.

Influential books in my life:

Berlin, J. (1987). *Rhetoric and reality: Writing instruction in American colleges, 1900–1985.* Carbondale, IL: Southern Illinois University Press.

Crowley, S. (1998). *Composition in the university: Historical and polemical essay.* Pittsburgh, PA: University of Pittsburgh Press.

Donovan, T., & McClelland, B. (Eds.). (1980). *Eight approaches to teaching composition.* Urbana, IL: National Council of Teachers of English.

Elbow, P. (1981). *Writing without teachers.* New York: Oxford University Press.

Lincoln, Y. & Guba, E. (1985). *Naturalistic inquiry.* Newbury Park, CA: Sage.

McCrorie, K. (1970). *Uptaught.* New York: Hayden Book Co.

North, S. (1987). *The making of knowledge in composition: Portrait of an emerging field.* Portsmouth, NH: Heinemann Boynton/Cook.

Russell, D. (1991). *Writing in the academic disciplines, 1870–1990: A curricular history.* Carbondale, IL: Southern Illinois University Press.

Shaughnessy, M. (1977). *Errors and expectations.* New York: Oxford University Press.

PAUL KEI MATSUDA

I'm no longer a graduate student, but I continue to draw on my own experience to help other graduate students engage in various professional activities, including writing for publication. Currently, I am Assistant Professor of English at the University of New Hampshire, where I teach various writing courses as well as graduate courses in composition, rhetoric, and applied linguistics. While I was a graduate student, I published in journals such as *Academic Writing*, *College Composition and Communication*, *Composition Studies*, the *Journal of Second Language Writing*, and *Written Communication*. I've also coedited a few books, including *Landmark Essays on ESL Writing* (Erlbaum, 2001) and *On Second Language Writing* (Erlbaum, 2001). I'm a die-hard night owl—I usually stay up until 4 a.m. writing, but sleep until around noon whenever I can. I spend a lot of time on the Internet, creating webpages and occasionally writing personal essays in Japanese. When I'm not writing or teaching, I enjoy cooking, watching Japanese TV shows, and listening to Japanese pop music.

This is not a book, but it has had a significant impact on my attitude toward research and publication—especially the part where Bernstein and Woodward go through a huge number of library check-out records:

Coblenz, W. (Producer), & Pakula, A. J. (Director). (1976). "All the president's men" [Film]. Burbank, CA: Time Warner Company.

SANDRA LEE MCKAY

I began my professional writing with a book on writing (*Writing for a Specific Purpose*, with Lisa Rosenthal, Prentice-Hall). I wrote the book for an undergraduate writing class that I was teaching at the time. I found that these students often had difficulty writing because they felt they had no audience or purpose for their writing. My plan was to give them an audience and purpose by providing them with an imaginary voice and purpose based on writing tasks they might face in their professional life. Although I still firmly believe that writers need to have a clear sense of audience and purpose to write well, I realize now that no one can give another person these things.

As for my own audiences and purposes in writing, most of my writing has been based on my teaching. Many of my books were written on topics and for students I was teaching at the time at San Francisco State University, whether it was a writing, sociolinguistics, or TESOL methodology class. More recently, my purposes in writing have come from a need to formulate my philosophical stance regarding the teaching of English. For example, my most recent book (*Teaching English as an International Language: Rethinking Goals and Approaches*, Oxford University Press) was written largely because of my experiences of teaching English in a great variety of countries including Hungary, South Africa, Chile, Singapore, Japan, Thailand, Hong Kong and the Philippines. These experiences led me to believe that it is time for the way English is taught to reflect the fact that English is a language that no longer belongs to the West or to so-called native speakers of English.

I am certain that new experiences I have will lead me to again begin a new article or book in the need to clarify my own thoughts and, in the process, I hope to make some contribution to my professional community.

An article that has inspired me is that by Shen, which opened my eyes to the issue of culture, identity, and writing:

Shen, F. (1989). The classroom and the wider culture. Identity as a key to learning English composition. *College Composition and Communication, 40*(1), 459–466.

A book that has influenced my approach to the teaching of writing:

Kern, R. (2000). *Literacy and language teaching.* Oxford, England: Oxford University Press.

BRIAN MORGAN

As my mom and dad like to remind me, around the age of four I seemed to have developed an acute sense of fairness demonstrated by several short-lived attempts to leave home with a large bag of sandwiches in protest to the parental injustices I perceived. Over time, I transferred this awareness on to broader concerns, gradually becoming fascinated by and alert to the potency of language in the shaping of social realities. This awareness remains a significant influence on how I approach L2 writing pedagogy. Another formative aspect has been music. For most of my life I have been performing and composing music to some extent and often find myself listening to the soundscape of ideas as much as reading their content. The unfortunate side to this is that the writing and revising process can be painfully slow—and notably "unproductive" in terms of academic career enhancement. The upside is that I've come to appreciate and value the pleasure that texts can bring to both writers and readers, even when their intentions are serious. These two lifelong influences, the critical–social and the aesthetic–expressive (or self-indulgent!), can create personal dissonance; harmonizing them in print remains an enduring challenge.

Influential books related to L2 writing (three I've been using recently):

Benesch, S. (2001). *Critical English for academic purposes.* Mahwah, NJ: Lawrence Erlbaum Associates.

Collins, P. (2001). *Community writing: Researching social issues through writing.* Mahwah, NJ: Lawrence Erlbaum Associates.

Pennycook, A. (2001). *Critical applied linguistics: A critical introduction.* Mahwah, NJ: Lawrence Erlbaum Associates.

BONNY NORTON

In the context of an insanely busy life in the Department of Language and Literacy Education at the University of British Columbia, writing represents both opportunity and challenge. The opportunity is to use the written word to help make sense of my life as a researcher and teacher. Without the opportunity to reflect on educational issues that are important to me, I feel I have little control over my life. The challenge, of course, is to make time to write, time that is often "stolen" from other demands and commitments. Worse, I cannot write if my life is in chaos! So I have to "clear my desk" literally and figuratively in order to organize my thoughts. I am constantly thankful that I have access to word processors, printers, and a good paper recycling program.

Academic writers who inspire me are those whose writing is both informative and engaging. Barbara Tuchman is one of my favorite authors, as are Oliver Sacks and Stuart Hall. I loved *Galileo's Daughter* by Dava Sobel, and I'm currently reading *A Primate's Memoir* by Robert Sapolsky. Where's that comfortable chair?

Books and chapters that have inspired me:

Hall, S. (1992). The question of cultural identity. In S. Hall, D. Held, and T. McGrew (Eds.), *Modernity and its futures* (pp. 273–325). Cambridge, UK: Polity Press.

Sacks, O. W. (1989). *Seeing voices: A journey into the world of the deaf.* Berkeley, CA: University of California Press.

Sapolsky, R. M. (2001). *A primate's memoir.* New York: Scribner.

Sobel, D. (1999). *Galileo's daughter: A historical memoir of science, faith, and love.* New York: Walker & Co.

Tuchman, B. W. (1978). *A distant mirror: The calamitous fourteenth century.* New York: Random House.

ANETA PAVLENKO

At the point of submitting this biographical sketch, I still see writing as fun and revisions as an enjoyable collaborative process. I am still working at Temple University with wonderful students and colleagues. I aim to offer my students multiple opportunities to develop into academic writers, including the recently created Working Papers. As my chapter already provides the reader with a very good idea of who I am and what I do, I would like to use this sketch to acknowledge the coconstructed nature of my academic biography and to thank several individuals who helped me enter the scholarly community: Howard Marblestone (who trusted that I could do graduate work); Jim Lantolf (who encouraged me to explore and branch out in all possible directions, and who just let me be myself); Barbara Legendre (who, simply speaking, taught me how to write), the editors of *Bilingualism: Language and Cognition* (François Grosjean and Judy Kroll), *Applied Linguistics* (Claire Kramsch), *The International Journal of Bilingualism* (Li Wei), and *Multilingua* (Richard Watts); my anonymous reviewers; and, of course, an outstanding community of friends, peers, coauthors, and coeditors who continuously offer me their valuable feedback and advice and provide me with an inspiration: Adrian Blackledge, Jean-Marc Dewaele, Scott Jarvis, Yasuko Kanno, Michele Koven, Ingrid Piller, Bob Schrauf, and Marya Teutsch-Dwyer. And last but not least, I receive daily help and support from the two most wonderful men in the world, Doug and Nik. Their faith in me and my work, belief in untraditional arrangements (where a woman writes more than she cooks and cleans), willingness to take over household responsibilities, and amazing sense of humor allow me to continue my scholarly pursuits without guilt-tripping at every step.

Among the books that inspire my writing pursuits and remind me that second language users can be legitimate writers are:

Antin, M. (1912/1969). *The promised land.* Princeton, NJ: Princeton University Press.
Codrescu, A. (1990). *The disappearance of the outside.* Reading, MA: Addison-Wesley.
Danquah, M. N. (Ed.). (2000). *Becoming American: Personal essays by first generation immigrant women.* New York: Hyperion.
Hoffman, E. (1989). *Lost in translation. A life in a new language.* New York: Dutton.
Kellman, S. (2000). *The translingual imagination.* Lincoln, NE: The University of Nebraska Press.
Mori, K. (1997). *Polite lies: On being a woman caught between cultures.* New York: Henry Holt.
Novakovich, J., & Shapard, R. (Eds.). (2000). *Stories in the stepmother tongue.* Buffalo, NY: White Pine Press.

My favorite book that challenges traditional women's narratives is:

Heilbrun, C. (1988). *Writing a woman's life.* New York: Ballantine Books.

I also deeply believe that no woman in academia should find herself without:

Toth, E. (1997). *Ms. Mentor's impeccable advice for women in academia.* Philadelphia: University of Pennsylvania Press.

MIYUKI SASAKI

My life is quite typical of many other EFL learners in that I started to study English when I was 12 in the highly controlled Japanese educational system. I never used English as a means of communication until I went to the University of Michigan as a senior-year exchange student. I majored in English education as an undergraduate student at Hiroshima University, and in TESL–applied linguistics as a graduate student at Georgetown University and the University of California, Los Angeles. Now that I have studied English for almost 30 years, it is truly embarrassing to confess in this essay how much of a struggle I still have to go through to write just one paper in English. In spite of all of my past ESL and EFL teachers' well-meaning advice of "trying to think in English when writing in English," I simply cannot think in English when I write in English, which might severely slow down my English writing process (but I honestly can't help thinking in Japanese, my first language, when I have to write a complex research paper). In this essay, I also broke my own taboo of not publicly talking about my private life, especially about my children. I still feel hesitant about making family life an excuse for unproductivity as a researcher. But I am now grateful that the editors made me break this taboo by giving me the opportunity to write about my life, not only as a researcher, but also as a whole person. I sincerely hope that they are right in predicting that my story will be interesting and helpful to at least some readers.

Key books that have inspired me greatly about writing:

American Psychological Association. (1994). *Publication Manual of the American Psychological Association* (4th ed.). Washington, DC: American Psychological Association.
Kawakita, J. (1967). *Hassouhou* [Abduction: Ways of producing new ideas]. Tokyo: Chuoukouronsha.
Kinoshita, K. (1981). *Rikakei no Sakubun Gijutu* [Writing techniques for science writing]. Tokyo: Chuo Koronsha.
Tachibana, T. (1995). *Boku wa Konna Hon wo Yondekita* [The books I have read]. Tokyo: Bungeishunjuu.

STEPHANIE VANDRICK

I was born in Canada, grew up in India, went to college in Michigan, have spent my whole teaching career in San Francisco, and am married to an Iranian-American, so in a sense a career teaching ESL seemed and seems like a good fit for me. At the University of San Francisco I teach ESL, writing, literature, women's studies, and combinations thereof. I most often write about feminist and critical pedagogies, identity issues in ESL, and the use of literature in ESL classes.

I have always been a voracious, actually addicted, reader, and have always been fascinated with the power of narrative and stories for education, entertainment, illumination, and comfort. My academic writing has always tended toward the qualitative–essayistic rather than the quantitative, and I have welcomed the increasing (albeit still controversial) acceptance of writing on social and political contexts of teaching. In trying to bring together various aspects of my background and interests, I have recently begun experimenting with writing personal–professional narratives such as those the other contributors and I have written for this book.

A few of the books on writing that have inspired me:

Lamott, A. (1994). *Bird by bird: Some instructions on writing and life.* New York: Pantheon.
Welty, E. (1984). *One writer's beginnings.* Cambridge, MA: Harvard University Press.
Woolf, V. (1929). *A room of one's own.* New York: Harcourt Brace Jovanovich.

APPENDIXES

Summary of Basic Steps in Journal Article and Book Publishing

JOURNAL ARTICLES

- Choose an appropriate journal.
- Follow manuscript guidelines carefully.
- Submit as clean a draft as possible to the current editor of the journal. Depending on the journal, you might need to send the manuscript electronically, with or without a hard copy and floppy disk sent separately.
- Send your manuscript to only one journal at a time.
- If the journal is refereed, the editor will decide whether to send your article out for review. If the journal is not refereed, the editor will make decisions.
- If you receive reviews, pay attention to (but do not be bound by) the (sometimes conflicting) suggestions. Note that "revise and resubmit" is not a rejection. Decide whether to revise and send to the same journal, revise and send to another journal, or not to revise, but send to another journal.
- If you revise and send your article to the same journal, write a careful cover letter in which you address all the points made by the reviewers, explaining what you changed in your manuscript and why you did not make other suggested changes.
- Understand that the editors may still decide to reject your manuscript even after you have revised it.
- Be patient with possible long delays at each stage. From start to finish, it may take 1 to 3 years to see your article in print.

BOOKS

- Identify several publishers that seem to have a line of books that are compatible with your book plan. (A good place to do this is at professional conferences where there are publisher displays.) Write query letters explaining your book briefly and requesting to be sent book prospectus guidelines if the publishers seem interested.
- Prepare your book prospectus carefully, according to each publisher's guidelines. In almost all cases this will involve your identifying a market, discussing competing and compatible books, and providing a strong rationale for why you think your field needs this book.
- Send in the prospectus to the current acquisitions editor. Usually you will also need to send a draft of the introduction to your book, a complete table of contents, and one or two chapters. In most cases you do not need to send an entire draft.
- You may send your prospectus to multiple publishers.
- If the acquisitions editor decides to send your prospectus and chapters out for review, there may be a space of several months while reviews are done.
- Study reviewers' suggestions carefully and write a detailed response to the reviews, explaining where you agree, disagree, and why.
- If the book looks promising (e.g., professionally important and a potential money maker), the acquisitions editor will recommend to an acquisitions committee that you be given a contract. Royalties typically range from 5%–10% and are difficult to negotiate upwards. Read the contract carefully and be realistic about the eventual length of your book and timelines for completing it.
- Revise the chapters you sent as needed, draft the others, and submit as clean a manuscript as possible, following all details and conventions of style and formatting. (This will save a great deal of hassle down the road.) The full manuscript may or may not be sent out for review.
- Check with your acquisitions editor about the details of production. At the very least, you will have a great deal of detailed work to do once you receive a copyedited version of your manuscript to check carefully, and later the page proofs, to check equally carefully. Do not rely on a production editor to catch all mistakes. Authors are ultimately responsible for all details of their books, including typos that were not caught.
- If you have strong feelings about a cover design, communicate your ideas to the production editor.
- Be realistic about the time required, from start to finish, to get your manuscript into print. Depending on the publisher and type of book, this could be 2 to 4 years.

B

Sample Book Proposal Guidelines

Lawrence Erlbaum Associates, Publishers

HOW TO PREPARE A PUBLISHING PROPOSAL

In preparing your proposal, bear in mind that the publisher needs to know as much as possible about your book, its scope, its intended audience, and how the publisher can promote the book to that audience. The publisher also needs to be convinced that you can write with authority, accuracy, and clarity, and that you can present what you have to say in a way that will be of use, of interest, and of importance to your readers.

With this in mind, your proposal should include four items:

I.   A PROSPECTUS describing your intentions;
II. A detailed TABLE OF CONTENTS;
III. From two to four SAMPLE CHAPTERS that demonstrate the clarity and precision of your prose and the appeal of your expository strategy; and
IV. An up-to-date VITA.

Such a proposal should provide Lawrence Erlbaum Associates sufficient evidence for a publishing decision.

I. The **PROSPECTUS** should include the following:

1. **Brief Description**: In one or two paragraphs, describe the work, its rationale, approach, and pedagogy.
2. **Outstanding Features**: List briefly what you consider to be the outstanding, distinctive, or unique features of the work.

3. **Competition**: Consider the existing books in this field and discuss their strengths and weaknesses individually and specifically. This material is written for reviewers and not for publication, so please be as frank as possible. You should describe how your book will be similar to, as well as different from, the competition, in style, topical coverage, and depth. If significant books are now available, you should explain why you choose to write another book in this area. Please mention all pertinent titles, even if they compete with only a part of your book.

4. **Apparatus**:
a) Will the book include examples, cases, questions, problems, glossaries, bibliography, references, appendices, etc.?
b) Do you plan to provide supplementary material (solutions, answers, workbook, laboratory manual or other material) to accompany the book?

5. **Audience**:
a) For whom is the book intended (the lay public, professionals, students, etc.)?
b) In what discipline or disciplines?
c) Is it primarily descriptive or quantitative, elementary or rigorous, etc.?
d) Prerequisites, if any (mathematical level, if any applicable)?

6. **Market Considerations**: What kind of person will buy the book, and why? What new information will the book give them to justify its cost? What is your estimate of the total market for the book? If you are aware of professional organization or mailing lists that would be useful in promoting the book, please mention them.

7. **Status of the Book**:
a) What portion of the material is now complete?
b) When do you expect to have your manuscript completed?
c) How long a book do you plan (in double-spaced typed pages)?
d) How many and what sort of figures (e.g. drawings, half-tones, charts, etc.) do you plan?

8. **Reviewers**: We may use reviewers of our own choice, but we will also try to include some whose opinion you feel will be valuable. Can you suggest any? If the book has several distinct markets, try to recommend at least one reviewer for each. Naturally, we do not reveal the names of our reviewers without their permission. If you desire, we will submit the material to the reviewers anonymously.

II. The **TABLE OF CONTENTS** should be complete and detailed. Explanatory notes should be included as necessary. This enables the reviewers to understand the structure and content of the manuscript.

III. **SAMPLE CHAPTERS** should be in sufficiently good condition to allow a valid assessment of your capability, but they need not be in final form. You should include rough sketches of all necessary figures. Ideally, about one-fourth of the work should be submitted, but the chapters need not be in sequence. It is advisable to submit any chapter that is particularly innovative. The material submitted should reflect your writing style and pedagogy in the best possible light.

IV. A **VITA** outlining your education, previous publications, and professional experience is needed.

With this material in hand, we can make a prompt publishing decision on your proposal, and both you and we can be certain that we are in agreement on the nature of the book contracted. Please feel free to call us if you have any further questions. Good luck and we look forward to receiving your material.

C

Sample Journal Article Guidelines[*]

* Check recent issue for current names and addresses of editors.

TESOL *Quarterly* Information for Contributors

EDITORIAL POLICY

TESOL Quarterly, a professional, refereed journal, encourages the submission of previously unpublished articles on topics of significance to individuals concerned with the teaching of English as a second or foreign language and of standard English as a second dialect. As a publication that represents a variety of cross-disciplinary interests, both theoretical and practical, the *Quarterly* invites manuscripts on a wide range of topics, especially in the following areas:

1. psychology and sociology of language learning and teaching; issues in research and research methodology
2. curriculum design and development; instructional methods, materials, and techniques
3. testing and evaluation
4. professional preparation
5. language planning
6. professional standards

Because the *Quarterly* is committed to publishing manuscripts that contribute to bridging theory and practice in the profession, it particularly welcomes submissions drawing on relevant research (e.g., in anthropology, applied and theoretical linguistics, communication, education, English education [including reading and writing theory], psycholinguistics, psychology, first and second language acquisition, sociolinguistics, and sociology) and addressing implications and applications of this research to issues in the profession. *The Quarterly* prefers that all submissions be written so that their content is accessible to a broad readership, including individuals who may not have a familiarity with the subject matter ad-

267

dressed. As an international journal, *TESOL Quarterly* welcomes submissions from English language contexts all over the world.

GENERAL INFORMATION FOR AUTHORS

Submission Categories

TESOL Quarterly invites submissions in six categories:

Full-length articles. Contributors are strongly encouraged to submit manuscripts of no more than 20–25 double-spaced pages or 8,500 words (including references, notes, and tables). Submit three copies plus three copies of an informative abstract of not more than 200 words. If possible, indicate the number of words at the end of the article. To facilitate the blind review process, write the authors' names only on a cover sheet, not on the title page; do not use running heads. Submit manuscripts to the editor of *TESOL Quarterly*:

```
Carol A. Chapelle
203 Ross Hall
Department of English
Iowa State University
Ames, IA 50011-1201 USA
```

The following factors are considered when evaluating the suitability of a manuscript for publication in *TESOL Quarterly*:

–The manuscript appeals to the general interests of the *Quarterly*'s readership.

–The manuscript strengthens the relationship between theory and practice: Practical articles must be anchored in theory, and theoretical articles and reports of research must contain a discussion of implications or applications for practice.

–The content of the manuscript is accessible to the broad readership of the *Quarterly*, not only to specialists in the area addressed.

–The manuscript offers a new, original insight or interpretation and does not simply restate others' ideas and views.

–The manuscript makes a significant (practical, useful, plausible) contribution to the field.

–The manuscript is likely to arouse readers' interest.

–The manuscript reflects sound scholarship and research design with appropriate, correctly interpreted references to other authors and works.

–The manuscript is well written and organized and conforms to the specifications of the *Publication Manual of the American Psychological Association* (5th ed.).

Reviews. *TESOL Quarterly* invites succinct, evaluative reviews of professional books. Reviews should provide a descriptive and evaluative summary and a brief discussion of the significance of the work in the context of current theory and practice. Submissions should generally be no longer than 500 words. Submit one copy by e-mail to the reviews editor:

> Roberta Vann
> rvann@iastate.edu

Review articles. *TESOL Quarterly* welcomes occasional review articles, that is, comparative discussions of several publications that fall into a topical category (e.g., pronunciation, literacy training, teaching methodology). Review articles should provide a description and evaluative comparison of the materials and discuss the relative significance of the works in the context of current theory and practice. Submissions should generally be no longer than 1,500 words, with the number of words indicated at the end of the article, if possible. Submit two copies of the review article to the reviews editor at the address given above.

Brief Reports and Summaries. *TESOL Quarterly* also invites short reports on any aspect of theory and practice in the profession. Manuscripts that either present preliminary findings or focus on some aspect of a larger study are encouraged. In all cases, the discussion of issues should be supported by empirical evidence collected through qualitative or quantitative investigations. Reports or summaries should present key concepts and results in a manner that will make the research accessible to the *Quarterly*'s diverse readership. Submissions to this section should be 7-10 double-spaced pages, or 3,400 words (including references, notes, and tables), with the number of words indicated at the end of the report, if possible. Longer articles do not appear in this section and should be submitted to the editor of *TESOL Quarterly* for review. Send one copy of the manuscript to:

> Carol A. Chapelle
> 203 Ross Hall
> Department of English
> Iowa State University
> Ames, Iowa 50011 USA

The Forum. *TESOL Quarterly* welcomes comments and reactions from readers regarding specific aspects or practices of the profession. Responses to published articles and reviews are also welcome; unfortunately, the *Quarterly* is not able to publish responses to previous exchanges. Contributions to the Forum should generally be no longer than 7–10 double-spaced pages or 3,400 words, with the number of words indicated at the end of the submission, if possible. Submit two copies to the editor of *TESOL Quarterly* at the address given above.

Brief discussions of qualitative and quantitative **Research Issues** and of **Teaching Issues** are also published in the Forum. Although these contributions are typically solicited, readers may send topic suggestions or make known their availability as contributors by writing directly to the editors of these subsections:

```
Research Issues

Patricia A. Duff
Department of Language and Literacy Education
University of British Columbia
2125 Main Hall
Vancouver, BC V6T 1Z4 Canada

Teaching Issues

Bonny Norton
Department of Language and Literacy Education
University of British Columbia
2125 Main Hall
Vancouver, BC V6T 1Z4 Canada
```

Special-topic issues. Typically, one issue per volume is devoted to a special topic. Topics are approved by the *TESOL Quarterly*'s Editorial Advisory Board. Readers wishing to suggest topics or make known their availability as guest editors should contact the editor of *TESOL Quarterly*. Issues generally contain invited articles designed to survey and illuminate central themes as well as articles solicited through a call for papers.

General Submission Guidelines

1. All submissions to *TESOL Quarterly* should conform to the requirements of the *Publication Manual of the American Psychological Association* (5th ed.), which can be obtained from the American Psychological Association, Book Order Department,

PO Box 92984, Washington, DC 20090-2984 USA. Orders from the United Kingdom, Africa, Europe, or the Middle East should be sent to the American Psychological Association, Dept. KK, 3 Henrietta Street, Covent Garden, London, WC2E 8LU England. For more information, e-mail order@apa.org or consult http://www.apa.org/books/ordering.html.

2. All submissions to *TESOL Quarterly* should include a cover letter with a full mailing address, both a daytime and an evening telephone number, and, when available, an e-mail address and fax number.

3. Submissions of full-length articles, Brief Reports and Summaries, and Forum contributions should be double-spaced and should include two copies of a brief biographical statement (in sentence form, maximum 50 words) plus any special notations or acknowledgments.

4. *TESOL Quarterly* provides 25 free reprints of published full-length articles and 10 reprints of material published in the Reviews, Brief Reports and Summaries, and Forum sections. Manuscripts submitted to the *Quarterly* cannot be returned to authors. Authors should be sure to keep a copy for themselves.

5. It is understood that manuscripts submitted to *TESOL Quarterly* have not been previously published and are not under consideration for publication elsewhere.

6. It is the responsibility of the author(s) of a manuscript submitted to *TESOL Quarterly* to indicate to the editor the existence of any work already published (or under consideration for publication elsewhere) by the author(s) that is similar in content to that of the manuscript.

7. The editor of *TESOL Quarterly* reserves the right to make editorial changes in any manuscript accepted for publication to enhance clarity or style. The author will be consulted only if the editing has been substantial.

8. The views expressed by contributors to *TESOL Quarterly* do not necessarily reflect those of the editor, the Editorial Advisory Board, or TESOL. Material published in the *Quarterly* should not be construed to have the endorsement of TESOL.

Informed Consent Guidelines

TESOL Quarterly expects authors to adhere to ethical and legal standards for work with human subjects. Although TESOL is aware that such standards vary among institutions and countries, authors and contributors are required to meet, as a minimum, the conditions detailed below before submitting a manuscript for review. TESOL recognizes that some institutions may require research proposals to satisfy additional requirements. To discuss whether or how your study met these guidelines, e-mail the managing editor of TESOL publications at tq@tesol.org or call 703-518-2525.

As an author, you will be asked to sign a statement indicating that you have complied with Option A or Option B below before TESOL will publish your submission.

   A. You have followed the human subjects review procedure established by your institution.

   B. If you are not bound by an institutional review process, or if it does not meet the requirements outlined below, you have complied with the following conditions.

Participation in the Research

   1. You have informed participants in your study, sample, class, group, or program (a) that you will be conducting research in which they will be the participants or (b) that you would like to write about them for publication.

   2. You have given each participant a clear statement of the purpose of your research or the basic outline of what you would like to explore in writing, making it clear that research and writing are dynamic activities that may shift in focus as they occur.

   3. You have explained the procedure you will follow in the research project or the types of information you will be collecting for your writing.

   4. You have explained that participation is voluntary, that there is no penalty for refusing to participate, and that the participants may withdraw at any time without penalty.

   5. You have explained to participants if and how their confidentiality will be protected.

6. You have given participants sufficient contact information to reach you for answers to questions regarding the research.

7. You have explained to participants any foreseeable risks and discomforts involved in agreeing to cooperate (e.g., seeing work with errors in print).

8. You have explained to participants any possible direct benefits of participating (e.g., receiving a copy of the article or chapter).

9. You have obtained from each participant (or from the participant's parent or guardian) a signed consent form that sets out the terms of your agreement with the participants and have kept these forms on file (TESOL will not ask to see them).

Consent to Publish Student Work

1. If you will be collecting samples of student work with the intention of publishing them, either anonymously or with attribution, you have made that clear to the participants in writing.

2. If the sample of student work (e.g., a signed drawing or signed piece of writing) will be published with the student's real name visible, you have obtained a signed consent form and will include that form when you submit your manuscript for review and editing.

3. If your research or writing involves minors (persons under age 18), you have supplied and obtained signed separate informed consent forms from the parent or guardian and from the minor, if he or she is old enough to read, understand, and sign the form.

4. If you are working with participants who do not speak English well or are intellectually disabled, you have written the consent forms in a language that the participant or participant's guardian can understand.

Statistical Guidelines

Because of the educational role *TESOL Quarterly* plays in modeling research in the field, it is of particular concern that published research articles meet high statistical standards. The following guidelines are provided to support this goal.

Reporting the study. Studies submitted to *TESOL Quarterly* should be explained clearly and in enough detail that it would be possible to replicate the design of the study on the basis of the information provided in the article. Likewise, the study should include sufficient information to allow readers to evaluate the author's claims. To accommodate both of these requirements, statistical studies should present the following

1. a clear statement of the research questions and the hypotheses being examined

2. descriptive statistics, including the means, standard deviations, and sample sizes, necessary for the reader to correctly interpret and evaluate any inferential statistics

3. appropriate types of reliability and validity of any tests, ratings, questionnaires, and other measures

4. graphs and charts that help explain the results

5. clear and careful descriptions of the instruments used and the types of intervention employed in the study

6. explicit identifications of dependent, independent, moderator, intervening, and control variables

7. complete source tables for statistical tests

8. discussions of how the assumptions underlying the research design (e.g., random selection and assignment of subjects, sufficiently large sample sizes so that the results are stable) were met

9. tests of the assumptions of any statistical tests, when appropriate

10. realistic interpretations of the statistical significance of the results, keeping in mind that the meaningfulness of the results is a separate and important issue, especially for correlation

Conducting the analyses. Quantitative studies submitted to *TESOL Quarterly* should reflect a concern for controlling Type I and Type II error. Thus, studies should avoid multiple *t* tests, multiple ANOVAs, and so on. However, in the very few instances in which multiple tests might be employed, studies should explain the effects of such use on the probability values in the results. In reporting the statistical analyses, authors should choose one significance level (usually .05) and report all results in terms of that level.

Likewise, studies should report effect size through such strength of association measures as omega-squared or eta-squared along with beta (the possibility of Type II error) whenever this may be important to interpreting the significance of the results.

Interpreting the results. The results should be explained clearly and the implications discussed such that readers without extensive training in the use of statistics can understand them. Care should be taken in making causal inferences from statistical results, and correlational studies should avoid such inferences. The results of the study should not be overinterpreted or overgeneralized. Finally, alternative explanations of the results should be discussed.

Qualitative Research Guidelines

The following guidelines are provided to ensure that *TESOL Quarterly* articles model rigorous qualitative research.

Conducting the study. Studies submitted to *TESOL Quarterly* should exhibit an in depth understanding of the philosophical perspectives and research methodologies inherent in conducting qualitative research. Utilizing these perspectives and methods in the course of conducting research helps ensure that studies are credible, valid, and dependable rather than impressionistic and superficial. Reports of qualitative research should meet the following criteria.

1. Data collection (as well as analyses and reporting) aims at uncovering an emic perspective. In other words, the study focuses on research participants' perspectives and interpretations of behavior, events, and situations rather than etic (outsider-imposed) categories, models, and viewpoints.

2. Data collection strategies include prolonged engagement, persistent observation, and triangulation. Researchers should conduct ongoing observations over a sufficient period of time so as to build trust with respondents, learn the culture (e.g., of the classroom, school, or community), and check for misinformation introduced by both the researcher and the researched. Triangulation involves the use of multiple methods and sources such as participant observation, informal and formal interviewing, and collection of relevant or available documents.

Analyzing the data. Data analysis is also guided by the philosophy and methods underlying qualitative research studies. Researchers should engage in comprehensive data treatment analyzing data from all relevant sources. In addition, many qualitative studies demand an analytic inductive approach involving a cyclical process of data collection, analysis (taking an emic perspective and utilizing the descriptive language the respondents themselves use), creation of hypotheses, and testing of hypotheses in further data collection.

Reporting the data. Researchers should generally provide "thick description" with sufficient detail to allow readers to determine whether transfer to other situations can be considered. Reports also should include

1. a description of the theoretical or conceptual framework that guides research questions and interpretations

2. a clear statement of the research questions

3. a description (a) of the research site, participants, procedures for ensuring participant anonymity, and data collection strategies and (b) of the roles of the researcher(s)

4. a description of a clear and salient organization of patterns found through data analysis (Reports of patterns should include representative examples, not anecdotal information.)

5. interpretations that exhibit a holistic perspective, in which the author traces the meaning of patterns across all the theoretically salient or descriptively relevant micro- and macrocontexts in which they are embedded

6. interpretations and conclusions that provide evidence of grounded theory and discussion of how the theory relates to current research/theory in the field, including relevant citations—in other words, the article should focus on the issues or behaviors that are salient to participants and that not only reveal an in depth understanding of the situation studied but also suggest how it connects to current related theories

D

Journal and Book Publisher Contact Information

The following list of websites of selected journals and book publishers in language education is by no means exclusive, and we encourage readers to note which journals and publishers publish the articles and books they find most helpful and take into consideration that information when deciding where to submit their own manuscripts.

JOURNALS

Applied Language Learning
http://pom-www.army.mil/atfl/ap/aj/

Applied Linguistics
http://www3.oup.co.uk/applij/scope/

Asian Journal of English Language Teaching
http://www.cuhk.edu.hk/ajelt

Canadian Modern Language Review
http://www.utpjournals.com/cmlr/

College Composition and Communication (CCC)
http://www.ncte.org/ccc/

ELT Journal
http://www3.oup.co.uk/eltj

English for Specific Purposes
http://www.elsevier.com/

Foreign Language Annals
http://www.actfl.org/

International Journal of Applied Linguistics in Language Teaching (IRAL)
http://www.degruyter.de/journals/iral/

JALT Journal
http://www.jalt.org/jj/

Journal of Language, Identity, and Education
http://www.erlbaum.com/Journals/journals/JLIE/jlie.htm

Journal of Second Language Writing
http://icdweb.cc.purdue.edu/~silvat/jslw/index.html

Language Learning & Technology
http://llt.msu.edu/

The Language Teacher
http://www.jalt-publications.org/tlt/

Linguistics and Education
http://peabody.vanderbilt.edu/depts/tandl/faculty/Bloome/Journal.html

Modern Language Journal
http://www.blackwellpublishers.co.uk/journals/MLJ/descript.htm

System
http://www.elsevier.com/inca/publications/store/3/3/5/

TESL-EJ
http://www-writing.berkeley.edu/TESL-EJ/

TESL Canada Journal
http://www.tesl.ca/journal/

TESL Reporter
http://www.byuh.edu/courses/lang/teslr.htm

TESOL Journal
http://www.tesol.org/pubs/magz/tj.html

TESOL Quarterly
http://www.tesol.org/pubs/magz/tq.html

Written Communication
http://www.sagepub.co.uk/

BOOK PUBLISHERS

Boynton/Cook/Heinemann
http://www.heinemann.com/

Cambridge University Press
http://uk.cambridge.org/

Lawrence Erlbaum Associates
http://www.erlbaum.com/

Longman
http://www.longman-elt.com/

Mouton de Gruyter
http://www.degruyter.de/mouton/

Multilingual Matters
http://www.multilingual-matters.com/

National Council of Teachers of English (NCTE)
http://www.ncte.org/

Oxford University Press
http://www.oup-usa.org/

Routledge
http://www.routledge.com/

TESOL
http://www.tesol.org

E

Selected Resources on Writing and Publishing

American Psychological Association. (2001). *Publication manual of the American Psychological Association* (5th ed.). Washington, DC: American Psychological Association.

Becker, H. S. (1986). *Writing for social scientists: How to start and finish your thesis, book, or article.* Chicago: University of Chicago Press.

Booth, W. C., Colomb, G. G., & Williams, J. M. (1995). *The craft of research.* Chicago: University of Chicago Press.

Braine, G. (1998). Academic publishing: Suggestions from a journal editor. *The Language Teacher, 22*(9), 5–8, 43.

Calkins, L. (1986). *The art of teaching writing.* Portsmouth, NH: Heinemann.

DeNeef, A. L., & Goodwin, C. D. (1995). *The academic's handbook.* Durham, NC: Duke University Press.

Elbow, P. (1981). *Writing without teachers.* New York: Oxford University Press.

Elbow, P. (1981). *Writing with power: Techniques for mastering the writing process.* New York: Oxford University Press.

Gebhardt, R. C., & Gebhardt, B. G. (1996). *Academic advancement in composition studies: Scholarship, publication, promotion, tenure.* Mahwah, NJ: Lawrence Erlbaum Associates.

Germano, W. P. (2001). *Getting it published: A guide for scholars and anyone else serious about serious books.* Chicago: University of Chicago Press.

Goldberg,, N. (1986). *Writing down the bones: Freeing the writer within.* Boston: Shambhala.

Goldberg, N. (1990). *Wild mind: Living the writer's life.* New York: Bantam.

Henson, K. T. (2001). Writing for professional journals: Paradoxes and promises. *Phi Delta Kappan, 82*(1), 765–768.

Henson, K. T. (1998). *Writing for professional publication: Keys to academic and business success.* Boston: Allyn & Bacon, Inc.

Holmes, V. L., & Moulton, M. R. (1995). A guide for prospective authors. *TESOL Journal, 4*(4), 31–34.

Huff, A. S. (1998). *Writing for scholarly publication.* Thousand Oaks, CA: Sage.

Jalongo, M. R. (2001). *Writing for publication: A practical guide for educators.* Norwood, NJ: Christopher-Gordon Publishers.

Klausmeier, H. J. (2001). *Research writing in education and psychology: From planning to publication.* Springfield, IL: Thomas.

Luey, B. (1995). *Handbook for academic authors* (3rd ed.). New York: Cambridge University Press.

Meloy, J. M. (2001) *Writing the qualitative dissertation: Understanding by doing.* Mahwah, NJ: Lawrence Erlbaum Associates.

Olson, G. A., & Taylor, T. W. (1997). *Publishing in rhetoric and composition.* Albany, NY: State University of New York Press.

Parker, F., & Riley, K. (1995). *Writing for academic publication: A guide to getting started.* Superior, WI: Parlay Enterprises.

Toth, E. (1997). *Ms. Mentor's impeccable advice for women in academia.* Philadelphia: University of Pennsylvania Press.

Vandrick, S. (1996). How does your article grow? From idea to publication. *IEP Newsletter, 13*(3), 10–11.

Williams, J. (1995). *Style: Toward clarity and grace.* Chicago: The University of Chicago Press.

Williams, J. M. (1999). *Style: Ten lessons in clarity and grace.* Boston: Addison-Wesley Longman, Inc.

Ziegler, A. (1981). *The writing workshop.* New York: Teachers & Writers Collaborative.

Zinsser, W. K. (2001). *On writing well: The classic guide to writing nonfiction* (25th Anniversary Edition). New York: Harper Trade.

Author Index

Subject Index